THE ROLE OF THE LOCAL ELDER

Other Books by Dan Day

Being Saved When You're Feeling Lost

A Guide to Marketing Adventism

Hanging On by Your Fingernails

Kids, Teens, and Wives

Straight Thinking in the Age of Exotic Beliefs

THE ROLE OF THE LOCAL ELDER

Applying Best Practices for Congregational Leadership

Pacific Press® Publishing Association

Nampa, Idaho | www.pacificpress.com

Cover design by Gerald Lee Monks
Cover design resources from iStockphoto.com—Pobytov/831548450, CdeBruijn/177016280

Copyright © 2018 by Pacific Press® Publishing Association
Printed in the United States of America
All rights reserved

The author assumes full responsibility for the accuracy of all facts and quotations as cited in this book.

Scripture quotations marked KJV are from the King James Version.
Scripture quotations marked TLB are from *The Living Bible*, copyright © 1971 by Tyndale House Foundation. Used by permission of Tyndale House Publishers Inc., Carol Stream, Illinois 60188. All rights reserved.
Scripture quotations taken from *The Message*. Copyright © 1993, 1994, 1995, 1996, 2000, 2001, 2002. Used by permission of NavPress Publishing Group.
Scripture quotations marked NEB are from the *New English Bible*, copyright © Cambridge University Press and Oxford University Press, 1961, 1970. All rights reserved.
Scripture quotations marked NASB are from the NEW AMERICAN STANDARD BIBLE®, copyright © 1960, 1962, 1963, 1968, 1971, 1972, 1973, 1975, 1977, 1995 by The Lockman Foundation. Used by permission. www.lockman.org.
Scripture quotations marked NIV are from THE HOLY BIBLE, NEW INTERNATIONAL VERSION®. Copyright © 1973, 1978, 1984, 2011 by Biblica, Inc.® Used by permission. All rights reserved worldwide.
Scripture quotations marked NKJV are taken from the New King James Version®. Copyright © 1982 by Thomas Nelson. Used by permission. All rights reserved.
Scripture quotations marked NLT are from the *Holy Bible*, New Living Translation, copyright © 1996, 2004, 2015 by Tyndale House Foundation. Used by permission of Tyndale House Publishers, Inc., Carol Stream, Illinois 60188. All rights reserved.
Scripture quotations marked Phillips are from The New Testament in Modern English by J. B. Phillips, copyright © 1960, 1972 J. B. Phillips. Administered by the Archbishops' Council of the Church of England. Used by permission.
Scripture quotations marked RSV are from the Revised Standard Version of the Bible, copyright © 1946, 1952, 1971 by the Division of Christian Education of the National Council of the Churches of Christ in the U.S.A. Used by permission.

Additional copies of this book are available for purchase by calling toll-free 1-800-765-6955 or by visiting http://www.adventistbookcenter.com.

Library of Congress Cataloging-in-Publication Data
Names: Day, Dan, 1943- author.
Title: The role of the local elder : applying best practices for congregational leadership / Dan Day.
Description: Nampa, Idaho : Pacific Press Publishing Association, 2018.
Identifiers: LCCN 2018023221 | ISBN 9780816364169 (pbk. ; alk. paper)
Subjects: LCSH: Elders (Church officers)—General Conference of Seventh-Day Adventists. | General Conference of Seventh-Day Adventists—Government.
Classification: LCC BX6154 .D355 2018 | DDC 262/.146732—dc23 LC record available at https://lccn.loc.gov/2018023221

September 2018

Contents

Foreword / 7

Preface / 9

Introduction
Discovering Best Practices for Adventist Leaders / 15

Chapter 1
Capturing the Opportunities in Local Church Ministry / 27

Chapter 2
The Story of the Local Elder in the Bible / 43

Chapter 3
The Elder as Shepherd and Teacher / 59

Chapter 4
How Nurture Results in Sustainable Church Growth / 79

Chapter 5
Providing Leadership Through Times of Crisis / 101

Chapter 6
Leading the Church Into Community Engagement / 119

Chapter 7
Skills for the Local Elder, Part 1 / 139

Chapter 8
Skills for the Local Elder, Part 2 / 171

Conclusion
Ministry of the Local Elder in This Crossroads Moment / 201

Appendix
Resources for the Training of the Local Elder in Adventism / 205

Foreword

Local elders play key roles in achieving congregational mission in any church setting, and they do this in a very special way in Adventist churches. They do this both through the support they give pastors in their ministries and in what they do to provide local leadership when no pastor is on the scene. Year-round, the local elder's leadership is the essential element that assures an impactful Adventist witness in our communities, as delivered by the entire membership of the church.

This book is about the local elder. It is part of an emerging commitment by the North American Division (NAD) to provide training resources for the leadership of the local congregation, especially for the local elder. We at the NAD have recognized for some time that a gap has existed between what we have understood about the importance of the role of the local elder and the resources we have provided to advance the needed training for pastors and elders. Along with this book—in addition to the associated course on the Adventist Learning Community website and a number of resources at our own Ministerial Association Elder's website—we are beginning to fulfill our commitment to carry out this training in an organized, systematic manner.

This is not to suggest that pastors have not been instructing local leaders. We know that excellent training has been delivered to elders by our pastors in many settings and will continue, whether or not these resources are available. But the challenge has been making those superb local resources available widely—and providing more specific resources that augment what is being developed locally. That is why we are in the process of developing many tools pastors can use in helping their elders maintain excellence.[1]

Part of the larger conversation that this book represents is being provided by Elder Dan Day. Dan spent many years as a pastor, so the work of the pastor in training elders was already familiar to him when he was asked to tackle the challenge this book represents. Having also spent many years as a writer and researcher—with more than thirty books and many articles in Adventist publications—Dan served as director of the NAD's Church Resource Center for many years, where he worked with pastors and other resource producers in developing a stream of useful tools for the local church. Now, as the director of special projects for the NAD, he works with our administrative team in the Office of Strategy and Research in sharing the larger story of Adventism in North America.

Church administrators at the NAD asked Dan to work with Ministerial in developing a course for pastors to use in training local elders, to be published by the Adventist Learning Community, which is the division's new online training center. In addition, he was asked to produce a book that could be used as a general introduction to the issues pastors and elders face in sharing the gospel in our local communities. This book would include the expected how-to segments to enhance the needed training, as well as a number of sections dedicated to the unique challenges of ministry in North America today. I am delighted to recommend *The Role of the Local Elder* to you. Its subtitle, *Applying Best Practices for Congregational Leadership*, captures the essence of our intent in developing these tools. This book is all about learning—and even expanding—best practices for leadership. It may not answer every question about the work of the local elder in today's setting, but it will provide not only a discussion of the various issues that contribute to the work but also references that lead to many books and articles that will add more information. On the NAD Ministerial Department's website, you can also find many additional resources to contribute to your training efforts. It is all part of a comprehensive effort to serve your needs.

The book is for many audiences in our churches: pastors, local elders, leaders in our various Adventist organizational institutions, and interested members who want to explore leadership, especially in the local congregation. It will have something to say to all. Welcome to the journey! We pray for your congregational success.

Ivan L. Williams Sr.
Director, NAD Ministerial Association

---

1. For further information, visit http://www.nadministerial.com/resources-for-elders/.

Preface

This is a book about the local elder; it is about the work elders do and the way in which their work influences the culture of the church. It is for the elder, the pastor, and for all those in the church who care about delivering grace-filled leadership and who want to see the Adventist mission in North America advanced. I intend the book to be a thoughtful but candid conversation about the local elder and local leadership in the church—lifting up the hood of the car so that we can see the engine underneath and have a chance to address openly what truly lies there. I want to discuss this without misleading oversimplification or mind-boggling complexity. And even though I may not be able to accomplish this as fully as I would like, given my own limitations as a communicator, I want you to know what I intend: I plan to tell the story broadly so that we are challenged to imagine the role of the elder and Adventist leadership through the filter of the big picture of contemporary Adventism in North America.

I do not claim to be an expert on eldership, let alone the broader aspects of Adventist leadership. Rather, I am an observer from the inside, who sees things happening and cares enough to speak out, like so many others in the church today. I was asked by the leadership of the Seventh-day Adventist Church in North America to study the role of the elder—what it has been and what it could be—and then write about it in the context of Adventist leadership. I was also asked to help produce online coursework for the Adventist Learning Community, along with other support resources supplied there and on the Ministerial website.[1]

As a part of this preface, I want to emphasize that the book you hold in your hands has been developed as part of the larger discipleship emphasis in

North American Adventism, which has been growing for several years. This is an emphasis the division has supported, in part, through the development of the new iFollow Discipleship Resource, which is available at AdventSource and includes books with subsidized prices, study guides, and more than one hundred free downloadable lessons on discipleship.[2] iFollow is an effort to support local leadership, not just by *describing* the existing role of the elder in the Seventh-day Adventist Church but by *equipping* him or her and discussing how the local elder can *expand* or *sharpen* his or her effectiveness in order to support the Adventist mission during these end times.

The book also emerges from some of the other work I have been doing with pastors and elders to lead toward more strategic efforts; this work is part of my job at the division offices as the director of special projects in the Office of Strategy and Research. This is part of a much larger collaboration between three parts of the division (the Ministerial Department, the Adventist Learning Community, and the Office of Strategy and Research) to serve local congregations more effectively.[3]

We have been collaborating in order to coordinate these new portals for elders. Great credit for the progress we have made should be given to those who have led out in making it possible, including Ivan Williams and his team from the Ministerial Department and the team at the Adventist Learning Community, where Sharon Aka has been my primary partner for bringing all this to life. Finally, I would note those who have facilitated this broad, collaborative emphasis, including Dan Jackson, the division president, and Paul Brantley, who serves as the vice president for the Office of Strategy and Research.

To help you understand what to expect from the book, it might be helpful to describe the steps I have taken in approaching this project. There are several major streams of input that fed into the book, including three clusters of insights. First, the NAD Ministerial Department recently conducted research with pastors and elders as part of a comprehensive effort to understand the current needs in local churches. This book reflects some of the research findings from that effort, as does the more extensive course. The findings also led directly to the materials available at the NAD Ministerial Department website, which are more problem-solving in character. (The research project on elders is only a small part of a broader effort by the NAD to understand better the needs of our local congregations.) I have been involved in a number of other research projects conducted with pastors and elders on church attitudes and expectations and other key issues in church life. These include research we did at the NAD Church Resource Center as well as more recent studies on how well our leaders and members believe the larger church is doing in responding to local church needs, chartered as part of the NAD Governance Committee process. Finally, these encompass efforts to determine how well local pastors feel they are being supported in achieving local mission, based on research the Office of Strategy and Research has carried out through organizations such as the Barna Group and Pew Research, along with direct studies with Adventists pastors and elders. This is all part of a growing effort to better understand what is happening at the local church so that we at the division might serve you better.

The second stream contributing to this book is a series of in-depth interviews I conducted with existing stakeholders. I sat down with a wide number of individuals who could be expected to contribute to the conversation, both at the Seventh-day Adventist world headquarters and in other locations. I specifically interviewed pastors, elders, administrators, and members of churches. I sat down with individuals with distinctive responsibilities over elders' ministries at several levels, including the General Conference, the North American Division, and union and conference levels. During these interviews, I attempted to listen carefully to the ideas and concerns presented by those deeply committed to the success of the work and tried to engage with people carefully on some of the more nuanced issues, letting them talk and then spending some time reflecting on these insights prior to beginning the book.[4]

One of the things I discovered during this process is that there are a number of varied understandings of the work of the elder. These are often tied to a wide assortment of other issues that might not seem relevant at first look, but they provide significant insights into Adventism during this crossroads moment. One of these is a concern some have over the perceived eroding authority of pastors, along with that of other denominational leaders. Another is the difference of opinion we have regarding the role of lay leadership in overall ministry. And still another is the importance of delivering a contemporary witness that may need to be adapted from what we have always done; this also involves more than a little disagreement over the role tradition should play in outreach to contemporary audiences. It is doubtful that we will resolve any of these complex issues in our discussion of elders; but in these pages, we will at least acknowledge that these problems exist and introduce some possible perspectives from which they may be approached at the local church level. Adventism in North America is not characterized by any version of uniformity; it is even more diverse than some of us are willing to admit. But I believe this diversity is a strength.

The third stream contributing to the book is the more traditional research that followed, including books, articles, sermons, and other published documents on elders, wherever they could be found. When I was asked to take on this project, I began a fairly aggressive exploration into the available written resources not only on elders themselves but also on all the issues that contribute to the discussion of the elder in Adventism. I first reviewed what is available from readily recognized Adventist sources. In some cases, I also spoke with resource producers to be sure I understood their intent in the developed tools. I wanted to clarify in my own mind what they had found along the way, as well as what they would recommend for the project I was beginning. For example, I met with some of the people responsible for the archives at the General Conference headquarters and sought clarity on how best to use the resources available there in tracing the history of how elders have been viewed at various stages in the denomination's development.

After that, I began researching books and articles available from non-Adventist sources. I continued doing this even when it became clear (as it often did) that they would require a bit of filtering in order to adapt the salient information to the unique Adventist setting.[5] Consequently, I spend more time explaining a few obscure evangelical concepts and nuances of language than you may require.

Finally, I want to affirm the General Conference Ministerial Department for the resources they have developed for elders, deacons, and deaconesses. If you are interested in what is currently available from them, you should visit the General Conference Ministerial website. Some resources will be free,

Preface

while others will require payment, which is used to fund continuing development. I not only want to emphasize the availability of these resources but also assert how helpful they are. They are *not* tailored specifically for Adventist churches in North America, let alone designed to fit our culture (or our variety of cultures). Rather, they have been developed for use in the world field, where a number of broader challenges exist, so in some ways, they fail to deal with certain challenges that are unique to North America.

I am not proposing that this book will be a complete tool on eldership, let alone one that will last forever. What I have set out to do in this book is to research best practices for the local elder, as well as I could identify them, and point at a few that are needed in North America.

This is already a longer preface than intended, so all that remains is for me to thank you for coming along on this journey. A better understanding of the role of the local elder in Adventism in North America is of vital importance, as is the larger issue of overall Adventist leadership. Please consider what has been written in these pages as no more than a starting place for your own journey of discovery.

Dan Day
Director of Special Projects
Office of Strategy and Research
North American Division of Seventh-day Adventists

---

1. The Adventist Learning Community is available at https://www.adventistlearningcommunity.com/. The Ministerial website is available at http://www.nadministerial.com/resources-for-elders/.

2. In terms of full disclosure, I was the executive editor for the development of the iFollow Discipleship Resource and continue to be a strong supporter of it, so you would expect me to say nice things about it. This resource is clearly not the only approach that could have been taken to support discipleship training, but it is being advanced as a good-faith effort, based on a broadly informed process of helping local members grow in Christ.

3. As part of this collaborative effort, other departments are contributing to the work as well, but it is the intentional effort of these three that we focus on in these pages.

4. As a way of referencing this process, I should note that it is the very nature of my

work at the NAD that requires me to follow this same process on the various projects to which I have been assigned. My job often entails approaching topics on which I have no extensive previous understanding, to which I am expected to bring a somewhat unbiased look. I do have some experience with elders as a pastor; but the extensive research I pursued did change my own perspectives in a number of significant ways.

5. I am well aware that a segment of the Adventist community is vigorously opposed to Adventists reading anything written by non-Adventists. As the director of the NAD Church Resource Center, I waged an ongoing battle against this viewpoint for years. Let me simply observe that Ellen White had an extensive library written by non-Adventists. Even though she had prophetic insights I do not have, I suspect she would advocate that we all read widely and well, because the better educated we are, the better equipped we are for ministry.

INTRODUCTION

Discovering Best Practices for Adventist Leaders

It is Sabbath morning on a weekend when the pastor is ministering in another church in his or her district. The congregation has completed Sabbath School and is now assembled for the worship service. There are far fewer than one hundred people in attendance (as is typical for the majority of Adventist churches in North America). Music has been playing, and people have been responding warmly; they are happy to be in church. But now the congregation quiets as the local elder steps to the pulpit with a Bible in hand. A sense of anticipation fills the room because it is the local elder who is about to preach, and the congregants expect to be given hope for daily living.

The elder opens his or her Bible, takes a deep breath, smiles widely, and then begins the sermon. The Holy Spirit fills the room with warmth and receptivity, allowing the audience to be blessed, and a distinctive openness to ministry is being bestowed on the entire spiritual community, preparing them for mission.

The scene just described is both very typical in North American Adventism and very important to our conversation about the local elder and local leadership in Adventism. The local elder is known and trusted by the members of the congregation. He or she is a long-standing member of the church—someone who understands the needs of this particular spiritual community because they are also the elder's needs. In short, the elder is a volunteer, not an employee of the church. That is why what the elder says during the worship service is expected to be especially important and relevant.

This appreciation for the ministry of the local elder does not lessen the congregation's recognition of and gratitude for the ministry of the pastor.

The pastor is the leader of the local church, and the elder does not in any way supplant that leadership. But the members of the congregation believe the elder knows them in their individual circumstances and cares deeply about what is happening in their lives. Moreover, they are convinced the local elder is focused on how they can become increasingly engaged in their relationship with Jesus and on delivering the distinctive Adventist end-time witness. The truth is, leadership from within is one of the most powerful forms of leadership, and the Seventh-day Adventist Church—wherever this scene is being repeated—is tremendously blessed by its local elders.[1]

This book takes a distinctive approach to the elder and leadership. (It is certainly influenced by my own spiritual walk, including some of the unusual pathways I have been on.) But it also places the conversation about the work of the local elder in the broader story of the Adventist end-time mission. As a result, even though the book will address in detail the specific job the elder may be called to perform, it is also about how the elder's leadership is to engage the entire church in delivering a consistent witness to the community through mission clarity, mission alignment, and mission accountability. These three primary elements may be new to you, but they shape how we integrate strategy with mission—and each of them is critical to success.

Mission awareness is emphasized by the degree to which the men and women within the organization (including the members of the local church) know and apply the overall corporate mission. Rehearsing the organization's mission statement until it is memorized is part of this, of course; but awareness of how the mission itself is to be achieved at their specific level is also essential. It involves understanding how the mission encompasses the character of the organization and how deeply it captures its personality. *What are Adventists here to do?*

Mission alignment is best revealed when all parts of the organization work closely together in leveraging their collective assets to accomplish the mission. This collaboration entails a clear line of sight between the organization's overall mission and the mission of each local congregation or organization and is best supported when the top leadership recognizes and rewards those who demonstrate the greatest commitment to advancing the common mission. Success is dependent on specific actions in order to achieve and maintain alignment. *How can Adventists all work collaboratively?*

Mission accountability is best seen when all parts of the organization not only commit to achieving the mission but are also held accountable for the mutually framed outcomes—including the deeply spiritual ones. These outcomes include the effective utilization of the resources that have been provided and the short-, medium-, and long-term expectations implied by the organization's collective understanding of the mission. This is not merely about counting. Rather, it is shaped both by measurable goals against which progress may be evaluated and clarity on how individual goals combine to provide the context for the largest organizational goals. *How do we know how we are doing, if we do not hold one another accountable?*

The three sides of a more strategic approach to mission are a bit technical, but I hope you will begin to see how these three large ideas about Adventist leadership are important to the work of the local elder. What we do in the local church is part of something both deep and profound that is happening in the church today, as we Adventists attempt to offer God a witness that is excellent in every way, including outcomes shaped by grace. How we lead as local elders, and in whatever other capacity we lead, makes a big difference in the impact we will have—especially in our current setting and with the people we are called to address within and near the church.

What we are being called to do is a stretch—advancing the Adventist mission in North America today is a tough nut to crack. The work of the local elder in this mission fits into a much larger conversation about the contemporary witness of the Seventh-day Adventist Church in North America and the world. But it is at the local level where the talk stops and action really begins—and where the mission of the church is applied.

Getting to church vitality

Let us begin by acknowledging who our elders are in the church and the circumstances within which they play their role in advancing the Adventist mission. Elders are local leaders, who adapt their efforts to what the local reality is. For example, Adventism in North America is largely a denomination of smaller, district churches that have fewer than one hundred members. These are congregations wherein the leadership that the local elder is capable of providing is particularly vital and in which amazing, untapped potential exists for mission extension.[2] This local potential is not always being fully addressed to face the challenge, of course; but that only helps to define the opportunity.

There are some larger churches in North America, of course, especially around our institutions, and we will try to keep them in the discussion as we move along. But the vast majority of pastors spend most of their lives in smaller congregations, and the majority of our local elders minister alongside them in these smaller settings.

I was recently at a conference workers' meeting with both pastors and elders in attendance. My office—the Office of Strategy and Research at the North American Division—was there to help pastors and elders learn better strategies for accomplishing mission. At one point in the meetings, a pastor pulled me aside for a brief conversation. He said to me, "The division is getting it wrong in a lot of what it sends out to the churches."

"What do you mean?" I asked.

"I've been a pastor for thirty years," the pastor responded, "and I've never had one hundred members in any of my churches." He gestured toward the pastors and elders who were engaged in small-group discussions. "And neither have any of the other guys here at the meeting. You guys at the division seem to be sending out stuff that only works in much larger churches, and you need to be preparing resources that are aimed more specifically at small churches, because that's the reality we face."

I told him we would take seriously what he said about the reality so many local pastors face, and I have subsequently thought about it a great deal and have shared his perspective with a number of administrators and resource producers. In addition, I started this book on the elder with the pastors and elders of smaller congregations in mind. Whether or not this pattern of ministry has been yours specifically, it represents a perception of Adventism in North America that we will acknowledge as we approach our discussion of the work of the local elder. By this, I mean that the elder is largely working in an intimate setting, surrounded by men and women he or she already knows. As a result, it is quite possible for a deeper, more personal ministry to be delivered, and that is one of the major perspectives for our conversation.

It is easy for some of us to forget that in the early Christian church—the setting many of us want to see emulated today—there were no megachurches where people could get lost in the shuffle. There were only small, intimate house churches, where every member was part of a vital faith community. It was Elton Trueblood, the famous Quaker author who wrote, "Perhaps the church, in many areas, must be smaller before it can be substantially stronger."

Think about that possibility for a moment, and imagine ways in which it might be true for Adventists today, even as we all seek to grow the church. Could it be possible that in some of these smaller settings we can most readily apply the dynamics of ministry success? The rate of growth for the church in North America—while impressive compared with some of the older, more mainstream denominations—is challenging in terms of how we accomplish mission. In an article by Petr Činčala, who is the director of the Institute of Church Ministry at Andrews University, Adventism is described as growing fairly rapidly as a worldwide movement, but the growth in North America is of a substantially different character. He writes, "Moreover, the growth in North America is predominantly through multiethnic groups, immigrants, and refugees. Recent figures show that that 52% of those baptized into the North American SDA church in 2015 were from ethnic minorities. If the trend continues, the rate of adding Caucasian members to the church will actually decrease."[3]

Now, Činčala and I are happy we are growing among these multiethnic and immigrant population groups, but the church must reflect on where some of our greatest opportunities lie and the places where we are investing our resources. While there are 1.2 million Adventists in North America today, there are more than 20 million worldwide.[4] In short, we are growing far more rapidly outside North America than inside. Moreover, the circumstances we are facing here and in a few other places, such as parts of Europe, where the complications of secular culture shape our witness, require some thoughtful contemplation because they depict a challenging future for the entire church—for us now and for everyone else just a bit further down the road.

Having said all that, this section of our conversation is about a moment of perspective. Even while fully embracing the ministry of the local elder in small churches—and having made a commitment not to forget how important this is—I am not arguing that we should remain *intentionally small*. Rather, I merely urge leaders in smaller churches to explore the benefits for witness that they may bring to the table, including the opportunities for more personal interaction among members and within the community. Additionally, I encourage pastors of small churches, along with their elders, to excel at capturing the possibilities that small churches provide, and I especially suggest we consider the qualitative side, along with the quantitative, when we address an Adventist vision of mission.[5]

As part of my work at the North American Division (NAD), I have served as one of the Adventist representatives on an ecumenical committee that does research projects each year on religious health in North America. In the group's recently completed annual survey, the primary topic being assessed was church vitality. That is to say, it was focused on what makes a church compelling for its members beyond mere growth in numbers. This is a perspective that may seem a bit odd to some of us, because we Adventists have typically equated mission largely with evangelism and church growth—where the focus is often perceived to be on numbers—rather than other elements of church vitality. But it is an important perspective for us to keep in mind as well when we are assessing mission success. For example, beyond how many new members we have, we need to consider the impact we are having on our communities, based on what they see in the church. How compelling is the story of Adventism that we are telling, in what ways does it witness to the loving character of God, and how we are serving people in need?[6] Furthermore, how might the local elder contribute to this broader view of overall church vitality and the degree to which it supports what we are preaching?

To put this into some context, there are a number of books available on the Christian market that argue that churches *should* be kept small in order to remain more faithful to their mission. One of the best of these is *The Strategically Small Church* by Brandon J. O'Brien, who was the editor of the now-defunct *Leadership Journal*. He values the small church because it is "intimate, nimble, authentic, effective."[7] His point is that the local church may be small in number of members, but its impact may still be large and profound because of the *quality* of the witness being delivered.

While there are some notable advantages to being small, emphasizing smallness for its own sake is not the intention of *this* book. I strongly support church growth, including the evangelistic emphasis in Adventism that has traditionally supported our activity and sense of achievement. But being small is not quite the handicap some would make it, and it presents some interesting opportunities that we should begin to celebrate. If you are the pastor or elder of a small church, rather than see size merely as a limitation, you should see the benefits and take full advantage of them. In support of this idea, I would direct you to an article in the February 2017 issue of *Ministry* magazine, in which David Klinedinst writes: "As I searched the Bible, it appeared to me that there were no paid pastors overseeing a congregation or house church and doing ministry for the people in the early New Testament church. Those who were paid by the tithe were sent out to evangelize and plant churches in unentered lands and cities. . . . The existing churches were left in the hands of capable lay people."[8]

Klinedinst goes on to depict the same pattern in the early Adventist church and offers some quotes from Ellen White in support of these locally managed congregations. Then he describes a couple of approaches we could take to more fully emulate this apostolic model in today's setting. And at the end of the article, he asks, "What would happen if more churches in North America followed these models? What would happen if we started gradually transitioning churches to be lay-led by trained, dedicated elders and deacons? Then the ministers could be sent to nearby towns and cities to evangelize and plant churches."[9]

I am not advocating for entirely lay-led churches, and neither is Klinedinst. It is true that the model Klinedinst is proposing is somewhat different from the one most Adventist conferences are following today, where the intent is to have churches led by pastors, even if the districts are large. But we should ponder the questions Klinedinst asks. What would happen if we started putting a greater emphasis on lay leadership of our churches, featuring the local leadership of the elder? How would it affect life in Adventism? Would we be happier, more engaged, and less fascinated with internal debate—the way it sometimes seems we are today? Or would it lead to catastrophe? Even in Adventism, growth in size is not incompatible with growth in depth of spirituality, but they are merely two sides of the same story about the Adventist mission. Moreover, leadership, in whatever specific model we embrace, requires collaboration.

The local elder and discipleship
In these pages, we will discuss how the local elder is a partner with the pastor in more strategic efforts that "move the ball down the field" for better ministry and more compelling outcomes. While our conversation in these pages will be largely *about* the local elder, it will at times be framed within the context of the larger North American religious scene. This will include the ways in which Adventism in North America faces some distinctive issues from those that Adventists are currently facing in other parts of the world.[10] We will, at times, also contrast what elders might have done in the past with what they may be called on to do today and in the near future. The conversation will be about how the church itself is changing and about how our approaches to ministry, even at the local level, must transform with it in order to be more effective in reaching contemporary audiences.[11]

At the core of this book is the idea that the elder has been called by God to engage with both the church membership and the community in ways that resonate with more contemporary audiences, without driving away current members. In order for the elder to do this well, he or she will likely need to employ some new methods and tools.[12] It is my intent in these pages to describe some of them and to hint at others we may need in the future.

Our current dreams of ministry in Adventism are sometimes interpreted through the rather extensive polarization that characterizes broader Christianity today, and it has entered our Adventist churches as well. This polarization causes some of us to see our mission through what some would call *fundamentalist* lenses—including a misguided pursuit of perfectionism. At the same time, others of us would imagine that God does not care about how we live or what we profess. Neither of these extremes is helpful in advancing the contemporary Adventist mission, so I will argue for a radical third lens through which we see God's dream for His church. This lens involves a rather significant reimagining of Adventism as a wholly redemptive community with a distinctive mission to contemporary audiences.

This third lens is an important part of how we might begin to reach some of the audiences that are often closed to us. I will also argue in favor of an Adventism that features our "better true stories."[13] This includes a witness that significantly enhances our effectiveness with audiences that might otherwise ignore us. In these pages, I will also advocate for *an Adventism that is at its best*. By this, I mean an Adventism full of men and women whose joy and grace lead us to pursue matters with integrity, generosity, and to have a commitment to social justice and give us a compelling end-time witness—one that simply makes more sense to contemporary audiences.[14] Finally, I will contend that the local elder is in many ways the one best positioned to lead out in this more comprehensive witness to contemporary audiences.

A book that is part of a larger story
At the very heart of this introduction is the idea that this particular book on the elder in Adventism has been written as part of a larger story. The book was written in conjunction with an online course for the local elder that is being offered by the NAD through the Adventist Learning Community, along with an expanding number of additional resources available through the NAD Ministerial Department. This is a multipronged effort, including distinctive elements that help in different ways to make the work of the local elder more successful in contributing to congregational success.

By the end of the book, you will hopefully capture a larger vision of what the local elder may be called to do in ministering to his or her congregation and community as part of God's larger end-time mission. One reality we have to acknowledge is that there are not as many Adventist resources on the elder as we might hope. There are *some*, of course, and the ones that we have are quite good, if a bit limited at times in addressing *context* as fully as needed in North America. There are also a number of conferences experimenting with broader approaches to the work of the elder, so we can expect more resources to become available in the near future. The Ministerial Department at the division is launching a new effort to put in place volunteer lay pastors. This is currently being approached in a very careful manner, due to some of the legal and insurance issues associated with it, but it has great potential for helping address the impending crisis we face as an increasing number of baby-boomer pastors retire.

In looking back at my own pastoral years, I am painfully aware of how little intentionality I gave to addressing the training of my own elders for best practices. I mostly expected my existing elders to mentor my new ones. In doing the research for this book, I have discovered that I was not alone. Learning by doing does not always fully prepare someone for actually excelling in an area of responsibility, and this sometimes even results in a kind of "knowledge drift," where each generation does slightly less than the previous one.

I would urge you to begin reading with a notebook and a pen or pencil in your hand so that you can log questions for which you do not find easy answers. If the pastor or other elders in your church cannot help resolve these questions, perhaps others in nearby churches can. Then you can make queries of Adventist resources on the internet at some of the previously mentioned sites. Also, the local conference leadership group should have someone who can help explore the matter, whatever it is. And because we are who we are denominationally, there is additional help from the several levels of governance above the conference.

A final word on organization

There are eight chapters in this book. The first six deal with the primary information an elder needs in order to get his or her mind around the history and mission of the elder. These six chapters combine both conceptual and practical information, telling a story that encourages a powerful service in our churches and communities. The nature of this material is such that it intentionally addresses larger issues of mission and should be of interest to pastors, elders, other leaders, and local church members who want to better understand the church in its present context and leadership in today's church. The last two chapters, however, represent a rather precise discussion of the specific tasks or skills the elder must master. These last two chapters are tied in a direct way to the *Elder's Handbook* from the General Conference. I have carefully taken into account what is written there and added contextualization for North American pastors and elders.

1. This does not in any way suggest that the pastor does not care for the members or that the pastor is not as committed or sensitive because he or she is an employee of the church. Rather, it is to put a distinctive focus on the ways in which the local elder—when he or she imagines what God can do—becomes a uniquely powerful agent for mission.

2. This tends to be true in North America as well as around the world. In some areas, the congregations are smaller, and in others, the congregations may be larger. But even when they are larger, the typical district is also larger.

3. Petr Činčala, "Building a Vibrant, Healthy, Growing Church" (paper, Adventist Society of Religious Studies, San Antonio, TX, November 18, 2016), 5, https://digitalcommons.andrews.edu/pubs/231.

4. Office of Archives, Statistics, and Research, General Conference of Seventh-day Adventists, "Table 4: Church Membership by World Divisions," in *2017 Annual Statistical Report*, rev. February 26, 2018, http://documents.adventistarchives.org/Statistics/ASR/ASR2017.pdf.

5. By this language, I am connecting our specific conversation about the local elder and the larger missional questions facing Adventism with Ellen White's teaching that our work is not just about baptizing more people, but it is also about telling a larger story of the character of God. Our mission, then, includes both quantitative elements (telling more people) and qualitative ones (telling a more compelling story of a loving Father).

6. While this is a topic that will be addressed later in more detail, I should acknowledge that I am writing from the perspective that one of the major contributions Adventism brings to the evangelical conversation is an emphasis on the character of God as a loving Father. This topic is fully explored by Ellen White throughout her great controversy theme. As a part of that emphasis, we see that actions taking place on planet Earth are only a portion of a larger conversation about who God is and how He desires to relate to us.

7. Brandon J. O'Brien, *The Strategically Small Church: Intimate, Nimble, Authentic, Effective* (Bloomington, MN: Bethany House, 2010).

8. David M. Klinedinst, "Back to the Future: Lay-Led Churches and a Return to Our Roots," *Ministry*, February 2017, 10.

9. Klinedinst, "Back to the Future," 12.

10. In discussing the book with several of its early advocates, it was affirmed that a broad approach to the conversation would be useful, including discussions about the elder as part of the larger Adventist community. Consequently, from the very early stages, the book was intended to fit the story of the local elder into the larger account of our end-time witness—not ignoring the essential local emphasis but adding how it fits into the larger issues facing Adventism.

11. My intent is not to advance change in and for itself but rather to urge that our resistance to change be tempered by a deep commitment to mission. What is "traditional" is no more or less right than what is "contemporary." What matters is what works.

12. We will frequently discuss the role of the elder in terms of ministry to contemporary audiences, which includes the diverse mind-sets found in the church and community. By this, I am not suggesting that ministry to more traditional audiences, such as

members of other churches who may be persuaded to become Adventists, is not relevant. Rather, I am acknowledging that God requires more from us than merely getting people to agree to a few distinctive doctrines. He is calling us to find ways to minister to those who operate in today's secular settings with a compelling gospel witness that makes the Adventist appeal attractive.

13. This particular language ("telling our better true stories") can be explored more fully in Bernadette Jiwa's game-changing book *Difference* (Australia: Story of Telling Press, 2014). Jiwa, an Australian marketing writer, urges us to understand the importance of reaching contemporary audiences by telling stories that resonate with the men and women in modern culture.

14. While this is most certainly a book on the local elder, it is also about how we can move from a merely parochial view of the church to one where we see ourselves as agents of change in a world that has been shaped by various forces, including traditionalism. The end-time witness of Adventism is to be of such a profound character that the darkness and hopelessness of secular life will be shown in stark contrast with the loving, joyous character that Jesus Himself displayed and calls us to demonstrate. Moreover, the local elder can become a key agent in God's end-time witness, both within and through the local congregation. This does not diminish the role other denominations may play in God's end-time work, but it merely explores the language Adventists have used for themselves in believing that the church, in some distinctive way, represents God's end-time "remnant" people.

CHAPTER 1

Capturing the Opportunities in Local Church Ministry

Therefore go and make disciples of all nations, baptizing them in the name of the Father and of the Son and of the Holy Spirit, and teaching them to obey everything I have commanded you. And surely I am with you always, to the very end of the age.
—Matthew 28:19, 20, NIV

As Adventists, we all value the contributions the elder has traditionally made in church life. We do not want to lose any of the value from that historical perspective. But it is also important for us to imagine who or what the elder could become in today's setting if the position's full potential as a culture-changing ministry were realized.

The premise in this book is that the local church is where ministry and mission are applied in the most direct ways, and it is where the Adventist end-time mission is accomplished. It is true that Adventists often describe ourselves in macro terms—as an entire denomination with a common mission that is addressed to the whole world. But even when we do this, the ministry of the local congregation is still where that mission engages the community and reflects a distinctive Adventist culture that is intentionally modeled after what we see in the New Testament. For these reasons, this first chapter is largely about the *setting* in which the mission is to be accomplished. It includes the ministry of the pastor, the local elder, and the members of the congregation to the broader community. It is also why the second chapter focuses on the elder in the Bible, especially in the early Christian church. The Adventist mission involves how the ministry of the local church intersects with the worldwide mission of the church—but may not always be quite the same.[1]

The role of the local elder in support of the local pastor, here in North America, is central to our conversation. But how does the elder make a difference in the local church at times when the pastor is not immediately on the scene? In what ways does the elder then lead the church in its witness to the community? How might this be different from times in the past—or even in other parts of the world—due to our complex contemporary setting in the West? These are all the questions we will consider in this first chapter.

It is essential that the *entire church* be engaged in order for the mission of the church to be advanced. There are plenty of books by pastors from many denominations, including ours, who confess that they came to realize this only late in their ministry and that they wish they had learned it earlier. At the NAD, some of our most recent research shows that pastors put the need for help in training elders how to *nurture* second only to the need for help in personal ministries.

As a denomination, we have a policy that pastors should be hired and managed by local conferences, rather than by more distant levels of the organization, such as the union or the division. In North America, the pattern of how we use district pastors is undergoing significant reengineering currently, with the result that some pastors who had two or three churches in their districts are now often being asked to cover even more. Also, in one conference where I recently made a presentation, we learned that a couple of years earlier they had more than sixty pastors at the same meeting, but now they had fewer than forty due to fiscal challenges. This is a trend that promises to accelerate, not decline, based on predictions concerning resources, in terms of both finances and personnel availability. Effective ministry leadership will increasingly fall on the local elder, who is selected by the congregation, and he or she must find ways of training deacons and deaconesses, along with other leadership roles.[2]

We began our conversation by acknowledging that every local elder and every church is unique in a number of important ways. This sense of individualized ministry—tailored to the local congregation—has been with us since apostolic times, established and then contextualized by the leaders of the early church. The role of the local elder in Christianity was defined and then spread around by word of mouth. It was then repeated in letters that were passed from church to church. In time, these letters were combined with the gospel stories that were also circulating, first in verbal form and then written form. These two streams of information eventually became the canon of the New Testament.

During many of these years, it was the traditions of the church that served to shape congregational life. These oral traditions continue to be important even when we have other resources available, such as policy statements. Essential to mission, however, is persuasive storytelling, where we tie policy to outcome in a dynamic, collaborative effort to tell our distinctive story.

Discussing the local elder as a lay pastor
In this book, the term *lay pastor* is used sometimes to describe the local elder.[3] Not every group in Adventism may be comfortable with this language. To some, the terms *lay* and *pastor* may not seem to belong in the same sentence because the ordination issue—specifically as pertaining to female pastors—may be of such great concern that we are sensitized to the language, or we may simply feel that pastors require a different order of respect from other members.

I support respect for the pastor, of course; I was a pastor of a local congregation for many years and continue to serve in somewhat of a pastoral role at the division offices. But in many of the passages of the New Testament describing the leadership of the early church, the term *elder* could easily be translated as "lay pastor," since the contemporary concept of the pastor (as a paid employee of a larger denominational organization) simply did not exist and would not for centuries.[4] And I have spent considerable time in conferences where people have begged me to develop these materials with a consciousness of what is really happening in our churches—they are increasingly dependent on these lay pastors and want them to be properly honored for the incredible volunteer work that they do, often while holding down other jobs.

My interest is not in developing conflict over terminology but in helping you to enhance your *strengths*, not just correct your weaknesses. In his remarkable book *Church Unique*, Will Mancini writes, "The problem with this is simple. If your primary focus, or paradigm for effectiveness, is trying to enhance your limitations, you will end up worse off than when you started. You will be immensely more effective if your focus is on discovering and developing your strengths."[5]

When Jesus commissioned His disciples, He sent them out to "make disciples" of people in "all nations" (Matthew 28:19, NIV). This was a broad mission. It anticipated that the story would be told persuasively and in context for many different language groups and cultures—a process commonly known as "contextualizing the gospel," which means figuring out the best ways to reach those making up a given community. In some cases, those groups needed to learn a new language. The early believers were to make persistent attempts to understand how to communicate with people in varied locations and whose backgrounds did not necessarily prepare them to understand the rather radical witness Jesus was delivering. Today in North America we similarly have many local elders whose primary language is not English and whose context is quite different from that of their communities. While I do not have the background or skill to contextualize this for you, I can tell a story broad enough to include you and affirm your exciting effort to minister in your setting.[6] Evangelical scholar Soong-Chan Rah comments on the evident decay evangelicals are seeing in traditional membership and writes about hope for the church: "Contrary to popular opinion, the Church is not dying in America; it is alive and well, but it is alive and well among the immigrant and ethnic minority communities and not among the majority white churches in the United States."[7] This challenging language is the other side of the comment we read earlier that simply described how these new groups are coming to dominate much of the conversation in North America. The point is that these immigrant and ethnic minority groups are not only here but flourishing.

In many ways, the current situation parallels the early Christian church, as it was established in Israel first and then went to Asia Minor and beyond. It started with those who mostly spoke Hebrew or Aramaic and then moved on to those who spoke Greek or other languages. The gospel first came to the Jews. And those Christian Jews, rather predictably, believed they were called only to reach other Jews. But that understanding of mission was inconsistent with God's larger plan for the spread of the gospel. This soon resulted in the first missional crisis of the early church.

Remember, Jesus said that He was sending His Spirit to equip the disciples to make a compelling witness to people in all cultures; a witness stated in such broad terms that those audiences would be able to understand and embrace the gospel. He was sending them on a journey that would require the disciples to adopt an understanding of what God was doing for *an entire world* in need. He was forcing them outside the narrow confines of their culture and asking them to think bigger. Peter, who was one of the very first of these Jewish Christian disciples, struggled to understand this larger, more contextualized model of Christianity. As many of us today still do, he fought against it. But eventually, God got through to him, and Peter accepted it and wrote the following: "Your life is a journey you must travel with a deep consciousness of God. It cost God plenty to get you out of that dead-end, empty-headed life you grew up in. He paid with Christ's sacred blood, you know. He died like an unblemished, sacrificial lamb. And this was no afterthought. Even though it has only lately—at the end of the ages—become public knowledge, God always knew he was going to do this for you" (1 Peter 1:18–20, *The Message*). Think about what Peter is saying here: God *always* knew how broad the mission of His church would be. It was aimed not just at the Jews but also at men and women in all cultures. And it is the same mission He has given to Adventism today as well.

When Adventism began, the church members also had limited aspirations, based on their cultural expectations. They believed in what was called the *shut-door theology*, which meant that only those believers who had come out of their churches during the Millerite movement leading up to 1844 could be saved. It was a number of years before they saw the error in this interpretation of Scripture and began sending missionaries to the rest of the world. Like the early Christians in Jerusalem, Adventists needed to understand that the precise words of Scripture must be understood in context and must be filtered through contemporary mission.

Matthew 28:19, 20 represents a powerful affirmation of the fact that God is taking a personal hand in the character of the witness He asks us to deliver. He is not satisfied with a pale imitation of Christianity, focused only on theology or even rules and behavior. Rather, God wants to see in our lives a powerful testimony to His presence, expressed in our arms being open to others in the community. In the book *Elders in the Life of the Church*, a rather lofty portrait of the local church is painted: "The Lord's church, His bride, is comprised of not merely a list of individuals who are redeemed and being sanctified. Rather, in the society of the saints is something that seems more human than in the life outside of it. Furthermore, its radiance should shine out of our life together."[8]

When an author talks about the church as "something that seems more human than in the life outside of it," he is talking about mission. He is declaring a bold vision for how our common humanity shapes our witness and is discussing the generosity, humility, and compassion we should all display as followers of Jesus, which should be expressed in ways that make sense to our complex and varied audiences that are often made up of people with little interest in traditional religion. The language describing the impact of "our life together" is especially meaningful because it describes the ways in which church members should interact with one another to establish a witness that reveals what God wants us to display to the world.

The local elder in North America
What if we allowed God to take us on the journey to excellence that the apostle Peter described in terms of what God always knew He was going to do for us and in us? How might the role of the elder grow, along with the impact of ministry?

It is true that Adventism has grown into an organizational structure of significant size and complexity when compared with what it was in the very early days of the church. If the apostles were to look on it today, they might be quite surprised. There are many layers of leadership in the Seventh-day Adventist Church: the local church leadership, the conference, the union, the division, and the General Conference. Still, there is heavy lifting to do in God's remnant church, and we need capable hands doing it.

But here is the problem: all the available research confirms that Christian churches in North America are in deep trouble across the board (Protestant, evangelical, and Adventist). For example, in the book *Why Nobody Wants to Go to Church Anymore*, Scott Thumma tells us that nearly four thousand churches close their doors every year in North America, compared with only one thousand new ones that open their doors, and most of those that do are very small.[9] In many ways, the contemporary church is going backward, and the research also shows that megachurches are growing at the cost of other smaller churches.

The Barna Group, whose research into church life has recently been extended to include Adventist congregations, says that "three out of every five young Christians (59%) disconnect either permanently or for an extended period of time from church life after age 15."[10] We are losing 59 percent! The single most influential book that has been written recently on the state of the church in North America is David Kinnaman and Gabe Lyons's book *unChristian*. (Kinnaman is not only a respected researcher but also the president of the Barna Group.) They write, "Our research shows that many of those outside of Christianity, especially younger adults, have little trust in the Christian faith, and esteem for the lifestyle of Christ followers is quickly fading among outsiders. They admit their emotion and intellectual barriers go up when they are around Christians, and they reject Jesus because they feel rejected by Christians."[11]

Did you get that? These younger audiences reject Jesus because we, as His representatives, are perceived as *rejecting them*. This should give us pause. It says that we are losing credibility with an entire generation—not because they are only interested in sex, drugs, and rock 'n' roll, but because *we* are not reflecting a redemptive witness to them. Kinnaman and Lyons go on to say, "To engage nonChristians and point them to Jesus, we have to understand and approach them based on what they really think, not what we assume about them. We can't overcome their hostility by ignoring it. We need to understand their unvarnished views of us."[12]

These words should challenge us. But we need to be very careful in our reaction. Some of us would argue that Christianity continues to be a powerful force in our culture and we point out how many people say they go to church fairly regularly. The polls suggest that most people in North America claim they are Christian, which seems positive. But there are indications that those who actually attend a Christian church each weekend is far below what pollsters report.

> According to both Gallup and Barna, 43% of American adults attend church on a typical weekend. . . .
>
> . . . The actual rate of attendance from "head counts" is less than half of what the pollsters report.[13]

Going back to *Why Nobody Wants to Go to Church Anymore*, I want you to ponder this scary sentence: "There's no easy way to say this, but it needs to be said: The American church is broken."[14] This brokenness is illustrated in a remarkable book by Alan Roxburgh on renewing the culture of the church, and it speaks to the crisis: "The situation is particularly challenging for those Protestant churches that are the inheritors of the European reformations of the sixteenth century and European migrations that followed. These Eurotribal churches, until recently the dominant form of church in North America, still represent a major form of Christian life. However, a way of being, leading and organizing the church is unraveling. The unraveling metaphor proposes that existing ways of being church are less and less able to provide meaningful ways of shaping people's religious life."[15]

What Alan Roxburgh is telling us here is that how we "do church" in North America is not working any longer for a growing number of people, especially in particular age groups. The strands of interrelationship that hold members safely in the church are *unraveling*, and we Adventists must examine ourselves and the life in our churches to see what might be unraveling in our ranks as well. As the local elder, your job is not only to support the "paid professionals" but also to provide a personal, local example of what Jesus wants to do in our lives. We also have to consider what steps we might take to address this decline. Fortunately, research helps us understand what is happening. For example, the studies reveal four big factors these people say are behind their decisions to leave the church:

"I feel judged." Gabe Lyons and David Kinnaman's groundbreaking research confirms that 87 percent of young non-Christian Americans label Christians as judgmental.[16] Whether it is tied to behavior, looks, clothes, choice of friends, or lifestyle decisions, the church is seen as acting as judge and jury. And in our contemporary setting, people find this judgment (or perceived judgment) extremely difficult to endure.

Some of us may believe that judging others is a good thing to do and that these secular audiences *need* to be judged (and condemned). I get that; but even when we feel justified, what we cannot deny is the negative outcome. The fact is people who feel judged leave the faith community and rarely come back. Is there another pathway available to us?

"I don't want to be lectured." Young people today have stories they want to share. But they believe there is no place in the typical church for their questions, their doubts, or their stories. People want to be able to express themselves without coming under criticism when they speak up.

Again, some of us may feel entirely justified in lecturing them, because we believe we possess the truth and are well equipped to deliver it. We assert that we are mature and know more than they know. But we also have to take ownership for the outcome of our actions. And we need to ask ourselves if there are better ways to share beyond merely lecturing.

"Church people are a bunch of hypocrites." Postmodern men and women expect people in the religious community, who set the bar so high, to make at least a sincere effort at hurdling it themselves. Many of us in the church portray ourselves as bastions of morality, even when we know that the statistics show we are really not so different from the profiles of other members of society. But what matters is that these younger audiences perceive the church as a place where we focus on pointing fingers, rather than being generous, compassionate, and humble. Stories flourish of the lavish lifestyles of famous preachers or the abuse of children by religious leaders. And even in Adventism, there is a growing concern among some members that our lack of transparency in denominational activities and policies may hide ugly truths that would embarrass the church were they made public.

"Your God is irrelevant to my life." Today a growing number of people feel increasingly unmoved in the typical church environment. The church service itself is one of the places where this disconnect is most obvious. The statistics confirm that a rising number of our own members do not experience God in the typical worship service. They tell us they want to leave the worship experience with hope for daily living, and they ask us, "How can the churches be relevant when they don't seem to be in touch with the raw, everyday lives of the communities around them?"

This theme is particularly revealed in the success of some Christian television ministries, where people with little or no theological education—let alone spiritual character—are able to attract huge followings by giving people just a little hope for daily living. The criticism that preachers in Adventist churches are not delivering relevant sermons is one we commonly hear from younger audiences, and it contributes to why they say they are leaving.

Speaking to basic needs in North America
Even in the face of all the data on how traditional religion is declining,[17] I believe that the best days of the church lie ahead of us. But we can be successful only if we are walking down gospel pathways and not wandering off into the weeds, as some of us are doing.[18] The good news is that researchers have already gone before us and have identified what people in our communities really want out of life. The research says the basic needs of people in North America include the following:

- the need to believe life is meaningful and has purpose;
- the need for a sense of community and deeper relationships;
- the need to be listened to and heard;
- the need to feel one is growing in faith; and
- the need to be appreciated and respected.[19]

These are the very things the church already offers when we were being *our best selves*. So why is it that so many people are leaving?

Let me ask you a serious question: Could it be that we are not telling the story we think we are? Consider this: When you, as a local elder, are asked to preach, why not find some way to be sure these five needs are addressed in your sermon? When you are visiting, why not talk about these things? When you are interacting with the church in board meetings and the community in your daily interactions, why not make sure these are the things you are determined to emphasize? We do not negate what is distinctive about the Adventist witness by doing these things.

What all the recent research says to us is that people outside the church are not angry at God. They are not even indifferent to Him. The impulse for faith is not absent from their lives. But they are suspicious of the traditional church, in all its profession of righteousness and lack of humility. They are tired of the way religion has been packaged and delivered. In many instances, we in the church have been hesitant to tell the story of a loving God in ways that common, ordinary people can find relevant to their lives. Instead of moving through the community in redemptive ways by showing people we care and that we are eager to help, too often we settle for delivering what is easy for us to do, rather than trying new things that open new possibilities. I am urging local elders to take this to heart. The larger church must do so as well, but we are the ones who can really do something to change perceptions.

Telling our better true stories
As noted in the introduction, Bernadette Jiwa, an Australian marketing and branding author, contributes to our understanding of how we can successfully move into this new world of "nonreligious customers." She writes, "Perhaps it's time to get comfortable with the fact that if we want to change the world, we need to stop being afraid to tell better true stories."[20] Think about that idea for a moment, and consider its relevance for Adventist ministry and the work of the local elder. Ask yourself, *What are Adventism's "better true stories"?* Could we focus more than we do on why we live longer than many other people? Could we become far more engaged with the community, allowing our values to help others live more satisfying lives? Could the welcoming environment of the church be seen as an unusual strength in today's cold, heartless world?

Again, what are our "better true stories"? Could we change the emphasis in the stories we have been telling? One of the most exciting things happening recently in Adventism is the series of health-service events that have been going on in places such as San Francisco, San Antonio, and Los Angeles. Thousands of Adventist volunteers and their friends have come out to provide free health and dental care to the neediest populations. In Los Angeles, for example, more than eight thousand people received care in one day.[21] Imagine the impact on these people and the powerful witness for the values of Adventism that these events represent. Imagine the stories these people will be sharing with others.

Remember the story of the blind man in the New Testament? After Jesus healed him, all he could say was, "I don't know. One thing I do know. I was blind but now I see!" (John 9:25, NIV). In these end times, a key to our future success as Adventists is to stop being afraid to tell "better true stories." We Adventist local elders have *many* "better true stories." We have a witness to deliver to our communities that has a compelling character, and we ought to be known for telling these stories.

It takes time to change people's perceptions of us, but here is a reality check: There are people who represent Adventism in such destructive ways that Adventists are seen as a bunch of kooks, conspiracy theorists, and dispensers of bile and hatred. In order to offset these people, we must begin telling more hopeful stories. Local elders have an opportunity to tell far better stories, with far more positive impact.

The impact of Adventist diversity
In addition to the big themes presented so far, I need to add one last perspective on Adventist diversity. This is a positive quality of our denomination and we should celebrate it more fully. In researcher Diana Eck's rather shocking book *A New Religious America*, she writes:

> There are more Muslim Americans than Episcopalians, more Muslims than members of the Presbyterian Church USA. . . . We are astonished to learn that Los Angeles is the most complex Buddhist city in the world. . . .
> . . . Make no mistake: in the last thirty years, as Christianity has become more publicly vocal, something else of enormous importance has happened. The United States has become the most religiously diverse nation on earth.[22]

In Alan Roxburgh's book, mentioned earlier, we read another brief segment that deserves our consideration: "A new immigrant Christianity is emerging that will bring with it practices, values and theologies that won't fit neatly into the notions of Christian life familiarly shaped by the European reformations in terms of their polities, theologies and forms of communal life. The Protestant churches find themselves needing to travel in yet another altered religious landscape."[23] And if this need to "travel in yet another altered religious landscape" is true about Christianity as a whole, it is doubly true for Adventists. Changes in our culture are a compelling denominational reality for us. The story of Adventism's spread across the world (and how many Adventists from other countries have come to North America to contribute to our culture) is another of those "better true stories." Our Adventist values have transformed us so that we now need to add our diversity to the list of things that make the Adventist witness in these end times so effective.

Resisting the temptation to merely battle culture
There are so many good things happening in the church today that we dare not allow ourselves to be distracted by the few that cause us to shake our heads a bit and wonder if we have lost sight of our values. Clearly, God has called us to be local elders in challenging times. Do we merely sit on the podium every week, offering prayer or taking up the offering? Or are we captured by a new vision of servant ministry, where we allow God to do a "new thing" in our lives, as the prophet Isaiah described: "Behold, I will do a new thing; now it shall spring forth; shall ye not know it? I will even make a way in the wilderness, and rivers in the desert" (Isaiah 43:19, KJV).

It was Ellen White who wrote these words to us: "We need to branch out more in our methods of labor. Not a hand should be bound, not a soul discouraged, not a voice should be hushed; let every individual labor, privately or publicly, to help forward this grand work. Place the burdens upon men and women of the church, that they may grow by reason of the exercise, and thus become effective agents in the hand of the Lord for the enlightenment of those who sit in darkness."[24] Ellen White is promising us that local elders are not limited by our lack of professional training in ministry, but that we "may grow by reason of the exercise" of leadership and that by stepping out in faith—even when we do not feel as though we are entirely up to it—we may "become effective agents in the hand of the Lord."

This book is about helping that happen in your life and mine—and in our Seventh-day Adventist Church. The story of the local elder can make a powerful witness for hope and wholeness. And it is time for us to step up to the plate.

The Role of the Local Elder

1. This dissimilarity is not in the kind of mission or of quality but of specifics. While others can support and contribute, the local church engages with the community.

2. I often describe the role of the elder in terms of serving in order to demonstrate God's grace. We will not all see the role of the elder in these terms. But Adventists, in rather unique ways, have always understood that describing the character of God is central to our distinctive mission in the great controversy. We do not see ourselves merely as warriors in today's "culture wars" but witnesses to a loving Father.

3. Some contemporary Adventist communities find the term or phrase *lay pastor* a bit troublesome, due to a desire to put more authority in the hands of pastors. My use of the phrase is based on an increasing number of congregations that do not have a full-time pastor, in which the local elder will of necessity carry out many of the pastoral responsibilities.

4. In a later segment of the book, we will see that the term *pastor* meant something different to early Adventists than what it means today. In the early years of the church, the minister was really the leader of the "evangelistic machine," by which those who had accepted the Sabbath used every means possible to add to the number of believers.

5. Will Mancini, *Church Unique: How Missional Leaders Cast Vision, Capture Culture, and Create Movement* (San Francisco: Jossey-Bass, 2008), xxiii.

6. The role of the pastor is seen slightly differently in some of the major cultural groups in North America. There may well be a descending order of authority, with some groups placing a higher sense of power on the pastor, and other groups envisioning his or her role more in terms of a facilitator or coach. In many situations, the elder will take his or her lead from how the last pastor saw his or her role.

7. Soong-Chan Rah, "The End of Christianity in America?" *Patheos*, August 6, 2010, http://www.patheos.com/resources/additional-resources/2010/08/end-of-christianity-in-america.

8. Mark Dever, foreword to *Elders in the Life of the Church: Rediscovering the Biblical Model for Church Leadership*, by Phil A. Newton and Matt Schmucker (Grand Rapids, MI: Kregel, 2014), 9. What is of particular interest is that the writing of this book coincides with a debate within the Baptist Church regarding whether the local elder should be added to the organizational structure of the church, which typically has had only pastors and deacons. The book is part of an effort to overcome obstacles to the emerging practice of electing local elders in Baptist churches, which is why it is important for us.

9. Scott Thumma, "A Health Checkup of U.S. Churches" (presentation, Future of the Church Summit, Group Publishing, Loveland, CO, October 22, 2012), quoted in Thom Schultz and Joani Schultz, *Why Nobody Wants to Go to Church Anymore* (Loveland, CO: Group Publishing, 2013).

10. "Six Reasons Young Christians Leave Church," Barna Group, September 27, 2011, https://www.barna.com/research/six-reasons-young-christians-leave-church/.

11. David Kinnaman and Gabe Lyons, *unChristian: What a New Generation Really Thinks About Christianity . . . and Why It Matters* (Grand Rapids, MI: Baker Books, 2007), 11.

12. Kinnaman and Lyons, *unChristian*, 16.

13. David Olson, "12 Surprising Facts About the American Church" (PowerPoint presentation, Mission America Annual Conference, Kansas City, MO, 2007), slide 3.

14. Schultz and Schultz, introduction to *Why Nobody Wants to Go to Church Anymore*.

15. Alan Roxburgh, *Structured for Mission* (Downers Grove, IL: InterVarsity Press, 2015), 13, 14.

16. Kinnaman and Lyons, *unChristian*, 34.

17. If you want to know more about this, I recommend a recent book: John Dickerson, *The Great Evangelical Recession* (Grand Rapids, MI: Baker Books, 2013).

18. "Wandering off into the weeds" is to allow our attention to be distracted from the central themes of the gospel to some of the more fascinating "off roads" we have taken, such as our preoccupation with perfectionism and our willingness to embrace shortcuts to spiritual vitality.

19. George Gallup Jr. and D. Michael Lindsay, *The Gallup Guide: Reality Check for 21st Century Churches* (Loveland, CO: Group Publishing, 2002), 12–14.

20. Bernadette Jiwa, *Difference* (Australia: Story of Telling Press), 22.

21. Andrew McChesney, "Mega-Clinic Provided 'Miraculous' $38.4 Million in Services in Los Angeles," Adventist News Network, May 19, 2016, https://news.adventist.org/en/all-news/news/go/2016-05-19/mega-clinic-provided-miraculous-384-million-in-services-in-los-angeles/.

22. Diana Eck, *A New Religious America* (San Francisco: HarperCollins, 2002), 2–4.

23. Roxburgh, *Structured for Mission*, 19.

24. Ellen G. White, "The Duty of the Minister and the People," *Advent Review and Sabbath Herald,* July 9, 1895, 2.

CHAPTER 2

The Story of the Local Elder in the Bible

But let your minds be remade and your whole nature thus transformed. Then you will be able to discern the will of God, and to know what is good, acceptable, and perfect.

—Romans 12:2, NEB

As the apostle Paul suggests in Romans 12:2, knowing what is "good, acceptable, and perfect" does not come naturally to us but depends on our minds being "remade" and our "nature thus [being] transformed." This *restoration* of the way God made humans is viewed somewhat skeptically by some evangelicals, who find this process unlikely, given our sinful nature. But Adventists have always viewed God's intention to restore us to a deeper humanity, with greater compassion, forgiveness, and humility, as part of the gospel promise and as something we expect God to do in our lives.

In this sense, the Bible was given to us not only to tell us about God's act of redemption but also to provide us with hope and the promise of wholeness. These are some of the reasons why, in our conversation about the local elder, we can profitably discuss the unique witness we Adventists are called to deliver in the end times and the distinctive perspective on that witness that the local elder is capable of delivering.

In the New Testament setting, the local elder is depicted as the mainstay in congregational life. The pastor—as we see the role in traditional Protestant or Adventist churches—had not yet been invented. And when the distinctive pastoral role as we know it was introduced during the Reformation, it was still in some ways similar to the role of the Catholic priest that existed at the time, which represented a mingling of Jewish and pagan priestly roles. Only in fairly recent times has the role of the pastor taken on the more truly pastoral character that it holds in Adventism and the rest of Protestant Christianity.[1]

In the early Christian church, there were three key leadership roles. First, there were *apostles*, who went around establishing what were typically house churches. Once these small clusters of believers were established, the apostles left the area to continue their work elsewhere. Then, there were two local roles: *elders* and *deacons*, who were chosen from among the membership to provide ongoing, sustainable leadership, including, in the elders' case in particular, what we today would term *pastoral care*. The apostle, such as the apostle Paul, would remain in contact with the local churches he had founded, both through letters that went back and forth and through visits to him from members, and even through brief return visits when possible, such as when Paul and Barnabas were collecting funds for the needy church in Jerusalem (Acts 24:17). But the sustainable leadership of the local church was left to the elder or deacon.

During this early church period, the Bible itself did not exist in the form we are familiar with now. Most people could not read or write, and they depended on the verbal presentation of the Gospels and on storytelling based largely on the Old Testament and had the letters of the apostles read to them by the few in the congregation who could read. Even the four Gospels—Matthew, Mark, Luke, and John—were first part of an oral tradition that circulated among the churches. Later they became bound with the letters of the apostles and the book of Acts to form the earliest New Testament canon.

Why we need to understand the elder in the Bible
When we begin thinking about how the local elder may accomplish all the things that God wants him or her to do in the church and community, we realize that we are not talking about typical corporate activity or even the tasks of a community organizer. Instead, we have moved into an area where we are exploring the seemingly miraculous events displayed in the Bible's stories—and what only the Holy Spirit can do. This is a matter of directed spiritual growth and is not just about study and comprehension, or even historical patterns. Rather, it is about *spiritual enlightenment* and *inner transformation*.

In matters of spiritual life, something beyond what deliberate practice offers is required for us to experience the inner transformation God promises. I am certainly not implying that careful study is unimportant and efforts at comprehension are not necessary when we begin this conversation about the local elder in the Bible; rather, we want to learn as much as we can about the forces that led the church down the paths it has taken organizationally. But even these productive efforts result in the desired insight *only* because the Holy Spirit is active in our lives, helping us understand what we find in the Bible.

Let us begin this discussion of the elder in the Bible with how the language is used in the Old Testament.

The elder in Old Testament times

In the Old Testament days of Abraham, Isaac, and Jacob, God used the patriarchal system as the basis for decision making within the family and for all other leadership purposes as well. In that time period, the elders were the heads of the family or tribe. An elder was someone with experience and wisdom who also happened to lead a family group. Other terms of leadership were also used at various times during the Old Testament period: prophets, judges, and kings, for example, were also part of the Old Testament leadership tapestry, as were the Levites, or priestly caste. At one point, God spoke to Moses and said, "Bring me seventy of Israel's *elders* who are known to you as leaders and officials among the people. Have them come to the tent of meeting, that they may stand there with you. I will come down and speak with you there, and I will take some of the power of the Spirit that is on you and put it on them. They will share the burden of the people with you so that you will not have to carry it alone" (Numbers 11:16, 17, NIV; emphasis added).

Clearly, even at this early point in biblical history, the title *elder* was being used in missional terms, which is to say it was about facilitating God's mission. It was all about an experienced person who could alleviate the "burden" that Moses was carrying so that the mission could be advanced more effectively. The concept of splitting the work into units that various individuals might carry successfully is one from which we can all learn, especially today when collaboration is increasingly the key to success when ministering to contemporary men and women. Even in developing strategies and resources for ministry, we need to keep in mind that our members want to be cocreators with us.[2]

On a parallel track, one of the challenges in drawing material from contemporary writing on church leadership is that many of us have had our ideas shaped by leadership styles and training programs that were once in vogue but are no longer as effective for current audiences. In a rather remarkable book on creating churches that unchurched people would love to attend, Andy Stanley tries to redirect our attention to methods to increase our faith. He lists five of what he calls "faith catalysts." These include practical teaching, private disciplines, personal ministry, providential relationships, and pivotal circumstances.[3] What Stanley is reminding us of is that the task of the local elder in achieving the Adventist mission cannot be done just by working harder. Rather, it has to be done by *working smarter*, working *more personally*, and is tied to *relationships* and circumstances where we allow God to lead us into *a positive congregational life.*

Those who are attempting to lead churches in some of the ways that prevailed in earlier times are not necessarily doing a poor job nor are they destined to fail.[4] But they are offering approaches that will more likely make the effort challenging and create unneeded potential obstacles for working with our younger members. One of the major themes in this book is that for the local elder to lead well, it may be necessary for him or her to help change the thinking of the congregation in some very elementary ways—and one of these is the matter of leadership styles. One of the very best books on this sort of change is Robert E. Quinn's *Deep Change*. In it, he writes about the deep change today's leadership requires: "Deep change differs from incremental change in that it requires new ways of thinking and behaving. It is change that is major in scope, discontinuous with the past and generally irreversible. The deep change effort distorts existing patterns of action and involves taking risks. Deep change means surrendering control."[5]

How we lead must be based on what works best today, not just what someone in charge believes. We need to shift our approaches, which, as Quinn indicates, involves both "taking risks" and "surrendering control"; some of us may not be entirely comfortable doing either. The Adventist leader must be willing to try new things. Leadership in the church is about *collaboration*—not heavy-handed direction.[6] When God said to Moses that He would "take some of the power of the Spirit that is on you and put it on them," He was describing broader access to the Holy Spirit for a larger group. As local elders, we need to share a substantial part of the work that the pastor has often been expected to carry in helping the congregation move the church toward a more effective ministry.

Even in this Old Testament scene of God speaking to Moses, we see the beginnings of a transition to a less centralized process. When God spoke about the role of Israel, he was not describing what the priests or kings would do, or even what the prophet would do, but what the *entire community* would do. In later prophetic writings, we read, "And they that shall be of thee shall build the old waste places: thou shalt raise up the foundations of many generations; and thou shalt be called, The repairer of the breach, The restorer of paths to dwell in" (Isaiah 58:12, KJV).

What should we take from this verse at the level of the local Adventist church, particularly when the church is led by an elder? For one thing, we cannot minister merely by standing at a podium, preaching on exotic theological themes. Rather, we do it by restoring and repairing, which means engaging with the community, displaying through our actions that we care about the people in the community. We lead best when we do it from inside the community, when we provide the sort of positive witness that validates all the theology we articulate and the high behavioral standards we espouse.

The elder in New Testament times

When Jesus walked the earth, most of the people who would have been termed *elders* in the religious community were actually opposed to Him. They were in league with the Romans in an effort to put Him to death. The leadership of the religious community then was largely made up of Pharisees. As we view their actions, we must see the contrast between being merely religious and being deeply spiritual. The Pharisees were serious religious leaders. When they followed Jesus around, seeking to trick Him into saying something they could use to get the Romans to crucify Him, they believed they were doing God's will. But the negative impact of these elders reminds us that being a religious leader—both then and today—does not necessarily mean you are a spiritual person. Sometimes it just means you have managed to persuade the people around you that you are orthodox in your beliefs and willing, or even *eager*, to take on leadership.

Still, neither being orthodox nor merely willing to lead equates to accepting God's call, let alone serving in His way. On the other hand, even though the religious leaders were conspiring to thwart God, His will was undaunted. Jesus *was* crucified but not until He had performed the ministry His Father had set out for Him. And the same is true today. While there will be moments of crisis in the church, including conflicts over theology or policy that rage from time to time, God's plan is relentless in its advance.

The debate over a more missional organizational structure began in the early Christian church when Paul and Barnabas were founding churches in Asia Minor. In the dispute that led to the Jerusalem council, we can see a pattern for what these churches would be like as they grew in size and mission. In Acts, we read, "They put fresh heart into the disciples there, urging them to stand firm in the faith, and reminding them that it is 'through many tribulations that we must enter into the kingdom of God.' They appointed elders for them in each Church, and with prayer and fasting commended these men to the Lord in whom they had believed" (Acts 14:24, 25, Phillips). In this passage, there are a number of features of the elder's work that help us identify how the early church was being set up by the apostle Paul:

First, a realistic plan was established for assuring mission success. New church members were urged to "stand firm in the faith," which implies that some in the church were falling away, as is expected with any organization that is in conflict with existing cultural patterns. In the same way, we understand that Adventism is for those who are prepared to face the world boldly and to take a few bumps and bruises along the way. The local elder should be a strong supporter of a structured approach to local ministry; he or she should embrace the sort of clear, strategic plans that my office at the division is urging and training pastors and elders to put in place. But that does not mean that the ways we have done things in the past are appropriate for the future.

In Andy Stanley's recent book, he criticizes pastors whose major intent is to get larger followings by offering what is sometimes called the "gospel of prosperity." He says that preachers' kids "know that the best performers usually build the biggest churches but not necessarily the healthiest ones. We aren't impressed with moving lights, slick presentations, 'God told me,' 'the Sprit led me,' or long prayers. . . . So this isn't a book about how to make your church *bigger*. You don't need me for that. If bigger is your goal, just start promising things in Jesus' name. Religious people love that stuff."[7] Stanley is arguing for quality over quantity. He is calling for a church that sees mission in broader terms than numbers only. It is about delivering a faithful witness to Jesus, where depth matters as much as size.

Second, we are called in Acts to "put fresh heart" into members. This is a really critical perspective for the local elder. We can never forget that everything we do should have the objective of putting "fresh heart" into the people we serve. Many church members and visitors come to church depressed and on the edge of despair, longing for someone to come to the pulpit and speak a word of hope to them. As local elders, we must understand that we are not in place to knock people down or drive them out. On the contrary, we are there to build them up for the lives they are living. Our job is to figure out how to provide positive hope to the distinct groups in our congregation and community so that we are taking them above the mundane and the controversial into new territory—where a dream for what church life could be like, when operating at optimum, is both offered and demonstrated.[8]

Third, there is a call in Acts for a more sustainable *kind of local leadership.* Experienced men and women in the early church were taking the long view, which led them into mentoring their successors. Paul was continually seeking younger men and women, such as John Mark, Titus, and Timothy, who would carry the work even further. In a denomination that was formed by young people, as our Adventist Church was, we should see this pattern of older leaders being replaced by younger ones as an exciting dynamic. But what we see too often is only an emphasis on experience and tradition, including a rather obvious fear that younger, more creative voices will depart from traditional, time-honored approaches. Moreover, some segments of the church today are made up of people who fail to demonstrate the grace of Jesus Christ. They have no idea the degree to which their negativism is undermining any efforts to welcome in or retain new members, let alone prepare them for leadership. And their lack of mere civility is devastating. But as a collective group of believers, we in the Adventist Church (especially our elders) must have the courage to offer a firm contrast in our own behavior. It is not somebody else's job.

In the book *Elders in the Life of the Church*, we read, "Who were the elders in the early church? It is easy to read our modern concepts of a senior pastor and his church staff into the New Testament pattern. But there were no professional theological schools to produce 'pastors' in the first century. The early churches selected men from within their membership to serve as elders."[9] The apostles did this when they were on the scene; but when they had moved on, it was the elders' job to put in place sustainable leaders who were trained for those leadership roles. And the same is true today.

Finally, there is a hopefulness on display in Acts, even during trying times. We know from historical records that being a Christian during New Testament times put a target on your back. In those days, agreeing to be an elder in a local church was not for the timid. These early leaders did not go into the local leadership role looking for trouble or trying to stir it up, but they knew they would not be able to avoid it. Still, they knew God would be with them whatever happened, along with the rest of the church family. This is one of the reasons why leading from within is so vital today. As elders, we are not just leading the church but also *part of the family*. And that is why we are now going to turn to an exploration of what were called *house churches*.

The elder in small house churches

Over the centuries, churches have been configured in many ways, from the very small churches of the New Testament to the vast cathedrals that characterized Roman Catholicism during the Middle Ages. This includes the megachurches we see today. In his very helpful article on the role of the elder in Adventism, Adventist researcher Monte Sahlin writes, "The early Christian church was organized around 'house churches,' small groups that met in homes. The Scripture references, when illuminated with evidence from archeology and history, fit into a picture I will possibly over-simplify here to distill the practical significance: 'elders' were the immediate pastoral leaders of the particular 'house church' groups."[10]

The Story of the Local Elder in the Bible

The early church was a house-church movement. The process of choosing elders—those who would lead these family groups from within—was a serious one that included fasting and prayer. "Paul and Barnabas handpicked leaders in each church. After praying—their prayers intensified by fasting—they presented these new leaders to the Master to whom they had entrusted their lives" (Acts 14:23, *The Message*). The local elder was not just the leader; he was a participant in whatever the church was experiencing. The other members of the church were family members to him. This portrays closeness and a sense of interdependence that is important to understand as we try to imagine what church was like during those times.

These churches existed to tell a story of God's interactions with humankind. There is a wonderful depiction of this in Frank Viola's book *The Untold Story of the New Testament Church*. He writes, "And this pattern reflects God's ultimate goal—which is to have a community on this earth that expresses His nature in a visible way. This theme of a God-ordained community constitutes a unifying thread that runs throughout the entire Bible from Genesis to Revelation."[11] This imagery of a "God-ordained community" that "expresses His nature" is at the core of our discussion of the local elder: God is seeking a community witness by Adventists in these end times, led by the local elder, where closeness, mutual interdependence, and a common sense of mission prevail and where its very existence testifies to the true character of God as a loving Father.[12]

The processes by which the New Testament canon was formed must be addressed if we are going to get a feel for the elder in his or her times.[13] Stephen Voorwinde, writing on the formation of the New Testament canon, states that Clement of Rome wrote about the importance of apostolic authority in about A.D. 96. In about A.D. 115, Ignatius of Antioch "stated that the teachings of the apostles are known through their writings."[14] What happened is that two groups of stories began to exist, side by side: one group containing the Gospel stories, and the other the letters of Paul and the other apostles. F. F. Bruce, one of the most highly respected historians of the New Testament times, writes, "So long as the fourfold Gospel and the Pauline collection circulated separately, one can hardly speak of a canon, even in embryo. The bringing together of the two collections into one was facilitated by the existence of Acts, the hinge which joined the two. . . . Acts provided the central structure of an edifice which now took on the shape of the canon as we have received it."[15]

The character of ordained local elders

To add some texture to the story we are telling about the elder in the early church, we will explore some of the challenges elders were called to address. In 1 Peter 5, we see Peter's concern that those who have been set aside to lead out in the local church would be asked to face some difficult moments: "I have a special concern for you church leaders. I know what it's like to be a leader, in on Christ's sufferings as well as the coming glory. Here's my concern: that you care for God's flock with all the diligence of a shepherd. Not because you have to, but because you want to please God. Not calculating what you can get out of it, but acting spontaneously. Not bossily telling others what to do, but tenderly showing them the way" (verses 1–3, *The Message*).

Peter is expressing his growing concern over the *character* of local elders. He is emphasizing the gentleness they need to bring to the tasks they take on. He urges elders to serve their churches and communities with "the diligence of a shepherd," which is to say that they will be the person who goes out in the stormy night and rescues the single lost sheep. He does not want them to engage in their work out of a sense of obligation but because of their relationship with God. He does not want them to be bossy or overbearing but to be tender in all that they say and do.

This leads to one final discussion about the characters of local elders. There are two key passages dealing with the qualifications of elders in the New Testament: 1 Timothy 3:1–7 and Titus 1:6–9. By putting these together, we can see that the qualifications given by the apostle Paul include a number of positive characteristics. A successful local elder would be blameless as a steward of God, above reproach; a faithful husband of one wife; temperate, sober, vigilant; sober minded, prudent; of good behavior, orderly and respectable; given to hospitality; able to teach; not given to wine; not violent, not pugnacious; patient, moderate, forbearing, gentle; uncontentious, not soon angry or quick-tempered; not covetous, not a lover of money; a good ruler over his own house—his children are faithful and not accused of rebellion to God; not a novice or new convert; in possession of a good rapport or reputation with outsiders; not self-willed; a lover of what is good; just, fair; holy, devout; self-controlled; and one who would hold firmly to the faithful message as it has been taught. All these descriptions begin to capture the spirit of the local elder.

In his interesting article "The New Testament Elders," David Huston writes, "Today elders are commonly thought of as lay-leaders, board members, or men who assist the pastor. But these ideas come from Catholic and Protestant tradition, not the Bible. In the New Testament, the elders were the pastoral leaders of a local assembly. Their task was to shepherd the church as overseers."[16] This biblical perspective of the elder as a pastoral figure is the one we have been building toward. Too many of us see the elder as the guy in the slightly rumpled gray suit who sits on the platform, fidgeting and uncomfortable; he gives the announcements and offers prayer or takes up the offering and has something to do with taking the Communion service to shut-ins. But in the New Testament, the elder's role is clearly far more pastoral and central to the life of the church.

Female elders in Adventism

Having said all that about the biblical description of the local elder, let us turn now to a final element in the broader conversation, addressing one of these qualifications in some detail. Some of the books and articles that have been mentioned earlier take a particular pathway with which I must take some exception. Some of the evangelical writers that have been referenced in this book would put women in a lower permanent ranking than men—and always subsidiary to them. They employ arguments that are also often used to support male headship, which emerged in the Calvinist tradition and continue in many Reformed circles. These ideas are also being advanced by some Adventists today.

The texts *do* say the elder should be the husband of one wife and he should be faithful to her; if we take the texts only literally, we must admit that they do not say the elder will be the wife of one husband and faithful to him. But beyond the appeal to literalism that some emphasize, what should we deduce from such statements? How should policies be written or theology constructed where gender is involved, based on our larger story about our loving Father?

This debate over the proper role for women in the church is not one we are going to resolve here (and certainly not by me). I have close friends on both sides of this debate, and I love them all. I happen to believe that when Paul said that in Christ we are no longer Jew or Gentile, slave or free, or male or female (see Galatians 3:28), he was establishing something significant. It was the equivalent of saying, "Jesus is above culture," and he is asking us to think bigger too.

It is true that Jesus only called male disciples and there are a few texts—when taken out of context—that seem to require women to take a back seat. It might make some kind of sense to extract general insights from these passages in support of male supremacy, but only if you are determined to project male prerogatives back into the story. In giving up on the whole male-female debate, along with the other things Paul notes, we begin to unravel oppression based on color, status, or gender so that people are treated in a more egalitarian manner.[17]

You do not have to agree with me. While culture is still a factor today, just as it was in Jesus' day—He sat down with the woman at the well, in violation of every cultural prohibition, and had a meaningful conversation—it is not OK to be ugly for religious reasons. I believe the apostle Paul was pointing us in a specific, more enlightened direction, asking us to dream with him this dream of a fairer future, where class, gender, and race are of no significance.

The world of the New Testament elder

Alexander Strauch[18] describes the New Testament elder in clear terms that cannot be misunderstood: "In contrast to all priestly or lordly titles, nothing in the title *overseer* (or *elder*) violated the local church's family character, humble-servant nature, or priestly and holy status. The fact that the apostles and first Christians used the term *overseer* as a synonym for *elder* demonstrates flexibility in the use of leadership terminology and the desire to communicate effectively among Greek-speaking people."[19]

Let us summarize a few of the things we learn about local elders from the New Testament record.

The New Testament elders were all local. The apostles, such as Paul and

Barnabas, were similar to today's evangelists. They helped establish churches and then moved on. Even now there is something about the leadership of a local volunteer that is different from that of a paid employee of the larger church organization. When I was a full-time pastor, I felt that I was a little on the outside edges of the church family, ministering to it, of course, but not really a part of it. I was loved by the congregation but not fully inside it because I was an employee of the conference, who had placed me there as their agent.

But as noted before, the local elder is at the heart of the church family. He or she lives there full-time and will experience the longer-term implications of the choices he or she makes. This makes a real difference in terms of the potential for collaboration.[20]

The elder was authorized by the local church through the laying on of hands. The ordination of elders was a form of authorization that enabled apostles, such as Paul, to keep moving ahead and planting new churches, trusting that all local challenges would be handled well by the community's elders and deacons—people who had been empowered to speak locally for the faith. There was more than a little bit of confusion for new members in regard to living as a Christian, given that many of them had been living by Greek cultural standards, which were often in sharp contrast with Jewish standards. These new Greek members had none of the God-given structure that Jewish believers had behind them in matters such as worship practices, marriage, diet, and conduct.[21] The elders were there to express good judgment on all of these issues.

Similarly, when the early pioneers of the Seventh-day Adventist Church instituted elders, it was for many of the same reasons. Adventism emerged as part of a powerful movement of religious fervor that birthed several of today's more exotic religious groups, such as the Latter-day Saints, along with a number of religious themes, such as Fundamentalism. People were coming into local Adventist congregations, claiming to be delivering instructions or new teachings from the leadership group of the church and then leading the members not only into error but also causing severe disruptions in the fellowship. George Knight writes, "James and Ellen White's early concerns regarding organization seem to be essentially the same. Both feared disorderly, fanatical, and unauthorized representatives within the budding Sabbatarian movement."²² In other words, the early Adventist leaders, like the early Christians, were concerned about extremists.

In summary

In the Bible, the elder is presented as a man or woman who has been selected from among the membership of a local church to lead the congregation. God developed in the church a more *distributed* approach to leadership than what people typically tended to create. The Bible shows a progression from more to less authoritarian models. Elders were to both teach and enhance the leadership of others in the congregation for the accomplishment of mission. In the New Testament, elders were selected to lead congregations with compassion and gentleness. The local elder was the leader in pastoral care, working to motivate and minister to the congregation.²³

This picture of the elder in the New Testament is not presented to suggest that we should do things in precisely the same ways. Our time is quite different, and adaptations are not only appropriate but also required. But there are essential qualities displayed in New Testament times that properly inform our conversation about the local elder. And we will be better elders if we study these qualities and seek to emulate them.

---

1. Because many of us do not have access to the inner workings of other denominations, a brief explanation may be helpful: in many evangelical churches (including most independent churches), pastors are hired by the local congregation and are managed through the church board. This board can typically fire them as well. This contrasts considerably with the Adventist model, in which pastors are hired and placed by conferences.

2. The concept of people in the church wanting to be cocreators with us comes from some of the newer management and information disciplines that have overtaken social media. We are quickly leaving the world where leaders create plans and followers just follow. We live in a world where those who are not traditionally seen as leaders are expected to contribute and collaborate. The degree to which we ignore this (or even deny it) indicates how unsuccessful we will be.

3. Andy Stanley, *Deep and Wide: Creating Churches Unchurched People Love to Attend* (Grand Rapids, MI: Zondervan, 2012), 109.

4. A reading of Adventist history reveals a stark contrast in how leadership was carried out during the early years and what is productive currently.

5. Robert Quinn, *Deep Change* (San Francisco: Jossey-Bass, 1996), 3.

6. Again, we do not have to like this change in leadership dynamics. We do not even have to believe it is a good idea. But we do need to understand how things have changed and prepare ourselves for ministry in our world, not the one we wish we still had. When we forget this, we create an environment in which it will be more difficult for our witness to be embraced. It is all about mission.

7. Stanley, *Deep and Wide*, 12; emphasis in the original.

8. Even though this segment is not about preaching, per se, it is often when the local elder gets up to preach a sermon that the greatest opportunity exists for him or her to deliver a positive, hopeful witness, not just by the words of the sermon but by the entire demeanor he or she presents. Do not take yourself too seriously. Allow the joy God has placed in your life to stream through you and brighten the lives of others.

9. Phil A. Newton and Matt Schmucker, *Elders in the Life of the Church: Rediscovering the Biblical Model for Church Leadership* (Grand Rapids, MI: Kregel, 2014), 50.

10. Monte Sahlin, "What Is the Role of Elders in Large Congregations?" (presentation, Sligo, Maryland, Seventh-day Adventist Church, January 1998).

11. Frank Viola, *The Untold Story of the New Testament Church* (Shippensburg, PA: Destiny Image, 2004), 20.

12. Mission, as presented in the New Testament, is rather comprehensively discussed in Clinton Wahlen, "Mission in the New Testament," in *Mission, Message, and Unity of the Church*, ed. Ángel Manuel Rodríguez (Silver Spring, MD: Biblical Research Institute, 2013).

13. The term *canon* has an interesting history. But for our purposes, it refers to the group of documents that the church came to recognize as Scripture. The process of achieving this recognition was slow, and several of the books in the New Testament, such as Hebrews and James, were not accepted into the canon everywhere until much later. The canon was not complete until the fourth century, and even today, the Roman Catholic Bible contains several documents that most Protestants do not believe belong in the Bible.

14. Stephen Voorwinde, "The Formation of the New Testament Canon," *Vox Reformata* (December 1995): 3, http://www.rtc.edu.au/RTC/media/Documents/Vox%20articles/The-Formation-of-the-NT-Canon-SV-60-1995_1.pdf?ext=.pdf.

15. F. F. Bruce, "Canon," in *Dictionary of Jesus and the Gospels*, ed. Joel B. Green, Scot McKnight, and I. Howard Marshall (Downers Grove, IL: InterVarsity Press, 1992), 95.

16. David A. Huston, "The New Testament Elders" (paper, Urshan Graduate School of Theology symposium, Florissant, MO, May 2, 2003).

17. By calling for an egalitarian approach, I realize am lighting a fire under some of us. The idea that people should be treated as people, regardless of their circumstances, just strikes us as wrong. We have worked hard to get where we are, and those who have been less successful (or those who have not given up as much as we have) should just get in line behind us. But our sense of priority may be askew. God's love is far larger than we admit.

18. Strauch has done useful work in many areas of describing the New Testament model, and I am quite comfortable quoting from him. I differ strongly from him in his rather literalistic emphasis on limiting the role of the elder to men and utterly excluding women.

The Role of the Local Elder

I understand why he does this, given his unwillingness to contextualize the New Testament's male-dominated culture. And he is quite candid in rejecting the idea of stepping outside the New Testament model in order to reach contemporary audiences, who he admits will find his stance unacceptable. Still, I persist in using a resource when what he says is helpful to our present topic.

19. Alexander Strauch, *Biblical Eldership* (Colorado Springs, CO: Lewis and Roth, 1995), 32; emphasis in the original.

20. This is emphasized in order to bracket other conversations about the importance of the role of the local elder. But this is in no way intended to diminish the designated role of the pastor in Protestantism, or specifically in Seventh-day Adventism. The historical pathways we have taken to arrive at our current models make sense in context. I am merely pointing to a possible expanded role for elders where circumstances demand it.

21. There are few areas of Adventist life that stir others' curiosity as much our approach to diet. The same fascination existed in New Testament times. In both settings, an interest in vegetarianism drew (and draws) less concern than our rejection of unclean foods. Indeed, the idea that in order to become an Adventist one must give up bacon or shrimp serves as a major obstacle for some potential members.

22. George Knight, *Organizing to Beat the Devil* (Hagerstown, MD: Review and Herald®, 2001), 34.

23. In the optional coursework associated with this book at the Adventist Learning Community website, there is a rather extensive resource dedicated to the role of the elder in Adventist history, which is approached in a somewhat similar fashion to this discussion on biblical history. For purposes of space, that resource is not repeated here.

CHAPTER 3

The Elder as Shepherd and Teacher

And now, a word to you elders of the church. I, too, am an elder; with my own eyes I saw Christ dying on the cross; and I, too, will share his glory and his honor when he returns. Fellow elders, this is my plea to you: Feed the flock of God; care for it willingly, not grudgingly; not for what you will get out of it but because you are eager to serve the Lord.
—1 Peter 5:1, 2, TLB

The two previous chapters of this book reviewed a few of the overall concepts shaping the work of the elder. They discussed the elder's role in leading the contemporary church; looked at some of the key elements in history that contribute to the role of the elder in the Bible, especially in terms of the New Testament; and discussed a few things about the impact of early Adventism.

In this third chapter, we will explore in more detail the various parts of what the elder actually *does* to help the church become what Jesus intended it to be in these end times. At the center of this conversation is the character of the witness the church is called to deliver, led by the pastor and elder, along with some of the tools that contribute to success. In the first part of the chapter, we will examine the elder as an *undershepherd*, assisting the pastor in his or her work of organizing the church for mission, and then sometimes serving as the *shepherd*—especially in a smaller church or a district church that has no pastor present for much of the time. In the second part, we will look specifically at the *teaching* role the local elder holds, helping communicate a larger vision of Adventism in these end times.[1]

Putting these two parts of the conversation first in the discussion of what the elder actually does indicates that they are in some ways the two most important functions of the local elder's work. Before this conversation begins, we must address something intimately tied to both shepherding and teaching and the intended outcome from both—and that is the matter of how we sustain members in a growing spiritual experience.

There is a difference between a member and a disciple. The process by which we become fully functioning Christian disciples can also be described as forming habits of grace. This means that what we as leaders of the church are attempting to do in ministering to our members—through shepherding and teaching—is to lead them deeper into the life of faith, which is associated with forming lifelong habits that help sustain them even in the darkest of times.

In the important book *Habits of Grace*, David Mathis describes his simple, compelling approach to these themes: "In particular, I am eager to help Christians young and old simplify their approach to their various personal habits of grace, or spiritual disciplines, by highlighting the three key principles of ongoing grace: hearing God's voice (his word), having his ear (prayer), and belonging to his body (fellowship)."[2] What Mathis is suggesting is that whatever approach we take to forming good habits that sustain us in our Christian experience, God's Word, prayer, and Christian fellowship in the church will be at the center. We can list as many spiritual disciplines as we want (many writings on the topic list as many as ten or more), but when we come right down to it, growth in Christ comes through studying the Bible, praying, and engaging with the church in ministry.

In this chapter, we will explore how we help our members form lifelong habits that enable them to survive contemporary life. This is not a complex or demanding process that only some form of super Christian may achieve. It is the Bible; it is prayer; and it is making the church a true family. But our hope is not just to be a skilled Bible reader, someone with gifts for prayer, or a faithful church attendee; our hope is to lead our members into a deeper relationship with Jesus. We are talking about *process* but also about *outcome*.

That said, the deeper relationship with Jesus we are addressing has context and structure. Peter urges the local church leader to "feed the flock of God" (1 Peter 5:2, TLB). This is Job Training 101 for the local elder: "Feed my sheep" (John 21:17, NIV). Peter is not speaking to Christians in general here. Instead, he addresses this "word to you elders of the church" (1 Peter 5:1, TLB). He is speaking to those who have been acknowledged as "elders of the church"—the lay members of the congregation who have accepted God's call to lead out in local ministry.

If you are a local elder, then in this passage of Scripture Peter is speaking directly to you. Peter is using a metaphor that was familiar to the audiences of his time, saying in essence: "Whatever else you do in church leadership, be sure to feed the flock." The implication, first of all, is that the flock *needs* feeding. The sheep are largely unable to feed themselves and will look to the shepherd to provide guidance in taking them to the places where food and water can be found.

The local elder will be asked to perform duties that may increasingly fall under the description of a lay pastor (the *pastoral* role comes from the background of sheepherding). But the relationship between the shepherd and undershepherd must be artfully defined. The pastor and elder support each other. They each bring a set of distinctive attributes that makes the contributions of the other more compelling.

The pastor in the North American Division

Our general approach in North American Adventism is to have salaried professional pastors in every church, even if the church is part of a district. These are men and women who have been exposed to broad theological training in undergraduate programs and then at the Seventh-day Adventist Theological Seminary at Andrews University, or at some other authorized pastoral training center in one of our colleges or universities.[3] But our preferences do not always prevail.

Another reality is that an increasing number of pastors who enter the flow of ministry in North America are coming through alternative channels. Not only are some being trained in regional educational facilities but some also come into pastoral work from other forms of denominational employment, such as literature evangelism, Bible teaching, chaplaincy, and church administration. A few have even been trained in other denominations and have become Adventists later in life.

One final factor affecting the expansion of the local elder's role is that we in North America are approaching a crisis point for full-time pastoral workers. Significant numbers of older Adventist pastors are retiring or are on the verge of retiring. And the number of young men entering the ministry is insufficient to fill the gap. This will result in fewer and fewer well-trained pastors unless we begin training more women to fill these roles or approve other models for ministry. Tied to this is the conferences' reduced ability to afford as many pastors as they once did, as costs for health insurance and retirement benefits escalate and generational dynamics result in fewer and fewer tithe payers. As the available funding shrinks, other options may have to be considered.

Some denominations have addressed similar crises by encouraging pastors to hold other full-time jobs while pastoring churches on the side. The opposition to this is quite strong in the current leadership of the Seventh-day Adventist Church, with good reason; but one wonders what the future will hold, given today's demographic and fiscal trends. At any rate, when we look at reasons why the church might expand the role of local elders, the availability of full-time, well-trained pastors has to be considered.

Feeding the sheep today
As already noted, the specific biblical mandate for the elder in local church leadership is to feed the flock. Jesus specifically asked Peter to do this, which may have influenced his later effort to urge elders to do so (John 21:17). But what sort of feeding is being referred to here? As mentioned in the previous chapter, the local church in New Testament times was a small house church, set up by an apostle who was passing through the area but was overseen by a elder who had been chosen by the congregation.[4] These shepherds were called to do whatever was needed to make sure the flock flourished and that the church was effective in its witness to the broader community.

We understand that the flock is not maintained just by eating grass. As Christian sheep, we are to minister to the community and to encourage one another. That certainly means doing whatever it takes to make sure that the flock survives in the face of challenges in the local setting, but the implications in the New Testament almost certainly mean that elders are also called to keep the flock *healthy*, which is a compelling metaphor. Feeding the sheep means keeping the membership healthy.

A healthy flock, then, would be well fed. It would be protected from the unique dangers in the environment. In addition, it would be a flock organized so that healthy social interactions occur. And making the leap to modern times, it would be one that achieves its mission—reaching out to the community in ways that accommodate the people's needs. One of the functions of the local elder is to become a "generalist" within the congregation.

Admittedly, the role of a shepherd is somewhat unfamiliar in our urban, fast-paced culture. We may have never seen a sheep close up (other than its contribution to a sweater), so it probably takes some effort to provide a contemporary filter.

In Old Testament times, young David was a shepherd, caring for his father's flocks. Shepherding was not a job for the most gifted or powerful young men in the family. Those men often trained to be soldiers and were sent off as soon as possible to bring glory to the family name. But during one of the times when the enemies of God's people—led by the giant Goliath—were about to overwhelm Israel, the young shepherd David emerges to fulfill a heroic role. The story is told in 1 Samuel:

> Saul answered David, "You can't go and fight this Philistine. You're too young and inexperienced—and he's been at this fighting business since before you were born."
>
> David said, "I've been a shepherd, tending sheep for my father. Whenever a lion or bear came and took a lamb from the flock, I'd go after it, knock it down, and rescue the lamb. If it turned on me, I'd grab it by the throat, wring its neck, and kill it. Lion or bear, it made no difference—I killed it. And I'll do the same to this Philistine pig who is taunting the troops. . . . God, who delivered me from the teeth of the lion and the claws of the bear, will deliver me from this Philistine."
>
> Saul said, "Go. And God help you!" (1 Samuel 17:33–37, *The Message*)

Notice Saul's rather stunned reaction to David's speech. While Saul thought David was a mere shepherd, in David's mind, protecting the sheep from the many dangers in the environment was part of his daily routine. He was simply saying to God: "Here am I, send me." David went, and the rest is history. Rather than a sword and shield, David used a sling and several river stones. Even though he had not been trained as a soldier, he had been trained as a protector—and he used what he had.

What we see in this story is that local church leadership requires a tenacity and creativity that few other roles within the religious community demand. The typical sorts of training that pastors receive, including the ability to read the Bible in its original languages and then delve into the depths of theology, are not offered to the average local elder, who may be an auto mechanic, a press operator, or a tax accountant. But here is the point: God has still led in the elder's life. God has been preparing for the challenges ahead, even when the person did not have any idea that being an elder might be in the future. And the way in which many of these practical experiences can substitute for some parts of the more formal pastoral training is something we need to take into account. Seventh-day Adventists are, in fact, the heirs of William Miller and the other early Adventist leaders who did not have formal training in theology, or any other leadership skill, but trusted in God's gifts.

Alexander Strauch writes the following in his book *Biblical Eldership*: "A major part of the New Testament elders' work is to protect the local church from false teachers. As Paul was leaving Asia Minor, he summoned the elders of the church in Ephesus for a farewell exhortation. The essence of Paul's charge is this: *guard the flock—wolves are coming*."[5] This thematic element—that we need to "guard the flock" because the "wolves are coming"—deserves some reflection. The apostle Paul wanted the early church to understand that there would be men and women coming into the church in the years ahead who would seek to lead it astray. They would try to lead it in ways that were contrary to the gospel he was preaching, and the local elders he was ordaining (in this case, in Ephesus) needed to understand how best to deal with them.[6]

There can be no question that in the end times local Adventist elders can expect similar attacks by men and women who would confuse our members and lead them away from the gospel. Theological "wolves" are coming to threaten Seventh-day Adventism. Ellen White writes the following:

Peter was inspired to outline conditions that would exist in the world just prior to the second coming of Christ. "There shall come in the last days scoffers," he wrote, "walking after their own lusts, and saying, Where is the promise of His coming? for since the fathers fell asleep, all things continue as they were from the beginning of the creation." . . . Not all, however, would be ensnared by the enemy's devices. As the end of all things earthly should approach, there would be faithful ones able to discern the signs of the times. While a large number of professing believers would deny their faith by their works, there would be a remnant who would endure to the end.[7]

With these words, Ellen White warns us that in these very end times there will be "faithful ones" who will stand up against men and women who argue that things should always be the same. Ellen White reminds us that the local church must be led by elders able to "discern the signs of the times." The sheep may be utterly helpless in the face of their own flawed tendencies (when other animals attack, sheep commonly stand and watch while other members of the flock are eviscerated, instead of running away, let alone mounting any sort of common defense). The shepherds are called to protect the sheep, but protecting the flock is not just about fighting off enemies. It also includes pursuing and rescuing lost or straying sheep. The thing is, sheep wander. Sheep get lost. Our job is to wrap our arms around them and deliver them from whatever comes along.

This brings me to a brief interlude in my story. If you are a younger Adventist reader, a question may have been building in your mind as you read the past few pages: *Does this imagery of a helpless sheep fit me?* Few young Adventist members believe they are as stupid or helpless as the sheep that have been depicted or that they need someone to come along and heroically rescue them. Therefore, those of us who are older should approach "protecting the flock" with more subtlety and nuance than we have in the past.

Among the greatest dangers to the younger sheep is the tendency some of us in leadership have to drift from the freedom of the gospel to the prison of various forms of legalistic and literalistic thinking. Instead of encouraging our members to be bold and joyous in Christ, far too many of us have our noses buried in rules and policies, determined to make sure everyone in the church toes up to the lines we have drawn, because, after all, they are just helpless sheep and need to be led.

In my office at the Seventh-day Adventist world headquarters, I shared a suite with a couple of other ministries, including Children's Ministries and *Message* magazine. The Children's Ministries office featured a huge poster on the wall portraying a young child with his hands raised in victory. The caption read, "Be bold for Jesus." I took more than a little motivation from that poster every time I walked out of my office. We all need to be a bit more "bold for Jesus." Our younger members need to be affirmed for what they bring to the table. We need to value their enthusiasm and find our own hope in supporting them.

Getting back to the sheep metaphor, contrasting the specific jobs of the pastor and the elder may help. While the role of the shepherd is sometimes to get ahead of the sheep and point the way, it is typically the job of the *sheepdog* to run along behind, nipping at the heels of slow sheep and running out to the edges to drive the wanderers back to the main body. (I am *not* arguing that pastors are to play this lead role, while local elders are to follow along behind, nipping at the heels of the members. I am not saying that. But I want you to keep these two distinct roles [shepherd and sheepdog] clearly in mind.) The sheepdog is small and fast and clearly understands that its role is not to lead from the front. As long as the sheep are heading in the right direction, the sheepdog pads along with them, serving as a reminder that they are going in the right direction and that they should keep it up. The sheep know by instinct where food and water are located, so they do not require much urging. But they *are* sheep, so every once in a while, a wayward sheep wanders off toward the edges. But correcting sheep has to be done without terrifying them so much that they just lie down and die.

The nipping that the typical sheepdog does must be carried out with a bit of humor and gentleness. It is *not* the sheepdog's job to cut out bad sheep and drive them away from the flock. The sheepdog does not decide when a sheep has been too much trouble for the shepherd to endure any longer. Some of us in the church today are occasionally confused over this aspect.[8] It is the sheepdog's job to protect the flock by gentle nudging, and if the dog drives the sheep, it is only to get them back to the center.

A church experience so good that people are drawn

Having worked beside many local elders, I know that one of their greatest frustrations with the larger church is when we do well-intentioned things that turn out to be less helpful than expected. For example, we may produce resources that do not work in the real world or write policies that hurt people. Here are a few ideas to enable your shepherding to have the best possible outcomes:

First, as a local elder, be upfront with your members about the dreams and hopes that motivate you. Everything we do is personal, whether we intend it to be or not. Some of us do not realize how much the world has changed and how difficult ministry is if we only use the approaches that once worked well.[9] For example, our members today generally do not know a great deal about how to reach secular people. There are many books and articles that offer suggestions on how to do this, and some of them have been cited already.[10] But our "better true stories" need to dominate our witnessing as we describe our faith in terms that resonate with contemporary audiences. We need to help our members understand how postmodern and secular audiences respond. This sometimes involves being upfront about ourselves and our own challenges. What works is personal; people respond not just to stories but to *our* stories.

Second, support positive approaches, based on hope and wholeness. As Adventists, we have tended to chide one another over what we need to be doing or how we need to be living so that Jesus can come. But when we describe mission largely in terms of our denominational journey, we sometimes obscure our witness. Reaching the contemporary unchurched *is* our contemporary Adventist mission. There is much in what we teach that coincides with the modern psyche, especially in terms of our witness to hope and wholeness, but we need to put in the time to understand our communities' needs and phrase our witness to them in positive terms that capture their imagination. There is so much positive stuff we could be doing, as opposed to merely attacking others for their lack of enthusiasm.[11]

Third, we need to maximize our members' gifts. Part of our challenge, as local elders, is doing community assessment, so we must understand the needs we are addressing in the community, including those of our own members. In either case, we need to focus on matching our members to the challenge. At the time of this writing, the churches in Los Angeles just finished a health fair, during which more than eight thousand people were given free dental and medical services.[12] Our members and friends were there to serve the community. Imagine the impact of this. These are the "better true stories" we should be telling. And our members are often capable of things we do not begin to dream they can do.

Finally, we need to help revitalize the church experience itself. The Adventist worship service is a time of conflict in many churches when it should be seen through the eyes of opportunity and mission. Contemporary worship styles are seen by many as disruptive, and various segments of the church fight vigorously to prevent them from being adopted. Others are deeply moved by some of these contemporary approaches and probably would not attend our services without some effort to change the traditional worship styles we have offered. We should find ways of sitting down together to create combined worship experiences that have elements that appeal to various audiences (as opposed to merely reacting to specific voices in the church). We can do this, and we must.

The Adventist elder as teacher

We now move to the second section of this conversation, emphasizing the role of the local elder as teacher. A passage of Scripture guides our conversation: "Let the elders who rule well be considered worthy of double honor, especially those who labor in preaching and teaching; for the scripture says, 'You shall not muzzle an ox when it is treading out the grain,' and, 'The laborer deserves his wages' " (1 Timothy 5:17, 18, RSV).

There are many ways to share the gospel, of course; and many ways for the local elder to present the distinctive teachings of Adventism, from the subtle to the overt. But our access to those ways must be filtered through our broad understanding of the Adventist mission in North America. We have to ask ourselves: Are we Adventists only here to deliver a message of warning about impending doom, or are we also here to demonstrate the positive truth of the gospel by the lives we live? Is it just *message* that shapes our witness, or is it a redemptive personal interaction too?[13] I am talking about the elements that make up better storytelling. And our real question has to do with what makes for good storytelling.

In the book of Mark, we find a depiction of Jesus' teaching efforts: "As he went ashore he saw a great throng, and he had compassion on them, because they were like sheep without a shepherd; and he began to teach them many things" (Mark 6:34, RSV).

This passage can be seen as a transition between shepherding and teaching. The disciples often called Jesus "Teacher," and it is clear by His daily routine that He saw His role in those terms. Moreover, He specifically said that He had come to teach us about the Father.[14] Mark inserts his own interpretation into the story at this point, telling us that he believed that Jesus taught these people the way He did because He saw that they were "like sheep without a shepherd." Mark is telling us that even though these men and women were seemingly religious people, they were somehow unfulfilled and poorly challenged by the teaching they were receiving from the religious leaders of the day. The people Jesus was addressing were apt to wander into confusion; they had difficulty getting their minds around matters of deep spiritual importance in the ways God wanted. Still, they were longing for something more personal—which they found in Jesus. Many of us may find ourselves among those in the crowd Jesus saw from the boat. We are Adventists. We are religious people. Yet we are unfulfilled in some ways, looking for something that touches us more deeply and equips us better for daily life.

Why was Jesus so touched? Because He loved the sheep and because they were *His* sheep, there was no limit to what He would have done to keep them safe. As local elders, the members of the Adventist Church in North America, along with the unchurched in our communities, are *our* sheep, and we, too, need to extend considerable compassion in reaching out to them. The solution Jesus found was in His effort to "teach them many things." In some ways, the role of the elder as teacher parallels this dynamic. We, too, are to be teachers who are driven by compassion, choosing to minister to people who are sometimes ungrateful and, at times, more than willing to act contrary to what we have urged.

In that sense, we are called to undertake the sometimes thankless task of teaching and then teaching the same things again, even when we know many in our audience are not really paying attention or are not likely to take what we have said seriously.[15] Additionally, we need to understand that we must sometimes "teach them many things," too, meaning that we must approach our members in a wide variety of ways, continually seeking methods that will reach them in all their diversity.

We take up this thankless task because Jesus is in our lives, placing His own compassion in our hearts. We do it because the sheep we serve are *our* sheep, and we have set our will to lead them on the pathway that goes to heaven, regardless of how poorly our efforts are appreciated or how constantly we need to repeat things they should have learned. As the apostle Paul puts it: "For the love of Christ leaves us no choice, when once we have reached the conclusion that one man died for all and therefore all mankind has died. His purpose in dying for all was that men, while still in life, should cease to live for themselves, and should live for him who for their sake died and was raised to life" (2 Corinthians 5:14, 15, NEB).

Serving others because Jesus' compassion is in our hearts describes the pattern the apostle Paul presented in 2 Corinthians 3:18, when he wrote that it is by beholding Jesus that we are changed. When we observe Jesus, allowing His Spirit to touch us, we are gradually being transformed into more sympathetic men and women who are able to do things that would have been impossible for us without His transformation. This includes local elders telling our "better true stories" in increasingly compelling ways, even when the task proves challenging.

My wife, Brenda, teaches music (piano and voice) to some fifty children and adults. She does this in our home, and I often get to listen in. One of the roles I play in the "family business" is that I get to hear what the children do not ever hear—which is to say, the things she would like to say to them when they do not perform well but restrains herself from saying. These include such phrases as, "He had two weeks to study that one page of music theory, and he hadn't opened the book!" Or, "She told me her child had studied every day, when it's obvious he didn't study once!" Now let me bracket this by saying that Brenda loves teaching her students, and it gives her great satisfaction to see how they progress.

Brenda would never say anything to discourage her students or embarrass their parents. But I have observed that teaching music is not all fun and games. So when I think of the role of the elder as teacher, I filter it through the view of the personal sacrifices required in order to do it well.

The parable of the mustard seed also reminds me of those music students: "The kingdom of heaven is like a mustard seed, which a man took and planted in his field. Though it is the smallest of all seeds, yet when it grows, it is the largest of garden plants and becomes a tree, so that the birds come and perch in its branches" (Matthew 13:31, 32, NIV). When I read this text, I think of those students who struggled to find middle C on the piano when they started, but who then go on, in just a few months, to play confidently and are well on their way to a lifetime of music enjoyment. And I think about the stone we have placed prominently in our front yard, which the students pass when coming for their lessons, that reads, "Teachers plant for eternity."

My point is that people in the church community expect local elders to do more than merely manage meetings. They expect more from us than to appear behind the pulpit from time to time to offer the announcements or deliver an occasional prayer. They are looking to us to preach when the pastor is not in residence and, even more, in every interaction to have something to say that touches their hearts and teaches them something of significance—something that impacts their daily lives and gives them hope for the coming week.[16] We want them to say, "When our local elder preaches, I am so blessed."

The elder and the use of the Bible

Let us now spend some time on how the local elder uses the Bible to lead members. In our Adventist culture, as "people of the Book," we expect our elder to be someone who uses the Bible carefully and with some skill. What this means, technically, is that we expect the elder to use good hermeneutics.[17] The elder should be able to build a seamless and biblical argument on whatever theme he or she is approaching. We expect the elder to be able to tell good stories and draw reasonable implications that reassure us that what we have always believed is still credible today. And even more, we expect him or her to do so in ways that honor the Bible, rather than misuse it.[18]

This is a tough demand. It involves allowing the authors of the various books of the Bible to speak in context, neither twisting passages of Scripture to defend our personal views nor dragging our members out to the edges of Adventist thought, as slaves to biblical literalism. Most of our local elders *do* use the Bible well, in the context of our distinctive Adventist culture, but there is also a need for us, as lay pastors, to be able to encourage members to think outside the box from time to time as well.

Here is the problem: if we do not stretch the minds of the members of the congregation, some key segments of the audience will be disappointed, including our younger members who have a tendency to see church attendance as a waste of time. So how do we preach or teach biblically and also teach in ways that touch the hearts of our harder-to-reach audiences? Here are some ideas:

First, we need to teach in ways that are faithful to our "better true stories." We need to admit that Adventists in North America are a rather unique group—perhaps even somewhat distinctive from Adventists in other parts of the world.[19] For example, we expect messages to be presented with intellectual integrity and consistency and that the ideas will be buttressed by support from the Bible and Ellen White.

Obviously, the age of our audience and other forms of segmentation within the culture provide some differences in style, and even somewhat in theme, but what we say in all settings should be more alike than different. It is important for what we say to feel relatively orthodox, but it needs to be an orthodoxy that centers on the gospel and takes into account what makes sense in contemporary terms.[20]

Next, we need to develop good overall storytelling skills. Jesus commonly taught through storytelling and did so for reasons that still apply. It is not just children who respond well to stories. We all find it easier to understand what is being presented to us as a lesson if it is delivered in a format that captures our imagination in the way stories do. Even the more detailed theological writings of the apostle Paul, for example, can be tied to the details found in Acts. Indeed, Ellen White's most compelling writings are her books on biblical history—her Conflict of the Ages series, starting with *Patriarchs and Prophets* and ending with *The Great Controversy*.[21]

It is true that after we tell the story, we need to be fairly explicit in drawing from the story the lessons we want to teach. The implications of a good story need to be emphasized in simple terms that hit home for people, rather than merely cited as biblical or theological proof. Good preaching is often centered on a good story, and the best preachers, songwriters, politicians, and teachers wrap their most persuasive ideas within stories.

Finally, our words must accurately reflect a true biblical worldview. This is said with a bit of tongue in cheek because the language of a "biblical worldview" is sometimes misused. We need to understand that a "biblical worldview" often merely implies "political correctness." For example, in his book on the spiritual health of evangelical Christianity, researcher Brad Waggoner makes the case that in order to be considered evangelical, a rather specific set of doctrines must be accepted: "The Christian faith has many important doctrinal components. Claiming to be a follower of Jesus Christ implies that a person embraces a Christian worldview. Over time, a strong correlation must exist between a person's claim to believe in Jesus and his or her understanding and belief in what the Bible teaches."[22] Waggoner goes on to list the tests he would give to the person who claims to be a Christian.

If a "biblical worldview" means whatever is popular in evangelical ranks, Adventists are in a bit of trouble because we may not quite mean the same things that some other evangelicals do, particularly in the areas of social justice and eschatology. But a *true* biblical worldview would be one centered on the story of a loving Father who sent His Son to die in our place. A true biblical worldview would be full of grace and generosity, rather than merely requiring rigid theological agreement. In these pages, I have made the case several times already that *balance* is the key for us in creating a healthy church.

Often, it is in the places where we *differ* from evangelical political correctness that the genius of Adventism can be found. What our members are seeking in increasing numbers is leaders who are bold and sensitive, conservative and responsive to contemporary issues. For our audiences, we need to teach in ways that show our awareness of their varied needs and respect their differing points of view. We also need the ability to say something that balances all these, and far more, with integrity.

We also need to be careful that our awareness of the diverse audiences sitting in the congregation is not paralyzing. It is not that we avoid controversy or offer only bland, safe interactions. I do not want to make you tentative. Rather, we must show intentionality in what we say and do, along with maturity that avoids some of the extremes that often tempt us. These alternative approaches should be acknowledged as contributing to our broader and yet-developing understanding.

Finding our place in the Adventist story
The Adventist elder is in a place of remarkable opportunity. Waves of thought on how to say or do things change from generation to generation, and sometimes new responses to questions are needed in order to meet the emerging opportunities—and a thoughtful elder can deliver this. As Adventist believers, we are not always going to be on the side of current thinking, and current thinking is not always better than traditional thinking. Instead of becoming frustrated by this complexity, we need to be creative in building new bridges that connect the old with the new, with language that attempts to broaden our story. When our younger members challenge us with tough questions, they are not looking for a way out of Adventism. *Rather, they are asking us to help them stay in Adventism.*

As David Kinnaman and Gabe Lyons put it in their book, *unChristian*, in describing what is so different about today's audience: "They do not trust things that seem too perfect, accepting that life comes with its share of messiness and off-the-wall experiences and people."[23] Responding well to this expectation of untidiness is something the local elder is quite capable of doing. But in order to do it, we must be willing to be stretched. The best way to teach is to smile and offer our best answer while admitting that we do not know everything and that we may need to bring it up to Jesus when we are all in the kingdom.

Enabling the Adventist local elder to teach well in a contemporary context is one of our most compelling Adventist challenges. The teaching role of the local elder is a unique opportunity to tell the story of a loving Father personally, in terms of our own experience of the goodness and grace of God. Achieving success in the teaching role is not about theological speculation or mindless traditionalism. Rather, it is about saying, "Look, all I know is that God has done some amazing things in my life, and I believe He wants to do them in yours as well."

1. It is important to contrast these two roles with the more structurally significant views that entered the church during the second and fourth centuries, when powerful church leaders began to be termed *bishops* and *popes*. For a more detailed discussion of this transition and its challenges, see Denis Fortin, "The Holy Spirit and the Church," in *Message, Mission, and Unity of the Church*, ed. Ángel Manuel Rodríguez (Silver Spring, MD: Biblical Research Institute, 2013), 320.

2. David Mathis, *Habits of Grace* (Downers Grove, IL: InterVarsity Press, 2015), 15.

3. At the present time, several of our denominational universities in North America are offering coursework that proposes to be similar in content and proficiency to that offered at the seminary at Andrews University.

4. There are many resources available on how the early Christian church was organized and the ways in which it functioned. Some of these resources are shaped by specific doctrinal or theological intent, but even those are usually helpful. I recommend, in particular, George Barna and Frank Viola, *Pagan Christianity?* (Carol Stream, IL: Tyndale, 2002); Frank Viola, *The Untold Story of the New Testament Church* (Shippensburg, PA: Destiny Image, 2004); Robert Banks, *Going to Church in the First Century* (Jacksonville, FL: Seedsowers, 1990); and Phil A. Newton and Matt Schmucker, *Elders in the Life of the Church: Rediscovering the Biblical Model for Church Leadership* (Grand Rapids, MI: Kregel, 2014). These are also listed in the appendix at the end of the book.

5. Alexander Strauch, *Biblical Eldership* (Colorado Springs, CO: Lewis and Roth, 1995), 17; emphasis in the original. Paul's message begins in Acts 20:17.

6. These people entered the church very soon after Peter and Paul wrote these warnings, and the struggle to maintain a clear gospel emphasis has been one that continues even to our own day.

7. Ellen G. White, *The Acts of the Apostles* (Mountain View, CA: Pacific Press®, 1911), 535, 536.

8. Church discipline is required, but some of us tackle the job with unappealing enthusiasm and pursue it aggressively when gentler, more persuasive approaches might work better.

9. During the early years of the church in North America and in Australia, the cornerstones of evangelism were lay members selling pamphlets on religious themes. In addition, when tent meetings were set up, the entire community came out. (This was obviously before television provided in-home entertainment.)

10. Some of the better books are the following: Thom Schultz and Joani Schultz, *Why Nobody Wants to Go to Church Anymore* (Loveland, CO: Group Publishing, 2013); Andy Stanley, *Deep and Wide: Creating Churches Unchurched People Love to Attend* (Grand Rapids, MI: Zondervan, 2012); Will Mancini, *Church Unique: How Missional Leaders Cast Vision, Capture Culture, and Create Movement* (San Francisco: Jossey-Bass, 2008); David Kinnaman with Aly Hawkins, *You Lost Me: Why Young Christians Are Leaving Church . . . and Rethinking Faith* (Grand Rapids, MI: Baker Books, 2011); and Thom Rainer and Eric Geiger, *Simple Church* (Nashville, TN: B&H, 2011).

11. In my job at the NAD, one of the challenges I have been given—and gladly accept—is to help develop an Innovation Center, where we will bring in people from various

settings to work on better ways to do ministry, seeking those key innovations that we will need for sustainable success.

12. Andrew McChesney, "Mega-Clinic Provided 'Miraculous' $38.4 Million in Services in Los Angeles," Adventist News Network, May 19, 2016, https://news.adventist.org/en/all-news/news/go/2016-05-19/mega-clinic-provided-miraculous-384-million-in-services-in-los-angeles/.

13. Please understand as we begin this section of our conversation that I am not at all seeking to diminish our delivery of the message. Rather, the message will be unheard and ignored by contemporary audiences if we do not substantiate its appeal by being winsome, engaged men and women.

14. Indeed, Jesus said there was coming a time when He would no longer use figurative language but would tell us plainly about the Father (see John 16:25). Indeed, I will make the case that it was the loving character of the Father that Jesus was most committed to sharing. One of the great challenges of Adventism in these end times, as especially represented through Ellen White's great controversy theme, is to demonstrate that the Calvinist and Reformed theology picture of the distant, cold God, who unilaterally decides who will be saved and who will be lost, does not in any way reflect the Father Jesus taught us to love.

15. The simple truth is that while we teach in order to help our members grow spiritually, we understand that it is the Holy Spirit that convicts, and we realize that we cannot be overly concerned about the result because what God asks of us is a faithful witness, delivered compassionately. What people do with what we say lies between them and God.

16. I will make this statement repeatedly. One of the major ways both pastors and elders shortchange Adventist congregations is our failure to use the worship service to give members hope for daily living. We preach on themes of interest to us, failing to realize that many of our members are on a knife-edge, coming to church hoping someone will reach out to them with a witness to God's power to make things better.

17. One definition of *hermeneutics* is that it is the study of how we form the beliefs we have, including what sorts of resources we use to defend those beliefs.

18. Many of us expect to find in our elders' preaching a confirmation of our certainties. We typically do not want to be challenged or offered new ideas. What we really want is someone to tell us that we have been right all along and someone who will defend Adventism's distinctive beliefs and assure us of our place on the train to heaven. This is not necessarily a bad thing, but it does limit our witness to some of our modern audiences, who are hoping that we will make some effort, at least, to help them find contemporary pathways to a life of faith.

19. As I say this, I need to be sure I qualify it by acknowledging that even in North America there are nuances about what it means to be an Adventist that require a regional understanding. In today's context, in particular, I should mention an emerging sense of distinctiveness among what might be termed *Western Adventists*, including the West Coast and a few segments just a bit farther east. *California Adventist* has always been a phrase we have understood, but a number of current issues, such as the role of women in the church, are combining to accelerate this distinctive perspective.

20. Orthodoxy is a concept that must be viewed from several perspectives. It entails support for traditional views, but for it to survive, it also requires a rigorous investigation that implies intellectual integrity and a fair analysis of alternative conclusions.

21. It was during Ellen White's sojourn in Australia, after the heated debate over righteousness by faith in 1888, that she wrote one of her most compelling books on Jesus—*The Desire of Ages*. And it was with this book in hand that she brought a call for organizational reform to the 1901 General Conference Session.

22. Brad Waggoner, *The Shape of Faith to Come* (Nashville, TN: B&H, 2008), 31.

23. David Kinnaman and Gabe Lyons, *unChristian: What a New Generation Really Thinks About Christianity . . . and Why It Matters* (Grand Rapids, MI: Baker Books, 2007), 23.

CHAPTER 4

How Nurture Results in Sustainable Church Growth

We recommend ourselves by the innocence of our behaviour, our grasp of truth, our patience and kindliness; by gifts of the Holy Spirit, by sincere love, by declaring the truth, by the power of God. . . . We are . . . the unknown men whom all men know; dying we still live on; disciplined by suffering, we are not done to death; in our sorrows we have always cause for joy; poor ourselves, we bring wealth to many; penniless, we own the world.

—2 Corinthians 6:6–10, NEB

In attempting to meet the needs of our distinctive audiences, including the diversity in our congregations, it is essential that the elder have a broad vision of what he or she can do in ministering to contemporary audiences. In David Kinnaman and Gabe Lyons's groundbreaking book, *unChristian*, they explain the importance of understanding our culture's increasingly diverse audiences, focusing particularly on our young adults: "In many ways, young people perceive the world in very different terms than people ever have before. For example, the lifestyles of Mosaics [millennials] and Busters [Generation Xers] are more diverse than those of their parents' generation, including education, career, family, values, and leisure. Young people do not want to be defined by a 'normal' lifestyle. They favor a unique and personal journey."[1]

The implication Kinnaman and Lyons make—younger audiences are seeking a "unique and personal journey"—shapes much that we say in these pages. The Barna research Kinnaman and Lyons share not only shows that contemporary audiences experience this much more diverse set of interactions in every aspect of life but also that our audiences are in many ways perceiving the world quite differently, including the very language we use to describe that world.

For example, when Adventists begin discussing *diversity*, we tend to think about the ongoing role of Regional Conferences, the lack of leadership opportunities for black pastors in the broader work of the church, or the lack of diversity on various conference, union, or division committees, where few women or people from a variety of ethnicities serve. These are important issues and require our ongoing attention. But we also need to change the contemporary metaphor for diversity: from the traditional "one to many" (one pastor speaking to many people) to "many to many," and even "many to one." This captures the impact of social media and the other changes taking place in modern culture that in many ways redefine what we mean by *diversity*. For contemporary audiences, it is all about cocreation and deeper collaboration, with new targets and strategies tied to fuller engagement.

In the first part of this chapter, we will focus on the expanding role nurture plays in creating and maintaining a healthy congregation when led by a healthy elder. If we do not learn how to put our arms around people—in approaches they find comforting and meaningful—we will continue to lose them. It is about changing our Adventist culture so that contemporary audiences see something in us that speaks to their deepest needs and that allows them to imagine their own spiritual growth taking place as part of the Adventist story.[2] In the second part of the chapter, we will look at a few specific ways in which this focus on nurture results in sustainable church growth. Healthy churches grow symmetrically and in ways that commonly result in high retention of members. So by addressing overall church health we are helping at both ends of ministry—getting and keeping the people we reach.

Choosing pathways toward a healthy church

In this book, I have used the metaphor of the healthy church frequently, intentionally leading us to the point where our conversation in this chapter will make the most sense. For some of us, the idea that the Seventh-day Adventist Church is still *becoming* what it will need to be in the end times may be disturbing. We would rather believe that we already are what we will need to be.

But if there is one key to this entire book, it is in understanding that what we are empowered to do as elders—leading the local congregation in our journey toward a *healthier Adventism*—is essential for these end times. Paul says in 2 Corinthians 6:6–10, "We recommend ourselves by the innocence of our behaviour"(NEB). He runs off a long list of what those who are living as mature, healthy Christians display in their lives. We see that he is talking both about process and outcome.

At issue, then, are the questions: How do we become healthier churches? Is it possible that not all Adventist churches can be called mature and healthy? Is it possible that some of us display characteristics in congregational life that could be termed unhealthy? I am not questioning whether these congregations can become healthy or whether they should not be involved in an effort to become so. But I am asking whether they there yet.[3]

Many of us have endured the hardship of attending—or growing up in—a church that is less than healthy in a number of different ways. And some of us have the bruises and scars to prove it.[4] Not only are members sometimes misused in churches of this complex character but the reputation of that sort of church also is typically quite negative in the communities surrounding it and is bad for the Adventist brand itself.[5]

God's dream for His church
Seventh-day Adventists emerged from the religious excitement of the mid-1800s with a somewhat distinctive understanding of God's dream for His end-time "remnant" people.[6] We believed God had called us into existence at a particular point in time in order to provide a unique witness. This unique witness included two essential elements: First, it focused on hope when it brought a set of distinctive restorationist beliefs and practices, including ideas and observances that we maintained had been lost for centuries. And then it focused on wholeness when it brought a set of engagements with the community that included better living elements and a far more compelling story about the character of God and His love for humanity.[7]

When the local elder is leading the congregation toward God's dream for His church, it becomes increasingly obvious to the community that something special is happening. Moreover, once this dream captures our imagination, the steps that lead to congregational growth are far less complex or demanding. We do not need to desperately twist arms or prove things. Rather, we present a witness so compelling that people just want the blessings of being healthy. If a church makes nurture a significant part of who the members are and how they minister, the impact is going to be felt in ways that commonly result in steady growth. The following are some suggestions on how we might do this:

First, we must intentionally move beyond artifice to transparency. The passage of Scripture that opened the chapter spoke of "unknown men whom all men know." Paul is describing the early Christian believers, who are portrayed as "poor" but "bring wealth to many." The early Adventist Church, in all parts of the world, was characterized by being largely made up of working people and those facing times of crisis. They reached audiences by leading men and women to Jesus and into the healthy warmth of the church. The apostle builds his case by emphasizing that the believers displayed no artifice in what they said and did but rather had a spirit of transparency that enhanced mutual benefit.[8] Everything changes when we become open and transparent, eager for everyone around us to succeed. For example, in the Georgia-Cumberland Conference, a group of elders emerged from the 2010 General Conference Session in Atlanta with a commitment to bring elders together for more collaborative efforts across ethnic and congregational lines. They created an elders' consortium to help empower elders in each congregation. While the program is still in its early stages, the intent clear: to help elders by enhanced fellowship and training, so they are better able to support their pastors and envision a larger mission that includes such things as reviewing church liturgies and sharing best practices.[9]

Many churches today tend to copy what seems to be working somewhere else in the hope that lightning will strike twice. This drove much of what we did at the NAD when we set up the Church Resource Center. We believed that if we could find churches doing good things and if we could then create structured programming based on it that we could make the same "magic" happen in other places. But over time, we learned that it is more complicated than at first glance. It is when we are positive in our interactions and transparent in our efforts that programming is transferable.

Then, we need to explore new and diverse forms of nurture. If we want to keep people in the church and motivate them to bring in others, our members need to find the local congregation to be intentionally nurturing in a wide variety of ways, full of all the "warm fuzzies" that we Adventists are not always good at delivering. No matter what we are teaching people, if we are not at the same time intentionally and passionately loving them, it is a wasted effort. A large part of Kinnaman and Lyons's book, *unChristian,* is dedicated to addressing six negative themes that Kinnaman's research found that contemporary audiences attribute to Christians. Many people see evangelical Christians as

1. hypocritical;
2. too focused on getting converts;
3. antihomosexual;
4. sheltered;
5. too political;
6. and judgmental.[10]

Note that all of these perceptions impede the sort of nurturing church that Jesus asked us to be. Kinnaman and Lyons write, "In studying thousands of outsiders' impressions, it is clear that Christians are primarily perceived for what they stand against. *We have become famous for what we oppose, rather than who we are for.*"[11]

Few matters are of more importance for the Adventist Church's success in these end times than offering a positive witness, based on who we are for, rather than merely what we are against. I would also argue that in churches where nurture is actually made central—where the members of the church are listened to, prayed with, made to feel important, and then set out on a path of ministry that keeps them engaged—good things happen.

In the book *Why Nobody Wants to Go to Church Anymore,* which we discussed in chapter 1, we saw four reasons people why leave the church:

1. "I feel judged."
2. "I don't want to be lectured."
3. "Church people are a bunch of hypocrites."
4. "Your God is irrelevant to my life."

Compare this list to the one we just read from Kinnaman and Lyons and note the rather obvious parallels. The hard-nosed things many of us are doing or saying just do not match up with the needs these people are expressing. *They want to be held and loved, not just judged or lectured.*

"Wait a minute with all this lovey-dovey talk, Elder Day," someone is saying. "You've forgotten that these people are sinners. They *need* to be lectured to and judged. Adventists are called to warn them, 'You're all doomed if you don't confess your sins and start keeping the Sabbath.' "[12] I am not suggesting that we should overlook sin or fail to practice the ways in which God wants people to live. In addition, I am not arguing about where we want to go but about *how we get there*. Conviction of sin is the Holy Spirit's work, not ours. When we try to convict others, we drive them away.

One of the best books describing this process of going from where we are to something better and healthier is Ed Stetzer and Mike Dodson's book *Comeback Churches*. In it, they analyze three hundred churches that were in trouble once but turned around. They write, "Over time, most churches plateau, and most eventually decline. Typically, they start strong or experience periods of growth, but then they stagnate. Patterns and traditions that once seemed special eventually lose their meaning. Churches that were once outwardly focused eventually become worried about the wrong things. They become more concerned about a well-used policy manual than a well-used baptistry."[13]

Could that be us? As a local elder, could that be you or your church? Are our traditions losing meaning for us? Are some of us worrying about the wrong things? Do policies seem to be more important to some of us than nurturing? Think about it. Look around you at what is happening in Adventism today before you answer. We are able to do many things well: We can preach. We can raise money. We hold great committees and provide thoughtful discipline. We can even hold great evangelistic meetings. But far too many of us are more than a little lost when it comes to nurturing and retaining our members.[14] We are not indifferent to keeping those we baptize—just not very good at it. When we at the NAD conducted surveys with pastors, asking them what they most needed from us, they told us repeatedly that what they needed was *discipleship-training resources*. They told us they were not keeping the people they were baptizing and begged us for help.

In addition, nurture must be lodged at the very heart our evangelism. Adventists want the church to grow. But how do we hold on to those we baptize? In answering this question, I would urge you to consider a pamphlet that was produced by Pacific Press and authored by Mark and Ernestine Finley, titled *7 Keys to Successful Church Growth*. They list the steps for successful church growth:

1. Spiritual renewal
2. Inspiring worship
3. Effective training
4. Community outreach
5. Systematic reaping
6. Planned nurture
7. Caring fellowship

"A Word From the Finleys" introduces the pamphlet, where they say: "The seven keys to successful church growth are universal principles that contribute to active, growing churches. When these Christ-centered principles are implemented in local congregations, church members grow spiritually, discover their spiritual gifts, experience the joy of witnessing, and are equipped to serve."[15]

That sounds like a healthy church, right? I want to draw your attention to the sixth of the seven keys the Finleys present—planned nurture. They write, "Nurture and follow-up were significant parts of the disciples' evangelistic strategy. When people accepted Christ, understood His Word, and were baptized, they were integrated into a nurturing body of believers. The book of Acts describes their experience in these words: 'And they continued steadfastly in the apostles' doctrine and fellowship, in the breaking of bread, and in prayers' (Acts 2:42)."[16]

Ellen White also speaks on the issue of nurture and on the role that the local church, led by the elder, should play in helping new members become established in the life of the church. She writes, "After individuals have been converted to the truth, *they need to be looked after.* The zeal of many ministers seems to fail as soon as a measure of success attends their efforts. They do not realize that these newly converted ones need *nursing,—watchful attention, help, and encouragement.*"[17]

Then, we must support ministries in the congregation that explicitly represent nurture. One of the best ways for the local elder to assist in cultivating a nurturing church is to support those ministries that already exist in the church, such as ministry to children, families, shut-ins, or the homeless and hungry. When I was a young district pastor, one of my churches had a group of elderly women who met each week to make quilts. I was told that the previous pastor in that district met each Wednesday and quilted with the women. I was a young pastor, not long out of the seminary, and I just could not see myself quilting. In retrospect, I probably made a mistake in not making more of an effort to support the ladies because one of the ways we nurture is by our presence.

As local elders, we may not feel we have much to offer in a particular nurturing moment. But people can see that we care just by our investment of time, whether it is visiting someone in the hospital, taking someone to lunch, or even attending a baseball game where someone's children are playing. People who are laboring in various ministries notice when we are there. It helps them feel appreciated and valued, and nobody can do this better than the local elder.

Also, nurture is advanced by establishing a strong visitation program. When we spend time with people in their homes, we understand better what is happening in their lives. It is true that members are becoming less comfortable with a person from the church just dropping by, so visitations may need to be scheduled. But before we visit our members, we should take the time to think through what may happen. We should never be "on a mission," which is to say a targeted schedule that we are unwilling to adjust. We should be prepared, friendly, and interested in what is going on in the lives of our members.

In visitation settings, we are nurturing by presence. Moreover, we should be open to allowing a moment to develop where we can help a member in some area of need that was not specifically intended.[18] While we do not wish to be intrusive in our visits, we do want to express the church's interest in that person's circumstances in personal ways, asking reflective questions and interacting with the family. We want our visitation to be memorable. We want our members to be able to say later on, "Wasn't that a good visit?"

It is not about how often you come by or how long you stay. Rather, it is about how nurturing you were.

Finally, nurture is sustained through providing intentional discipleship training. Becoming a nurturing church does not just happen. When we talk about a nurturing church, we are talking about an outcome that is supported by well-conceived discipleship programming. The how-to questions about running a discipleship-training effort are sometimes the very issues too many books and articles fail to address. Discipleship training is all about helping the local congregation experience a deeper, more focused approach to life and ministry.

In an effort to encourage discipleship training in the Seventh-day Adventist Church in North America, the NAD spent time over the past several years working to complete and bring to market the iFollow discipleship-training resource, which is currently available from AdventSource. This new resource is about helping new members become true disciples of Jesus Christ and settle into their faith. It is also about helping existing members fill in the gaps that may occur in their own understanding of being a disciple and leading them into true spiritual maturity. We intentionally created a program that has the inclusive values that reflect Adventism at its best, specifically community, capacity, freedom, service, and witness.[19]

Pathways to sustainable church growth

Of course, any program aimed at helping the church become more nurturing should also anticipate supporting a local commitment to helping members grow. When Adventists talk about church growth, we generally see it in terms of the gospel commission to make disciples. It is our mission to share the gospel so that the men and women in our communities come to accept Jesus as Lord and Savior within the distinct context of Adventism. But as we saw earlier in this chapter, when we think more deeply about evangelism, we realize we want to see sustainable growth in those who choose to follow Jesus. We want new members to stay in the church and contribute to its mission over the long haul. It is in the context of sustainability that research findings suggest that contemporary evangelical Christianity is broken—and that many of the elements that held churches together previously are unraveling.[20] These findings are especially troubling.

As Adventists, we would like to believe that none of that brokenness applies to us. But the research conducted by the NAD Office of Strategic Planning and Assessment shows that our circumstances are not too different from contemporary evangelical Christianity. Our young adults are leaving the church, and those who have remained express concern about the future and are beginning to demand a greater voice in decision making. In light of this, our contemporary Adventist mission must be seen in the broadest possible terms, not just in doing what we have always done but also in changing the overall character of the church so that we begin more systematically reaching more people.

Sustainable church growth is itself a bit more complex than some of us have imagined it might be. We thought we would just hand out copies of *The Great Controversy*, hold more tent meetings, and expand our NET events. We thought that if we poured enough money into church schools that the teachers and principals would eventually figure out how to keep our children in church. But finding a balance between an evangelism that is all about getting new members and a discipleship that is about keeping them is critical for a mature approach to church growth. So our conversation in these pages is not going to be just about growing bigger (or more quickly) but also about our members growing deeper in spiritual maturity.[21]

In one of the books I have read on reaching these same contemporary audiences, Andy Stanley talks about how difficult it is to keep something good going, even when everybody's intentions are lined up properly behind it. He writes, "One of the fundamental realities of organizational life is that systems fossilize with time. The church is no exception. Your church and my church are no exceptions. It takes great effort, vigilant leadership, and at times good, old-fashioned goading to keep a movement moving."[22] Stanley is citing a fact that sociologists and historians understand well: Organizations grow stale with time. They become increasingly preoccupied with restrictive policies and centralized authority. He is not saying we *cannot* revitalize a church that is coming under the rule of bureaucracy, but that doing so is difficult, requiring all sorts of collaborative efforts, including more than a little pushing in the best directions—and often by those at the local level—especially the elder.[23] In these pages, I have argued repeatedly for theological and cultural balance and for focusing our efforts on driving the church back to the center, where the more positive aspects of our witness are found, rather than dwelling on the negativism found at the extreme edges of the church. The strongest possible approach for growing the church is when we do it in a symmetrical way, patterning Jesus.[24]

During His ministry on earth, Jesus anticipated the need for a balanced approach, where an emphasis on the sheer numbers in church membership is filtered through a focus on sustainable spirituality. Jesus said to Peter,

"Simon, son of John, do you love me?"

Peter was upset that he asked for the third time, "Do you love me?" so he answered, "Master, you know everything there is to know. You've got to know that I love you."

Jesus said, "Feed my sheep." (John 21:17, *The Message*)

Jesus wanted Peter and us to understand that of all the things we can do for the Lord in these last days, nothing is of greater impact than working to assure congregational health, with a well-fed church and members developing personal walks with Jesus. He sent us out to make as many disciples as possible, of course; but He also wanted us to create an environment where disciples can grow in Him. Jesus wanted us to understand that church growth in Adventism is not an end in itself—where we focus on being so popular, or so strategic in our efforts, that everyone will want to join. Rather, it is a community, where growth is the by-product of a church dedicated to inspiring members with lives of service.

In their book *Comeback Churches*, authors Stetzer and Dodson speak directly to the typical debate in churches over whether to offer contemporary worship: "The wrong question is whether your church is 'traditional' or 'contemporary' and which is better. The real issue is whether your church is biblically faithful, acting as the presence of Christ in the community at large, able to relate Christ to people in culture, and is on mission."[25] Did you note the four critical sides of this conversation that Stetzer and Dodson describe? In order for a local church to be successful, first, the church must be faithful to the Bible; second, it must become the "presence of Christ in the community." Third, it must be "able to relate Christ to people" within the culture; and fourth, it must stay "on mission." This parallels what we Adventists in North America mean when we describe ourselves as advocates of hope and wholeness. It is not just what we are *doing* that matters or even what we are *saying*. Most of all, it is *who we are perceived to be* in the community.

One of the books I have found to be the most helpful in deepening my own understanding of this broader approach to discipleship is Jonathan Dodson's book *Gospel-Centered Discipleship*. In it, he writes, "Some disciples focus on piety, a category that includes spiritual disciplines and personal holiness. Others prefer to focus on mission, a category that includes social justice, evangelism, and cultural renewal. Gospel-centered discipleship radically alters our approach to both Christian piety and mission. Very often, pious disciples and missional disciples don't mix. Pious disciples tend to withdraw from the world (to draw near to God), while missional disciples tend to engage the world (to bring God near to it)."[26] At the NAD offices, we have been describing this broader approach with the phrase *transformational evangelism*. We certainly have Adventists whose major interest is piety. We have Adventists whose major interest is in compassionate service. And we have Adventists whose primary interest is evangelism. But we have rarely been able to integrate these for a common purpose. Instead, we create "silos" where each of us believe what we are doing is the most important, while discounting the others. When we look at the life of Jesus, we see that He was attempting to show how true discipleship includes *all* of these perspectives.

Developing a focus on God's grace
At one point in the life and ministry of Jesus, the disciples of John the Baptist were growing restless over mission progress. With John in prison, they were confused and uncertain, so John asked them to go see Jesus. When they arrived where Jesus was ministering, John's disciples brought with them the expectations of John's prophetic witness, which was based on Old Testament models. John called on people to repent of their sins and be baptized, which

is why they were a bit perplexed to find Jesus in the streets, being touched by sinners and healing people.

Jesus was providing a new filter through which Christian spirituality—and even Adventist spirituality—was being defined, involving compassionate service to humanity. In the process, Jesus was taking religion several steps deeper. Jesus was saying, "The life of faith isn't just about being a better Jew. Rather, it is also about allowing God's grace to transform us into people who care about others and who minister to their needs in ways that reveal God's grace."[27]

Jesus told John's disciples to look carefully at what was happening in His ministry and view it through Old Testament prophetic eyes, where Israel was called to be a nation of healers and restorers (Isaiah 58:12; 61:1, 2). Then Jesus asked them to go back to John with a story about what they were seeing, featuring this prophetic filter through which God's witness was being defined.[28] In ministering the way He did, Jesus intentionally put His church at odds with traditional religion of all varieties.[29] Jesus was putting the emphasis on delivering a redemptive witness to people, including those that the Jewish religion had typically rejected: the poor, those with diseases, and those on the edges of Jewish culture. Jesus was saying, "My church will grow through compassion, generosity, forgiveness, and healing."

If we want the Seventh-day Adventist Church in North America to grow in the way God intends, then we, too, must grapple with this new filter Jesus is providing. Adventism must begin to see itself more clearly as a *healing community* that reaches out to people in the places where they are hurting and ministers His grace.[30]

Acts of love
In discussing the role of the local elder, I have referred several times to the book *Why Nobody Wants to Go to Church Anymore*. The book makes the assertion that there are four acts of love that will make your church irresistible.[31] (These acts have been condensed for our purposes.)

***Act of love 1: Emphasize* radical hospitality.** Most Adventist elders, I am sure, would argue that our churches *are* hospitable. We promise the evangelist, for example, that if he comes and baptizes people, we will keep them. Within a year or so, however, many of these new members stop attending, not because the evangelist did not do his job, but because we have not done ours. How would radical hospitality be different from what we are typically doing? Our Adventist hospitality can only be called "radical" if we are doing the following:

Authentically welcoming others and being glad to be with them. This *authenticity* is the key. We cannot accomplish this by merely assigning a committee to it. Both the pastor and the elder have to preach it and live it, and the members have to become so deeply committed to it that when people come into the church they are wrapped up in love.

Being a friend, even when it is not our job. The fact is we typically think that being friendly is the job of the pastor or the greeter. But if we want to make a real impact, it can be in helping the church become friendlier by talking about it, conducting training, and using every other avenue available to us to show its importance. Connecting with people *is* the local elder's key mission.

Accepting people, even if we do not like what they are doing. We do not have to give up our distinctiveness or become just like others in terms of dress or practice in order to accept someone for whom Jesus died to save—and who deserves to be treated with respect, kindness, and generosity. As Adventists, we have sometimes pushed aside being accepting, in preference for being right.[32]

Seeing it as something that takes time. Our lack of patience is at the root of much that keeps us from performing radical hospitality. We are looking for quick fixes that get people rapidly into the baptistry. But we cannot be in a hurry when it comes to love and personal engagement.

Allowing it to be unnerving, surprising, and messy. Unconditional love involves reaching out to people with no expectation of receiving anything in return. The kind of church that grows is one where members are not counting, demanding, or expecting. Rather, the church focuses on loving people because God loved us and leaving the rest to the Holy Spirit. When we do this God's way, it is sometimes messy and slow. But straight lines are not part of real hospitality. Let God surprise you.

Act of love 2: Offer fearless conversation. One of our challenges today is finding ways to show people a God who is more accessible. Paul wrote to one of the churches, "I planted the seed in your hearts, and Apollos watered it, but it was God who made it grow" (1 Corinthians 3:6, NLT). We can share our witness, realizing that it is just one part of the story God is telling. It is fearless conversation because we have a story to tell in order for God to use it in His own ways. The apostle Paul once asked, "What shall we say about such wonderful things as these? If God is for us, who can ever be against us?" (Romans 8:31, NLT). So we may offer fearless conversation if we are doing the following:

Honestly seeking to understand where people are coming from. Some are extremely careless in bashing ideas that another person holds. Instead of trying to keep the relationship intact, some try to impose their worldviews on others.

Really listening before speaking. Listening is a lost skill for many of us. We just want to jump in with our opinions. We need to let people know we are listening by the thoughtful responses we make, including forms of nonverbal agreement. We can support what people are saying, even when we do not agree with every detail.

Asking great questions. Far too many of us are satisfied merely asking obvious and predictable questions. We need to show our real interest by asking questions that seek additional information or clarification. People want to engage their brains and hearts. We need to ask questions that are surprising, specific, and personal.

Allowing others to talk, even when we are a bit uncomfortable. So much of our time is spent trying to protect what does not need protecting. As local elders, we can step down from the pulpit while preaching and engage the congregation personally. Examples include speakers who invite members to text questions during the sermon and even answer.[33]

Offering nonjudgmental responses. Often, we will say things such as, "Great idea," praising someone who agrees with us, rather than, "Got it" or, "I'm following you." Let other people's judgment stand. We are fearless in a conversation through simple agreement, without the need to correct.

Trusting the Holy Spirit to be on our side. Too often in the church, we are not really asking our audience for their responses. We are afraid that something will be said that may thwart our intent. But if what we are doing is of God, He will assure its success. Our job is to believe God and then allow the Holy Spirit to drive the conversation where God wants it to go.[34]

***Act of love 3: Experience and express* genuine humility.** We express genuine humility if we are doing the following:

Being radically relational. This means recognizing that we are really all the same, even if we are at different places in our lives. We are all "Becomers."[35] It means being willing to engage with people who are quite different from us and being willing to put aside judgments long enough to emphasize the value of those we are engaged with.

Being open to learning from others with different beliefs. How can we be salt and light if we are unwilling to give others an honest hearing (see Matthew 5:13, 14)? We can learn things from *everyone*.

Being open to learning from people of different ages. Younger people bring a curiosity, freshness, and exuberance to life, while older adults offer wisdom and life experience. It is in our cross-fertilizing that the best ideas emerge. So try to find what is helpful in our interactions with those of a different age grouping.

Putting people first. How many times in church life do rules and policies take precedence over people? For example, Ellen White's most devastating criticisms were aimed at sitting General Conference presidents, who were resorting to political tactics that ignored the broader needs of members.[36] People have to come before policies.

***Act of love 4: Experience* divine anticipation.** Divine anticipation involves living within the mystery and wonder of God, rather than requiring the certainty of policy or tradition. Divine anticipation involves training ourselves to watch for God in action; it tends to be far too messy for some of us. We may be experiencing divine anticipation if we are doing the following:

Realizing God is actively involved—all the time. We need to tune in to what God is doing and align our own plans and practices with His. Far too often, we believe that making the right choice is entirely up to us. We will not see God's hand if we are not looking for it.

Grasping God's power. The power that brought Jesus back from the dead is the same power available to us today. Jesus said, "I tell you the truth, anyone who believes in me will do the same works I have done, and even greater works, because I am going to be with the Father" (John 14:12, NLT). Part of our call as local elders is teaching our churches to expect great things.

Accepting that there are things we cannot explain. We are often determined to have logical answers for everything. But in the Bible, we are reminded:

> "Do you think you can explain the mystery of God?
>   Do you think you can diagram God Almighty?
> God is far higher than you can imagine,
>   far deeper than you can comprehend." (Job 11:7, 8, *The Message*)

Trusting the Holy Spirit. We must find ways to talk about the leading of the Spirit that do not automatically imply fanaticism. Our fear of Pentecostalism must not blind us to the Holy Spirit. We have largely emphasized a head religion, but God needs heart religion too.

Expecting God to show up. God is with us through the entire process of life. He shows up when we are trying new things, learning from our failures, and even when people are standing around, saying, "I told you so." Remember that C. S. Lewis's autobiography was titled *Surprised by Joy*.[37] We should expect God to act in surprising ways.

Trusting God to do what only He can do. What God says He will do in the end times sometimes seems impossible in human terms. That is why we need to trust that He will take care of the impossible stuff. The end times are all about God doing His "new thing" and us following His lead (Isaiah 43:19, NIV).

Telling others in an authentic way what God is doing in our lives. We cannot prove anything to anyone, and especially not postmoderns. But we *can* testify to what God is doing in our lives. We can be God's expert witnesses to His power.

It is all about symmetry over size

The local elder in Adventism wants to see the church grow but not in ways that lack symmetry and are unlikely to last. As local elders, one of our jobs is to maintain this balance, and we must be very clear on where our emphasis is put. We must be deeply committed to being kind, generous, and forgiving. Churches grow when the communities around them perceive them as places where they can find shelter from the storm. We must stop driving them back out into the storm.

1. David Kinnaman and Gabe Lyons, *unChristian: What a New Generation Really Thinks About Christianity . . . and Why It Matters* (Grand Rapids, MI: Baker Books, 2007), 22. Kinnaman and Lyons's intent is to prepare evangelical Christians to engage with an entire generation of young adults who are leaving the church because they believe the church has lost its center. These younger people are saying, in essence: "Yes, we know what Jesus said and did, but we do not see that the contemporary church is reflecting what you say He represented. We're not rejecting Him, but we are rejecting you."

2. One of the major assumptions in the approach we are taking is that we do not merely allow our culture to develop out of our traditional beliefs and practices, but that it is intentionally shaped by our growing understanding of our mission. We do not merely seek protection within our own comfort zone but extend ourselves to reach our contemporary audiences with the good news of a loving God who has provided for our redemption.

3. I am not suggesting that there are no healthy members of these churches. There are usually more than a few—and many more who wish they could be. But the point I am making has to do with the general impression someone from the outside might form on attempting to engage with members. Are we intentional in ministering in effective ways to those in our community who do not come to the table with our own values and expectations? When they see problems in the community, do they see us working with others to address them? When they come to visit the church, are they wrapped in arms of love and made to feel welcome?

4. Not all these bruises are due to an abusive church. Many are due to abusive parents, schools, and the culture itself. But even in these cases, the church often could have intervened or provided hopeful services that could have lessened the effect. I personally spent many years ministering to younger Adventists whose ability to have faith in a loving Father was hampered by their own personal experiences.

5. Another characteristic of unhealthy churches is that they have made no efforts to quantify how the community perceives them through surveys and focus groups. They simply move along with the simplistic conviction that they have the truth and everything is fine. Sure, there are some costs involved in doing these things, but they are nothing compared to the costs associated with *not* doing so.

6. There is a rather fascinating conversation by Fernando Canale in his chapter "The Message and the Mission of the Remnant: A Methodological Approach," in *Message, Mission, and Unity of the Church*, ed. Ángel Manuel Rodríguez (Silver Spring, MD: Biblical Research Institute, 2013). He not only discusses the restorationist nature of Adventism but also makes a rather persuasive argument that the Adventist view on the remnant is pivotal in addressing the Roman Catholic and Protestant views of the sacraments, which he sees as a fundamental divergence from New Testament theology and is complicit in many of the systemic challenges of evangelical Christianity today.

7. I use the term *restorationist* to encompass the beliefs we felt called to restore within the Christian conversation, including things such as the Sabbath, which had been largely lost, and bring into even greater clarity certain matters of faith and practice, such as the soon return of Jesus, His ministry in the heavenly sanctuary, contemporary spiritual gifts, and healthy living. But I am also making the case that we Adventists were called into exis-

tence to bring back an understanding of the loving Father that had been largely forgotten during the Reformation debates, with both Luther and Calvin caught up in attempting to establish the power of God, rather than His love for us.

8. In case *artifice* is not a word you commonly use, it means "a clever trick or stratagem." It implies guile and craftiness, cunning and artful contrivance. In using the word, I am specifically contrasting it with Paul's phrase "innocence of our behaviour." Christians should not be sneaky but open and transparent.

9. For more information about the consortium, email mickeypervans@gmail.com or visit http://sdaec.net/.

10. Kinnaman and Lyons, *unChristian*, 29, 30.

11. Kinnaman and Lyons, *unChristian*, 26; emphasis in the original.

12. I am exaggerating in order to make a point, and I am fully prepared to be criticized for the extreme portrait of Adventism I have painted here; but you and I both know that there are Adventists who believe our mission is precisely to condemn sin wherever we find it and that nurturing is a waste of time.

13. Ed Stetzer and Mike Dodson, *Comeback Churches: How 300 Churches Turned Around and Yours Can Too* (Nashville, TN: B&H, 2007), 17.

14. Not all of us are comfortable admitting that this is true, of course. I remember reading the bumper sticker for one evangelical church that stated, "You will be loved at . . ." and the name of the church was inserted. When I first saw this, I thought, *If my church put out a bumper sticker like that, I'm not sure that we could live up to it*. What about your church? Are you sure visitors will be loved if they show up?

15. Mark Finley and Ernestine Finley, *7 Keys to Successful Church Growth* (Nampa, ID: Pacific Press®, 2015), 2.

16. Finley and Finley, *7 Keys to Successful Church Growth*, 27.

17. Ellen G. White, *Evangelism* (Washington, DC: Review and Herald®, 1946), 351; emphasis added.

18. As a ministerial intern, I was taught how to visit by a pastor who worked a tight schedule. He often lectured me on how a pastor needs to get in and out quickly so that he or she can visit as many homes in a day as possible. It was obvious to me even then that we were rushing through visits that should have had more time and care. We do not want to overstay, but we must be flexible.

19. If you would like to explore these values further, I recommend one of my books in the iFollow series: *A Deeper Look at Your Church* (Lincoln, NE: AdventSource, 2013), especially chapter 4, "What Does My Church Really Believe?"

20. See Thom Schultz and Joani Schultz, *Why Nobody Wants to Go to Church Anymore* (Loveland, CO: Group Publishing, 2013); Alan Roxburgh, *Structured for Mission* (Downers Grove, IL: InterVarsity Press, 2015), 13, 14.

21. The third element in church growth, which is not our focus here, is simply having a church that is so attractive that Adventists from other churches and other communities come to join our membership. Many churches grow in this way but doing so tends to mask other elements of church health.

22. Andy Stanley, *Deep and Wide: Creating Churches Unchurched People Love to Attend*

(Grand Rapids, MI: Zondervan, 2012), 55.

23. The implication is that a healthy church is one where members are asking, "How are we doing?" This is a church where criticisms are seen as opportunities to improve. To some Adventists, I realize the distinction between a healthy church and one successful only at the numbers level is disputable. But let us see if the case can be made effectively that church health is a major contributor to sustainable church growth.

24. Once more let me be clear: I support public evangelism, including the specific seven legacy evangelistic ministries that are sponsored by the NAD. They are working hard to deliver a creative witness to Christian audiences, focused largely on providing a kind of reaping ministry. I am, however, concerned that we in the church are sometimes anticipating that evangelists can reap what we have not sown at the local level. It is their job to offer a strong witness for what is distinctive about Adventism; in the local church, it is our job to show how that distinctiveness makes us appealing in day-to-day life. Our witness must not be limited to theological or historical distinctiveness but must also be tied to our distinctive values.

25. Stetzer and Dodson, *Comeback Churches*, 6.

26. Jonathan Dodson, *Gospel-Centered Discipleship* (Wheaton, IL: Crossway, 2012), 44.

27. There is a fascinating chapter by Ganoune Diop, titled "Adventist Mission Among World Religions: Some Theological Foundations," in *Message, Mission, and Unity of the Church*, ed. Ángel Manuel Rodríguez (Silver Spring, MD: Biblical Research Institute, 2013). Diop contrasts Adventist Christianity with Islam, specifically in terms of this distinctive filter Jesus delivers. He makes the case that "paradoxically, the biblical Jesus is missing in Islam. His dignity is diminished, His prerogatives usurped and attributed to others."

28. What Jesus was doing and saying was new only in the sense that the Jews had failed to understand God's intent for them, or had refused to accept it, and God was reiterating it once more through the life and witness of Jesus.

29. Virtually all religions sought to appease God. But Jesus said we should call Him Father. This is at the core of what Jesus meant when He said to His audiences: "You have heard of old, but I tell you . . ." It was not a new message but another call to a broader understanding of God's love and the mission that the religious community had failed to comprehend.

30. There are many books and articles on the history of the Christian faith that lump Adventism in with other restorationist communities, in a process going all the way back to groups even before the Reformation. Each of these groups was engaged with restoring parts of the Christian faith that had been corrupted during the medieval period. I am making the case, however, that while this "restorationism" is part of us, we are not really looking backward. Rather, we are looking forward into the bright future God plans, where our compelling witness attracts secular and postmodern audiences by its comprehensive appeal. Moreover, in our witness to God's grace, we are reiterating the gospel story that the Bible describes over and over.

31. Schultz and Schultz, *Why Nobody Wants to Go to Church Anymore*.

32. This will be among the most challenging change for some of us. Many have the idea that we might be tarnished by association, so we find it almost impossible to resist scolding others for behavior that we find objectionable—and feeling justified in doing it.

33. In some settings, I have seen this done directly by the speaker, using his or her phone. But in others, a moderator on the platform is used. The speaker may turn to the moderator at some point in the sermon and ask, "Do we have any questions yet?"

34. I understand how hard this is to do. We have been trained to set people straight. But discipleship training should help us better understand the step-by-step process that is required.

35. The term was coined by a group of authors in the 1970s and 1980s, such as Bruce Larson and Keith Miller. It was featured in Keith Miller's book *The Becomers* (Waco, TX: Word Books, 1973).

36. If you would like to read more about this, Gilbert Valentine has written a very fine book about how Ellen White engaged with a series of General Conference presidents: *The Prophet and the Presidents* (Nampa, ID: Pacific Press®, 2011).

37. C. S. Lewis, *Surprised by Joy* (New York: Harcourt, Brace and World, 1955).

CHAPTER 5

Providing Leadership Through Times of Crisis

If then our common life in Christ yields anything to stir the heart, any loving consolation, any sharing of the Spirit, any warmth of affection or compassion, fill up my cup of happiness by thinking and feeling alike, with the same love for one another, the same turn of mind, and a common care for unity.
—Philippians 2:1, 2, NEB

Church life is sometimes complex for the local elder. Things do not always go the way we had hoped. Plans do not always work out. People let us down. But it is when times of crisis come that the leadership of the church has an opportunity to grasp a tighter hold on God's hand.

In the first part of this chapter, we will address what should be done in advance of crises in order to make them more manageable. The second part deals with how the pastors and elders manage the crises. In Adventism, the pastor is expected to fix things. And if the pastor is not around, the local elder (or the head elder) will become the go-to person. Whoever the immediate leader is, the success or failure in meeting the crisis will largely depend on the church itself.

Congregational health: The overall key to crisis management

Philippians 2:1, 2 is one of many Bible texts discussing the dynamic of life in the early Christian church that challenge us to emulate those believers today. Paul describes our "common life in Christ," which means our shared experience of being part of a healthy church. He urges us toward that which "stir[s] the heart," expresses "loving consolation," and involves "sharing of the Spirit." He describes "warmth of affection" and "compassion" and tells us that if we will continue emphasizing all these things, we will fill up his "cup of happiness."

Let me now draw your attention to the 2005 best-selling book *Blink*, by Malcolm Gladwell. In it, he speaks of the phenomenon of "thin-slicing." Gladwell argues that what we call insight or even genius comes from our ability to sift "through the situation in front of us, throwing out all that is irrelevant while we zero in on what really matters."[1] Here Gladwell touches on the sort of thing a perceptive local elder does by intentionally sifting through all the information coming at him or her—especially during times of crisis—and identifying "what really matters," including what offers the potential for causing lasting damage or long-term benefits. We see in the Gospels that Jesus uses this same thin-slicing to open the eyes of Jewish religious leaders to what God considered really important:

> "The Spirit of the Lord is on me,
>   because he has anointed me
>   to proclaim good news to the poor.
> He has sent me to proclaim freedom for the prisoners
>   and recovery of sight for the blind,
> to set the oppressed free,
>   to proclaim the year of the Lord's favor." (Luke 4:18, 19, NIV)

Jesus was not arguing that ministry to those on the edges of society is the *only* thing we should be doing. But the religious leaders of His time had entirely misunderstood God's priorities. We also need to utilize this thin-slicing to better understand what is important for the local elder to do first in addressing a crisis. In this chapter, I am arguing that ministry priorities are set up by ensuring that the church is healthy, thus reducing the overall complexity of potential circumstances. Healthy churches led by healthy pastors and elders recover quickly in the face of crises and go on to better days, while unhealthy (or less healthy) churches tend to spiral out of control, causing additional challenges.

This first part of our conversation about the benefits of overall church health is phrased in terms of anticipating crises because we need to realize that we are *not* at the mercy of circumstances. For example, we can support the pastor so well that he or she will stay longer. We can do discipleship training so that our members grow in Christ. We can put a security system in place to lessen the potential for break-ins or vandalism.[2] But the local elder cannot *make* the church healthy by waving his or her magic wand. The elder *can* contribute to a bright future first by his or her own healthy approaches to being a balanced Adventist, awaiting the return of the Lord, and then by being ready to engage the membership in positive ways.

Healthy churches begin with positive approaches to what they have been called to do. I have always been impressed with what Walter Brueggemann, in his *Theology of the Old Testament*, calls a "credo of adjectives"; five positive perspectives about God that occur all through the Bible. He argues that the Bible reveals a God who is merciful, gracious, faithful, forgiving, and steadfast in love.[3] These adjectives give us clarity for the center of our conversation with our members and community. Adventists must describe God in this broader, more positive way, as opposed to merely a tired, petulant god. He is bigger than some of the common intentions we attribute to Him and seeks in us a broader sense of spiritual health that enables us to present Him—and embrace Him—as a loving Father, who wants to be in fellowship with us.[4]

There are a number of possible definitions of a healthy church that have been put forward over time. As we will see, none of these provides the whole story, but each deserves at least some consideration:

First, some would argue that a healthy church is a growing church. Many of us would agree that healthy churches do tend to grow. Under this definition, though, bigger churches are almost automatically in better shape than smaller ones. Growing churches frequently have more money available, a "better" pastor on-site, and a church plant already in existence or in the planning.[5] But as important as these are, are they enough to assure a healthy church?

What most of us know is that our larger churches are usually located near an Adventist institution—a school, hospital, or some other business that attracts Adventists. For many years, the Sligo, Maryland, Seventh-day Adventist Church was the largest congregation in the denomination because it was near the General Conference headquarters, Washington Adventist Hospital,

Washington Adventist University, and the many other Seventh-day Adventist organizations that existed to support them.[6] But does the clustering of many Adventists in one place assure that they will not become hostage to radical thinking or get so comfortable that mission is obscured?

Some would argue that a healthy Adventist congregation is one where there are no conflicts. If the waters are calm, we assume that other indicators of church health are also high. But are calm waters enough to create a healthy church? It may look like health on the surface, since the waters are calm, but the quiet church is not one without its complications. The absence of conflict is an appealing way to estimate church health. But health is a dynamic quality. It sometimes flourishes alongside conflict and, in fact, seems to stimulate growth. We need to be careful that we do not misread quietness for health.

We should also note that other kinds of churches exist with an appearance of calm. For example, in the Washington, DC, area, where I live, there are several churches that were intentionally founded by people who wanted to reject traditionalism in all forms. Their members chose nontraditional approaches for how they do worship, what kinds of music they experience, how the members look during worship, and what sorts of sermons they enjoy on a regular basis. In these sorts of places, the calm is based on the passionate commitment to everything that is new and emerging. But is a determination to be different in itself enough to create a healthy church?

Some would argue that a healthy Adventist congregation is one led by a very good pastor. We would all agree with the blessings a good pastor brings, along with a good pastoral family. There is strong evidence that as good pastors move from place to place the congregations they serve are nourished. It is also true that as pastors mature they tend to get better at many of the things that members find to be a blessing. This is one of our denominational strengths.

But we know that some pastors who were successful in one setting are less so in another and that in some settings a previously successful pastor actually gets into trouble or fails. The same preaching style that won accolades in one place falls on deaf ears in another. A healthy church, then, is clearly not *all* about the pastor. And while helping pastors grow in effectiveness is important, it may not always be the major controlling factor in church health.

Some would argue that the key for congregational health is the health of the larger organizations supporting it. In Adventism, this would typically require us to look at all levels: the conference and the union, along with the division and the General Conference. How healthy are the governance systems we currently have in place? To what degree are they supporting the local mission? Clearly, a balanced, Spirit-led denominational organization is a good thing. Sloppy or too highly centralized organizations may sometimes hinder success by intervening in disruptive ways.

But this assertion ignores the reality that church life is local and that denominational health sometimes fails to predict local church health. At this time, the NAD is looking at our current governance structure to make sure that it is not, in any way, inhibiting mission.[7]

Finally, some would argue that congregational worship styles are the key to success. It is sometimes argued that if the worship service is led by better performers (especially paid performers), with better sound systems, and lots of musicians and vocalists, then we will be better at achieving our mission to contemporary audiences, and the church will grow. But newness is not the only issue. Sustainability is often an issue that crops up in more innovative congregations, especially when particularly charismatic individuals leave the scene.

Also, the process by which spiritual maturity is inculcated and measured is of concern. Matters of *style* sometime mask a lack of *substance* under various approaches to worship, and many of the more innovative churches in the larger Christian community are beginning to question whether the more casual styles are really working as well as hoped.

As I have said several times, I am arguing that an elder's goal should not be a magic bullet or quick fix. Is it possible that no single definition of a healthy church would fit all circumstances? Is it possible that there is a benefit to be found in encouraging some level of diversity in approaches? Could two churches that are quite different from each other *both* be healthy? Or could two churches that are very much alike in many ways be quite different in terms of actual membership health? A healthy church is one that is meeting real human needs.

One of the major challenges facing many churches is that of making the Bible into a book of ideas—about which we can be right or wrong—rather than an invitation to a new set of eyes and a new way of looking at things that creates possibilities that were never considered before. This limited view (that it is all about being right or wrong) gives us little wiggle room when contemplating a brighter future. I argue from *hope*. I maintain that churches who have seemingly forgotten the key dynamics of the gospel can change from being unhealthy to healthy.

We all know that change is great in theory but frustrating when it is personal and we have to give up something that we value. In the book *Transformational Church*, there is a little pull quote on one page. It reads, "Churches do not change until the pain of staying the same is greater than the pain of change."[8] While I am uncomfortable with the manner in which this may impact change in Adventism today, I must confess that this pull quote is compelling. Simple inertia is typically in effect. It is often not until problems have grown to the point of disruption that most of us are willing to tackle them.

Commonly, in church life, we find ourselves digging a rut. Once we have done that, we then dig it deeper. Nobody has to tell us we are in trouble. It is just that changing is too full of unexpected possibilities and what we are currently doing is so familiar. The truth is we cannot choose whether change will come. It is coming pell-mell down the pike, rushing toward us whether or not we are ready for it. We *can* choose whether we are in a condition to endure it. We can influence what kind of impact it will have and whether the church is transformed in biblical ways by it.[9]

In another book about supporting these transformational churches, Jim Herrington writes, "It is about reaching a critical mass of believers who are so empowered by the gospel of Christ that they change everything they touch—family, workplace, schools, business. As this critical mass is achieved, the power of the living God brings significant changes in the problems that plague our cities today—poverty, crime, addictions, gangs, divorce, violence—and a dramatic increase in things that characterize the kingdom of God—mercy, justice, prosperity (especially for the poor) and compassion."[10] That is a powerful image of what might be possible. It offers us hope! The idea of reaching a "critical mass" of believers who are so engaged is incredibly promising as a part of our pursuit of a healthy Adventism.

Identifying the key elements in congregational success

In his book *Deep and Wide: Creating Churches Unchurched People Love to Attend*, Andy Stanley maintains that there are five faith catalysts. By this, he means that there are five parts of church life that can contribute significantly to creating a healthy church: practical teaching, private disciplines, personal ministry, providential relationships, and pivotal circumstances.

Stanley uses the whole book to describe how these faith catalysts contributed to his being able to come out from under the shadow of his famous father, television personality Charles Stanley, and establish a contemporary ministry that has grown tremendously, both in size and influence. The configuration Stanley provides may not work in every church, but I do want to loosely follow his outline for a while because it reflects so well what I have seen clearly in the needs of Adventist congregations as they seek to be healthy in the face of various crises.

First, we must stress the importance of practical teaching. What the local elder preaches whenever he or she steps into the pulpit needs to be of a practical nature. As part of my research for this project, I listened to a number of recorded sermons by seemingly eloquent Adventist preachers. I listened to sermons by local elders as well and spent time looking over the sermons I have preached. What I found is that far too often we fall into the trap of preaching what is merely of great personal interest to us. Instead, we should ask ourselves this question: *How does this help my members?*

You may remember that when Jesus gave the Sermon on the Mount, the disciple Matthew recorded the event: "When Jesus had finished saying these things, the crowds were amazed at his teaching, because he taught as one who had authority, and not as their teachers of the law" (Matthew 7:28, 29, NIV). I am not saying Adventists are like these "teachers of the law" or that we should expect to be able to preach like Jesus did. But according to Matthew, Jesus had a passion that the other teachers lacked and an ability to tell stories that could be applied in real-life situations. He was not satisfied to merely discuss what was theologically true or reflected religious orthodoxy. Rather, Jesus taught for a response. He was calling for a life change and so should we.

By "practical teaching," I also mean counsel that touches on what is happening in the world and includes suggestions on how we can help the church provide a more compelling witness to the community, starting with our own personal engagement.[11] What matters is that the person up front—pastor or local elder—is taking the time to ask people what they are doing in their lives and offering hope that God can make things better. It is about help for daily living in today's complex culture and words of hope to which the congregation can cling to all week.

Second, we need to embrace and teach private disciplines. This is an elder who has a personal devotional life; someone who is developing a sense of intimacy and accountability with God. If we exclude the intimacy in our relationship with God, we miss a critical element that can lead to our downfall.

During His sermon on the mount, Jesus said, "But when you pray, go into your room, close the door and pray to your Father, who is unseen. Then your Father, who sees what is done in secret, will reward you" (Matthew 6:6, NIV). This is one of the many places where Jesus calls us to maintain the private spiritual disciplines that change our behaviors. He tells us that what happens on the outside *comes* from what is going on in the inside. This matter of intimacy with God is one that Ellen White wrote about often. For example, she said, "We are living in the most solemn period of this world's history. The destiny of earth's teeming multitudes is about to be decided. Our own future well-being and also the salvation of other souls depend upon the course which we now pursue. We need to be guided by the Spirit of truth. . . . We should now seek a deep and living experience in the things of God. We have not a moment to lose."[12] Notice that her appeal was not for us to become more astute at making our doctrinal arguments but to seek "a deep and living experience in the things of God." This is personal and important.

In addition, we must emphasize the key role of personal ministry. During the early years of Adventism, we created models for activity that matched the existing culture. Adventists were so involved in this personal ministry that many, including Ellen White, were kicked out of their churches for constantly telling people about the soon return of Jesus. Recently, however, more and more Adventists in North America live in isolated communities that surround our institutions, where our contributions to ministry are limited to the money we put in the offering plate.

I am reminded of a scene in Matthew, in which Jesus was preaching and healing late into the afternoon, and His disciples came to Him and said, "It is late, and we're in a deserted place, so we should send these people off to the surrounding villages so that they can eat." Jesus was not having any of that and said: "*You* give them something to eat." The disciples were a little embarrassed by the implied rebuke, but they scrounged around among the crowd and found a couple of fish and a few loaves of bread. Jesus took it and blessed it. And then He broke the bread and took the fish and distributed it to the disciples, who handed it out. The result was that there was enough to feed more than five thousand men, along with all the women and children, and lots left over (see Matthew 14:15–21).

"You feed them" does not mean that Jesus expected the disciples to have the capacity to do this without His intervention. But it did mean they were to become personally involved, distributing the food with their own hands. When we only put money in the plate, we are missing both the blessing and the personal transformation that comes from being personally engaged with the people around us.[13] We do not have to do the same things, but we need to do *personal* things. During the early years of Adventism, the members were expected to go around the community selling pamphlets and books written by Ellen White and other Adventist authors. Some have described this time in the church as representing a "culture of counting."[14] Those days are largely gone, and the denomination has other ways of getting us engaged. But the need for personal involvement remains.

Then, we need to focus on experiencing providential relationships. *Providential relationships* are points in our lives when we are changed by key interactions with others. One of the most obvious of these is when a new pastor comes to a church and radical spiritual growth takes place. But sometimes pastors and elders are the ones who are changed.

Early in my ministry, I was invited to spend some time as the camp pastor at the Adventist summer camp in Yosemite National Park. For a number of years after that, I went to work at Camp Wawona for several weeks each year, serving alongside the camp counselors in ministering to God's children. Then I also went on to work with these same youth leaders in other settings, such as camp meetings and Weeks of Prayer at academies. In this, I was working alongside a group of academy and college students who became not only my lifelong friends but also partners in ministry.

My life would have taken a far different turn except for these providential relationships. In working with these young people in event after event, we were engaging with an entire generation of young Adventists in North and Central California. Even now, I am sometimes approached by some of the men and women who went through this time with me; they want to share how those providential relationships have continued to bless their lives.

In the book *Creating Community*, Bill Willits and Andy Stanley describe creating an effective adult group-study model, in which some of these providential relationships were fostered.[15] You cannot program these sorts of relationships, but you can create environments that are conducive. In *Deep and Wide*, Andy Stanley writes, "At least 90 percent of the adults we baptize thank specific individuals in their small groups for the roles they played in their coming to faith and their decisions to be baptized."[16]

Finally, we must take into account the impact of pivotal circumstances. The life of faith grows in response to specific sermons or events—such as Weeks of Prayer or evangelistic series—and encounters with specific books or things we see or hear through mass media that shape us into the people we become.

The impact of these pivotal circumstances is often tied less to the events themselves than to our interpretation of them. For example, according to biographer Walter Isaacson, Steve Jobs of Apple fame took the photo off the cover of a *Life* magazine—a portrait of two children in the war-torn region of Biafra—to his Lutheran pastor and asked whether God knew in advance what was going to happen to the children. When the pastor gave the sort of safe, theological answer many of us might give about God knowing everything, Jobs ended the conversation and never went back to church again. It was his interpretation of the pastor's response that undermined his faith.[17]

This shows the negative side of these events. But we all know of moments in our lives when a positive, dramatic event happened to us and changed things forever. Life is not just a steady flow into spiritual maturity. It goes by jerks and jumps—all of which contribute to making us into the men and women God wants us to be.

Addressing times of crisis

Now, we are going to turn and look at the actual moments when crises arrive. In spite of everything we do, sometimes things just go wrong. The phones begin ringing. At that moment, the local elder sees all the things he or she should have done better and earlier but did not. Everything now depends on what we do in the middle of the crisis—both to limit that damage and ensure the best possible outcome.

The apostle Paul writes to those of us facing crises: "Show yourselves guileless and above reproach, faultless children of God in a warped and crooked generation, in which you shine like stars in a dark world and proffer the word of life" (Philippians 2:15, NEB). In Ephesians, he adds, "Live like men who are at home in the daylight, for where light is, there all goodness springs up, all justice and truth" (Ephesians 5:8, 9, NEB). The apostle is telling us that honesty and transparency will often enable us to survive in moments of crisis, even when our first temptation may be to cover things up and hope they will just go away. This parallels what Paul wrote in 2 Corinthians 6:6–10: "We recommend ourselves by the innocence of our behaviour, our grasp of truth, our patience and kindliness; by gifts of the Holy Spirit, by sincere love, by declaring the truth, by the power of God. . . . We are . . . the unknown men whom all men know; dying we still live on; disciplined by suffering, we are not done to death; in our sorrows we have always cause for joy; poor ourselves, we bring wealth to many; penniless, we own the world" (NEB).

When taken together, these passages describe a way of interacting among the membership and in the community that features innocence, which is to say being without guile and wholly open, even when others in our faith community may choose to be evasive. These texts talk about living in the daylight, rather than withdrawing into the shadows. They urge candor and simple transparency.

Paul is not asking us to be heroes or to display unusual brilliance. Rather, he is merely asking us to trust in God's ability to change us so that we can "discern the will of God" and "know what is good, acceptable, and perfect" (Romans 12:2, NEB).

Now, let me be transparent. I realize that some in the church may be more than a little doubtful with what I wrote about innocence and transparency.

"You need to show some good common sense," they may be saying. Indeed, some may want to lecture me: "Son, you just aren't describing the real world, where you have to keep secrets and always protect yourself!" I get that. But I also know that the harder our hearts become, the less likely we are to see God perform His miracles in our lives.

When a situation at the local level becomes an issue, we do not want to feel victimized by circumstances or unable to provide a sustainable Christian witness.[18] Rather, we want to stand up and be bold for Jesus. It is not just about getting by but addressing these challenging moments in ways that reveal to all the people looking on that we are not just an ordinary group of people. Rather, we are offering a witness of God's love for humanity and His desire to fellowship with us. We are God's character witnesses or His expert witnesses, like those that are often brought into a courtroom to testify in a case. And we want to be sure that we are telling our "better true stories." We are to stand up for our values joyfully and willingly, so that others can't help but take notice.

As noted earlier in this book, research confirms that evangelicals have become known mostly for the things we are *against*, rather than for Jesus and the good news He came to announce. I am not arguing that we are intentionally presenting a witness that is unnecessarily complex or contrary to the gospel. But with the current polarization in the evangelical church at large—and also between various segments of Adventism—some of us lose sight of our larger mission to present the story of Jesus in compelling terms. And in our determined effort to drag the church back into some of the very arguments we have settled long ago, we are confusing our members and not giving them what they need to face these troubling times.

In Philippians 2:15, 16, the apostle Paul gives us our explicit mission and frames it with a specific character. He acknowledges that we live among "a warped and crooked generation" (NEB), which is to say we are surrounded by people who do not grasp the values God wants to us emulate. With greed, desensitization to cruelty and inequality, and preoccupation with obtaining more things, we live in a time when values are incredibly skewed.

As Peter warned, "Above all, you must understand that in the last days scoffers will come, scoffing and following their own evil desires" (2 Peter 3:3, NIV). When Adventists read that, we often filter the call to action through our traditional experience. We come out firing, denouncing worldliness in all its forms. But many of our postmodern young adults are intensely critical because of the blind eye they believe we have turned to what they see as larger issues, such as our destruction of the environment and man's inhumanity to man in such things as the sex trade. When God asks us to "shine like stars," He is not asking us to double down on our traditional areas of condemnation. Rather, He is asking us to go the extra mile in delivering a positive story that is full of hope. We are to present a witness of generosity and forgiveness—and tell a story that grows stronger in people's minds as we demonstrate its features in our personal lives. And by implication, we are to avoid settling for merely being attack dogs in evangelical culture wars.

Principles for surviving crises

Now we come to a few specifics. Any list of principles elders can adopt for surviving crises will be subject to what is happening in the local church at any moment. Every circumstance is unique in various ways. One size does not fit all. Still, we may find the following steps useful in finding God in all the darkness. Here are some things we can do:

First, your role as local elder is to stabilize the situation. You can do this by relying on God and His strength through prayer and then putting on the armor of God. Sometimes we cannot fix the crisis we are facing. That great pastor who left us for another church (and who we are certain can never be replaced) is gone. The church will survive until the next great one comes along only if the local leadership chooses to seek the best of what lies ahead and encourage members to remember that God is their surety. This "armor of God," referred to earlier, is described in Ephesians: "Stand firm then, with the belt of truth buckled around your waist, with the breastplate of righteousness in place, and with your feet fitted with the readiness that comes from the gospel of peace. In addition to all this, take up the shield of faith, with which you can extinguish all the flaming arrows of the evil one. Take the helmet of salvation and the sword of the Spirit, which is the word of God" (Ephesians 6:14–17, NIV).

Then, as the local leader of the congregation, show your members what courage looks like. Fear is part of life. But we can *choose* to have courage when our natural instinct is to run. As local elders, we can find ways to continue ministering in spite of whatever feelings we may be experiencing. For example, if the church has split over some theological or personal conflict, begin the laborious process of rebuilding confidence and optimism, assuring those around you that the future is bright and that a resolution will be found. As the local elder, your job is not to take sides or declare winners and losers, but to help the congregation stay positive and see where the brightest part of the future may lie. The Bible says, "Be strong and courageous. Do not be afraid or terrified because of them, for the Lord your God goes with you; he will never leave you nor forsake you" (Deuteronomy 31:6, NIV). I love this New Testament comment: "When they saw the courage of Peter and John and realized that they were unschooled, ordinary men, they were astonished and they took note that these men had been with Jesus" (Acts 4:13, NIV). As local elders, our primary job is to lead by example. That means staying calm and being patient.

Next, use your leadership role to teach the congregation to trust in God's promises. The Bible is full of promises for us to claim. For example, God promises us: "If you search with all your heart, I will let you find me, says the Lord" (Jeremiah 29:13, 14, NEB). One of my personal favorites reads, " 'For I know the plans I have for you,' declares the Lord, 'plans to prosper you and not to harm you, plans to give you hope and a future' " (verse 11, NIV). And my all-time favorite reads as follows: "Of one thing I am certain: the One who started the good work in you will bring it to completion by the Day of Christ Jesus" (Philippians 1:6, NEB). Jesus promised that even small steps can result in great things: "The kingdom of heaven is like a mustard seed, which a man took and planted in his field. Though it is the smallest of all seeds, yet when it grows, it is the largest of garden plants and becomes a tree, so that the birds of the air come and perch in its branches" (Matthew 13:31, 32, NIV).

Reciting promises gives members courage. Study them so that you will have them in mind when the crisis comes.

Then, look to God by teaching hope and wholeness. God wants us to turn to Him when the crisis arrives. We read in the New Testament: "Now the God of hope fill you with all joy and peace in believing, that ye may abound in hope, through the power of the Holy Ghost" (Romans 15:13, KJV). The sequence here is quite clear: it is God's intent to *give us hope as we strive for wholeness*. His very substance is hope, and He wants to see hope abound in our lives and for us to display it to others by the wholeness or balance we maintain. We need to look to God, trusting that He will find a way. In *The Message* Bible translation, we read Paul's witness to one of the churches: "We can't quit thanking God our Father and Jesus our Messiah for you! We keep getting reports on your steady faith in Christ, our Jesus, and the love you continuously extend to all Christians. The lines of purpose in your lives never grow slack, tightly tied as they are to your future in heaven, kept taut by hope" (Colossians 1:3–5, *The Message*).

In addition, begin building your own personal theology of suffering. When we are in trouble, God is not up in heaven, wringing His hands and saying, "Oh my, oh my." He is still in control over everything that happens. It is true that God sometimes uses these moments of crisis to drive us back into His arms. But He does it only so that we will understand that we cannot manage things on our own and so that we are able to see more clearly His deliverance in our own lives. Constructing a personal theology of suffering means taking the time to think about our present difficulties through God's eyes. Doing this gives us a new perspective on what God may find necessary to allow in order to break through our hard shells of indifference and pride.

As you think about this, I would encourage you to read Mark Townsend's book *The Gospel of Falling Down*.[19] He argues that it is when we are falling down that we can become most open to God's touch. There is intent that lies behind what we experience. We are often blind to this because we have not taken the time to understand that God believes our salvation is worth whatever it may take to get it accomplished. Moreover, God is in the difficulty with us.

Finally, choose the best pathway and then move ahead with boldness. As the local elder, you are not the pastor. But you are there, and God can use you. While the pathway you choose may later prove to be less than ideal—and you must be willing to make adaptations on the move—you cannot remain paralyzed. There are downsides to virtually all actions, and people may sincerely differ with you. When times of crisis come, even a few minor steps to address the issue assures the congregation that things are not being swept under the rug or totally ignored. In the same sense, it is often better to move the ball partway down the court, knowing it is not a total solution, rather than lingering overlong, hoping to find some miracle cure.

It is sometimes difficult to imagine a moment of crisis in the life of the church as a good thing. That is simply the final truth we have to accept about crisis: God uses moments like these not only to move the church ahead but also to help us, as individual church members, become more fully the people God intends us to be.

Of all the points I have tried to make during this brief discussion of responding to a crisis, the key one is that we, as local elders, need to provide consistent, faithful leadership in these moments. If the pastor is on the scene, he or she will most likely lead the effort. But even if the pastor is on the scene, it will often be the entire local leadership team that will be called into play. If the pastor is not on the scene—and you, as the local elder, are the only one able to address the situation—remember that the conference will have resources you can tap in order to help you. You are not alone in any of this.

---

1. Malcolm Gladwell, *Blink* (Boston: Little, Brown, 2005), 33.

2. There are resources that have been developed at various levels of the denomination that label themselves as crisis-management plans. I suggest that you contact your conference leadership and adopt such a plan. Beyond that, or even with such a plan in place, the overall church health is still key to making the elements work as they should.

3. Walter Brueggemann, *Theology of the Old Testament* (Minneapolis, MN: Fortress, 2005), 215.

4. Some readers may be offended with the implication that we Adventists sometimes offer a description of God that includes attitudes such as petulance. But when we limit our conversation to a few distinctive themes that we believe are more important to God than the big ones He has proposed, such as faith, hope, and love, we do Him an injustice. Our distinctive doctrines have to be understood as secondary to the core elements of our Christian faith—or better said, seen through our faith.

5. It is true that due to demographic forces, some big churches in time become largely empty or see the membership flatline or stagnate. The question is whether size itself contributes significantly to overall health or whether number growth may be asserted as a predictor of health.

6. Big churches bring their own set of challenges. One of the more interesting facets of this is in terms of once-large churches that have declined in size and what the factors

are that contributed to this. In their book *Simple Church* (Nashville, TN: B&H, 2011), Thom Rainer and Eric Geiger tell the stories of several of these larger churches that have declined. I know of no such similar study for Adventist churches.

7. The criteria for a healthy denomination may, in fact, be somewhat parallel to those for healthy churches. Clearly, the managing organization may penetrate too deeply into the local church or may be of little practical value in terms of being present when needed.

8. Ed Stetzer and Thom Rainer, *Transformational Church* (Nashville, TN: B&H, 2010), 18.

9. The point is that our goal is to allow change to drive us into a deeper appreciation of what God's dream for us actually is.

10. Jim Herrington, "Transformation: The Bottom Line," in *City Reaching: On the Road to Community Transformation*, by Jack Dennison (Pasadena, CA: William Carey, 1999), 106.

11. By calling for practical teaching, I am specifically talking about addressing the issues that touch the hearts of the members of our congregations and communities.

12. Ellen G. White, *The Great Controversy* (Mountain View, CA: Pacific Press®, 1911), 601.

13. A growing number of Adventists in local churches are becoming involved through short-term missionary efforts. This may not directly address our local mission to our communities, but I believe it is transformational for those who go and gives them stories to tell.

14. Benjamin McArthur, *A. G. Daniells: Shaper of Twentieth-Century Adventism* (Nampa, ID: Pacific Press®, 2016), 35.

15. Andy Stanley and Bill Willits, *Creating Community: 5 Keys to Building a Small Group Culture* (Sisters, OR: Multnomah, 2004).

16. Andy Stanley, *Deep and Wide: Creating Churches Unchurched People Love to Attend* (Grand Rapids, MI: Zondervan, 2012), 134.

17. Walter Isaacson, *Steve Jobs* (New York: Simon and Schuster, 2011), 14, 15.

18. We want to be transparent but also present the best possible information. In a sense, it is a sort of dance between the two values, as we try to avoid providing too much information, but at the same time making sure the information we do provide is accurate and faithful to the complexity of real life.

19. Mark Townsend, *The Gospel of Falling Down* (Hants, UK: O-Books, 2007).

CHAPTER 6

Leading the Church Into Community Engagement

The Spirit of the Lord is on me, because he has anointed me to proclaim good news to the poor. He has sent me to proclaim freedom for the prisoners and recovery of sight for the blind, to set the oppressed free, to proclaim the year of the Lord's favor.

—Luke 4:18, 19, NIV

Here we are at the final point in our conceptual conversation about the role of the local elder. In the next two chapters, we will look, in more traditional terms, at the details of what an elder does.

Earlier in the book, I directed you to what some have called "the freedom framework"—the five core values in Adventism: community, capacity, freedom, service, and witness.[1] These values address not only the fundamentals of our Christian faith but also our intentions for engaging with our neighbors. The first of these is *community*, and it holds that position for a reason: it is though our community engagement that we touch lives in ways that promise sustainable mission success.

We Adventists have sometimes viewed ourselves as being required only to proclaim an end-time message, delivered in propositional terms. But when we have done that, we have found to our own frustration that this approach has many weaknesses associated with it, including the feeling that we have nothing in common with those we are called to reach. Rather than allowing us to walk this path, God would have us reach out to our communities in the ways Jesus did, as word of His works preceded Him from community to community. Ellen White writes, "Wherever He went, the tidings of His mercy preceded Him. Where He had passed, the objects of His compassion were rejoicing in health, and making trial of their new-found powers."[2]

In this statement, Ellen White speaks of Jesus' "mercy" and His "compassion." Jesus' *words* had credibility within the community primarily because His *actions* were so compelling. The people who had been touched by Him, healed by Him, or in any other way ministered to by Him were the best storytellers for spreading His witness. "I was broken," they said to everyone they met, "and Jesus put me back together." In this, I am arguing in favor of *a ministry of engagement* that has the potential of God's "tidings of . . . mercy" to precede us, as they did with Jesus.[3] In order to tell this story well, my intent is to direct this chapter toward parsing some of our more compelling texts and quotes on our engagement with our communities.

There are things Adventists bring to the table when we minister through engagement that no one else can present with the same effectiveness. Both Jesus and the apostle Paul stressed the transformational role this offers, and others have seen it too. For example, in Jonathan Dodson's book *The Unbelievable Gospel*, he writes, "Paul was compelled to do all kinds of ministry in all sorts of circumstances, not to receive attaboys from God the Father, but because Jesus died to resurrect a whole new kind of humanity: 'If anyone is in Christ, he is a new creation. The old has passed away; behold, the new has come' (2 Corinthians 5:17). Paul isn't performing; he's truly living. He is living a whole new life that revolves, not around self, but around the Messiah who died and lives for him. His evangelism is utterly Christ-centered."[4]

Dodson is arguing for a contemporary Christian witness that reimagines its evangelism in terms that postmodern men and women are able to find compelling. He writes, "People who are influenced by postmodernism find modernist evangelistic methods off-putting and ineffective. People who are more sensitive to relationships are quick to discern that rational, presentational approaches no longer work well within postmodern culture, where people want to be known, loved, and respected, not informed and presented to."[5]

Can you begin to see why this perspective is so important for the ministry of the local elder? We struggle sometimes in grasping the implications of this change in our contemporary audiences. We fail to see the distinction Dodson is making. As a result, we are far too often our own worst enemies. We persist in doing only propositional evangelism, where we tell people what they ought to know, as opposed to understanding what they will respond to and using love and respect to reach them. By not telling our "better true stories"—the ones that capture the imagination of our audiences—and by allowing ourselves to settle for some of our "lesser stories," we are classed with others in the traditional religious community, who have nothing to say that is of interest to contemporary audiences.

Ellen White also speaks to our tendency to depend too much on our doctrinal certainties. She writes, "As a people we are certainly in great danger, if we are not constantly guarded, of considering our ideas, because long cherished, to be Bible doctrines and on every point infallible, and measuring everyone by the rule of our interpretation of Bible truth. This is our danger, and this would be the greatest evil that could ever come to us as a people."[6] In this statement of warning, Ellen White offers a rather startling commentary about how we typically position ourselves. She is telling us that "the greatest evil" that could ever happen to Adventists is that we begin to think that our doctrines and views are "infallible" and that we would believe that we should "measure everyone" by the "rule of our interpretation of Bible truth." Think about what she has said here, and imagine the implications. There is nothing wrong with having strong opinions, or even believing ourselves to be right on various religious themes. But present truth is only "present" when it takes into account the language and culture of the audience we are trying to reach. There is a great deal of danger associated with becoming so infatuated with ourselves and our traditional approaches—and so certain that we have the truth—that we stop listening to others or imagining whatever else God may choose to teach us about reaching people. Ellen White is not trying to take away our confidence or our established certainties, but she is reminding us to be *humble*, even when it comes to our own biblical interpretations—and not just humble by *saying* we are humble but in terms of being open to learning new things and reimagining how we need to approach new audiences.

It all starts with the example of Jesus

Jesus Himself gave us the model we will be exploring in this chapter. He announced His mission specifically in terms of ministry to the neediest parts of the community. As we see in Luke 4:18, 19 (NIV), He said He was here to "proclaim good news to the poor" and to "proclaim freedom for the prisoners." He said He would cause the "recovery of sight for the blind" and "set the oppressed free." And finally, He said He would "proclaim the year of the Lord's favor," which means He would spread abroad God's good news in the most positive terms.

So what does this mean to us as elders? If we are His disciples, it is our mission too. Right? These are all aspects of this ministry of engagement that we must embrace more clearly in the time of the end, making this emphasis even more central as end-time events develop and other venues of reaching people become less accessible.

Near the close of His ministry, we see that Jesus was not doubling down on theology. Rather, we see Him wrapping a towel around His waist and washing people's feet. We imagine Jesus walking in the streets, listening to people, tousling the hair of children, eating with people, and letting them touch Him—even some of the less savory among them. Jesus ministered in a very personal way. Sure, Jesus healed. Sure, He preached. But He also spent time making certain that people were noticed, encouraged, and most of all, *loved*.

Early on in Adventist history, the believers began to understand the example Jesus set, and they began practicing the ordinance of humility to remind themselves of what He did and how He wanted us to live in communion. Learning this history helped us understand the theology behind the ordinance of humility as well. We understood that we were not just an apocalyptic community but also a fundamentally *Christian* group, emphasizing ministries of compassion as evidence of our depth of spiritual service.

On the other hand, we have also had to face the fact that we are also like the disciples of John the Baptist, in that we are somewhat stunned to see Jesus in the streets, being touched by common men and women; and we are sometimes not so certain we can do that ourselves. Theoretically, we believe in humble service, but in reality, we would rather assign someone else to do it. We ask, "Isn't this the reason we put money in the offering plate, so the people in the church who like to do community services can do that?"

Jesus reminds us that Christianity is about humble service. It is about ministering to poor people, to people who are in prison, to social outcasts, and to people with terrible diseases. He emphasizes that it is about helping people who are being oppressed.

I have never actually heard an Adventist say, "Couldn't we minister to upper-class people? Couldn't we minister to people who smell better and don't have so many awful habits?" But I *have* seen the way we cringe and offer money for others to do it. "Surely, we Adventists could get the angel in charge to assign us a less offensive mission. I mean, after all, we've been proclaiming the Sabbath and the investigative judgment all this time without a complaint. Don't we deserve a break?"

I am exaggerating things a bit, I admit. But the problem is that some of us just cannot get the image of Jesus touching the lepers without flinching out of our minds. We cannot see Him addressing those who were demon-possessed with patience and kindness; sitting by a well with a woman of ill repute, regardless of what others thought; and going to meals with people who were considered the outcasts of society—where prostitutes could wash His feet and wipe them with their hair—without delivering a self-righteous sigh. It does not seem appropriate for good Christians to do that sort of stuff.

The fact remains that even though Adventists are well aware of the mission Jesus articulated for Himself and for us, we have somewhat adjusted how we apply it to better accommodate our preferences. For example, rather than going out in the streets as Jesus did, we have declared ourselves to be deliverers of the truth and defenders of apocalyptic imagery. We have followed the example of William Miller and his adherents: we have creative ideas on how the time of the end is supposed to work out (in great detail), and we think it would be great fun to hold seminars and workshops on these things. Maybe if we kept at it for a while, we could even fill stadia with audience members, like some of our evangelical brethren did when they were introducing the "four spiritual laws" for witnessing.[7]

In some ways, Seventh-day Adventists have already created a distinctive mission niche for ourselves: We are the people who set up tent meetings and get religious people to leave their churches and join ours. Right? Or we mail Ellen White's books to people and tell ourselves we are engaging with our community.

Sometimes we seem to have rewritten the mission statement that Jesus gave us—the one about taking care of the poor and the oppressed and visiting people in prison (see Luke 4:18). Teaching is good, but we cannot neglect serving others.

Addressing contemporary audiences

Our Adventist end-time mission is not *just* about poor people or those on the edges of society. It is also about reaching the secular and postmodern men and women who surround us in the community, along with people in other churches. On the one hand, God has not promised that He will change the world so that the people in our communities will suddenly want to listen to what Adventists have to say. On the other hand, He has asked *us* to speak to contemporary audiences in ways that make sense to them and in their own context. As the apostle Paul put it: "Let your conversation be always gracious, and never insipid; study how best to talk with each person you meet" (Colossians 4:6, NEB). Consider the rather detailed implications that come from this statement of mission:

First, the apostle Paul instructs us that local elders are to engage in conversation with the people in our communities. The thing about conversation is that it takes two people actually engaging with each other. We cannot hide in our Adventist enclaves—six miles from the nearest sin—but must position ourselves where people live and enter into meaningful discussion with them.

People must be addressed personally. We cannot do it by proxy. And if we just try to inundate them with our ideas on what they should believe or do, they will not listen. We *have* to begin meaningful conversation, coupled with long-term engagement.

Then, Paul tells us we always are to be gracious in our interactions. Behaving with grace is always a difficult prescription for Christians, even though we have been the recipients of God's grace and we ought to know a lot about it. Instead, we want people to sit still and listen to us. In spite of our requests, they keep squirming away, which tends to irritate us and make us suspend our commitment to grace.

Being gracious runs deep. It is not just about refraining from attacking people because they have the audacity to disagree with us but engaging them in ways that cause them to feel blessed. It means we have to listen to people, acknowledge when they say something worth hearing, and not intrude on their areas of sensitivity by our ignorance of their ideas or with undue aggressiveness.

In addition, Paul instructs us that we should avoid being insipid. No one likes being described as *insipid*. The apostle means that we should not *bore* people by our meaningless chatter.⁸ Rather, we should talk with them in ways that capture their imagination and resonate with them. When we listen to what our own young adults are saying about the church, we find that they call us judgmental, irrelevant, and hypocritical. We irritate them by not taking the time to learn how to discuss things in ways that resonate with them. In addition, we must learn how to text, use Facebook and Twitter, along with all the newer forms of social media.

Next, Paul tells local elders that we need to study *how to communicate better.* This emphasis on *study* indicates an intentionality that should force us to try to understand better what our audiences require of us before they are willing to interact with us. We need to seek to understand our culture in order to engage with it. As local elders, we need to take the time to read up, not only on current events, but also on sports, style, and opinion. This "studying" is aimed at making us more interesting people who understand our culture. We might even try asking young people in the church to teach us how to do this. They may be a bit shocked when we ask, but we need to use every avenue of study.

And finally, Paul urges us to do this with each person we meet. In other words, this implies that we are to have a broad witness—one that is applicable to many different people in many different settings, involving people who may need to be approached differently from one another. Our more contemporary audiences are especially concerned that we deal with them individually, based on our own experience with Jesus. In reaching modern people, a personal testimony is often the key. They do not care what the church believes. They only care about what we have *personally experienced.*

Remembering the Adventist mission
In his landmark book *Bowling Alone*, Robert Putnam discusses how all facets

of the North American lifestyle have become increasingly less engaging than they have ever been previously. He writes that by 1999 attendance at club meetings fell by 58 percent; family dinners came down 34 percent; and having friends visit declined by 45 percent. And he argues that social media has flooded in to fill the void left by our loss of personal engagement.[9]

The Adventist mission in these end times—the one the local elder is often challenged to fulfill and which he or she is to lead—is a big one, with a broad scope, and one that must take into account these changes in the social contract we all have with one another. The early Adventists couched their language in then-contemporary terms. What they said and did, then, *fit their times*. But we do not live in their times, and it is essential that we find current language and images to tell our story today.[10]

We are told that the light of truth advances constantly (Proverbs 4:18). Ellen White said some interesting things in regard to this. She wrote, "We shall never reach a period when there is no increased light for us."[11] And she also wrote that "in every age there is a new development of truth, a message of God to the people of that generation."[12] Think about those two statements, and imagine what they might mean for us today as we try to engage with contemporary audiences. We are supposed to continue learning, and we are to address our witness to each new generation in ways that connect with it. We are warned not to get so wrapped up in our traditions that we are unable to adapt to changing cultural realities. Let's refer one last time to Jonathan Dodson's book: "These shifts in the social landscape, from physical to digital, make deep relationships rare. This has a huge impact on evangelism. When it comes to talking about something as deep and personal as faith, we hesitate for fear of offending or losing a friend. We're on relational thin ice. Twenty-first-century Christians want people to know they are loved. Period. Without an evangelistic parenthesis."[13]

So what is it that we are supposed to do? If our current strategy of holding meetings where we make presentations about Bible prophecy is not effective for contemporary audiences, where should we turn?[14] Both the apostle Paul and Ellen White were very explicit here. As we just saw, Paul said we are to constantly reassess how we are attempting to reach people in their own context. As a result, we should begin connecting with people in ways that are personal and substantive. It is not that we should find better topics for our meetings but that we should find other ways of engaging with audiences. We should not expect presentations to take the place of our own personal witness. Will the reimagining of our approaches stretch us? Sure, it will. It is never easy to rethink what you have been saying or doing so that it speaks to new audiences. But it is the mission we have been given; and to the degree that we drag our heels at doing it, we are limiting our potential for supporting God in His work.

Jesus' method for achieving mission
You may have already anticipated where I am going with this—we must reimagine how we can connect successfully with postmodern and secular audiences. We will begin by taking a closer look at what Ellen White presented in terms of *Jesus' method* for reaching people.

Ellen White wrote the following in one of her most widely quoted statements: "Christ's method alone will give true success in reaching the people. The Saviour mingled with men as one who desired their good. He showed His sympathy for them, ministered to their needs, and won their confidence. Then He bade them, 'Follow Me.' "[15] Ellen White presents Jesus as providing a model we can follow in putting together a healthy approach to our communities. She tells us we will find greater promise of success in reaching contemporary people if we do a number of specific things. Let us take a deeper look at this model by reflecting on it, phrase by phrase:

First of all, Ellen White reminds us that Jesus "mingled" with people. This word, *mingled,* is one of the key activities we need to get our minds around if we want to reach contemporary audiences. This is the key word in any conversation about Jesus' method. Jesus not only talked about engaging with people, but He also *mingled* with them. Jesus wandered about in ancient Israel, talking with people, listening to them, having meals with them, and delivering a healing touch wherever it was needed. He did not hire somebody to do this for Him. Instead, He walked the streets and entered the homes Himself.

Mingling is a fascinating word that conveys a personal level of interaction that causes people to feel at ease. The root word *mingle* almost suggests that

Jesus spent idle time with people with no specific intent or objective. Young people now speak of "just hanging." Could Jesus have possibly been "just hanging" with people as He traveled across Galilee? Would He want us to do it, too, in our local settings? Could it be that in limiting ourselves to more structural evangelistic patterns we are missing something important?

Then, Ellen White tells us Jesus presented Himself in such a way that people understood that He "desired their good." This is almost as distasteful to some of us as "mingling." It suggests that we pay less attention to what *we* want to achieve and more to what *others* dream about and hope to achieve in life. We need to find out what people want in their lives. We have to ask more questions, rather than make more proclamations. We have to engage with people at a deeper and more personal level. In this description of the Adventist mission, Ellen White was talking about outcome, not strategy. The way Jesus interacted with people left them feeling both engaged and cared about. The people Jesus ministered to came to believe that He was more interested in their good than His own. And we must follow His example.

Then, Ellen White tells us Jesus "showed His sympathy." Sympathy is one of those words that has all sorts of other important stuff crammed inside it. We send people sympathy cards. True sympathy contains an element of passion. It includes empathy and commitment. It is about choosing to be part of someone's life. Jesus understood people's aspirations and knew that in feeding them, healing them, and taking the time to listen to them, He was making a lasting connection. He was identifying with humanity forever. Ellen White was saying in this quotation that we are to be *on the side of people*, letting them know by our words and actions that we will support them as they move ahead. Sympathy is not just about the head. It is about the heart too. It is affirming that "you are my friend; you are someone I care about, pray for, and celebrate."

Next, Ellen White tells us Jesus "ministered" to people's "needs." What the biblical record shows is that Jesus wandered around the community. He had some individual, heart-to-heart conversations. But He understood that His words would have far more meaning to people once they saw that their physical needs were being met. He did not say, "If you listen to Me, I'll feed you." Rather, He told His disciples to feed them first. This represents a broad-based commitment to addressing human need and is one of the reasons why early Adventists emphasized medical missionary work. It hints that before we launch a specific community-service program we should do some sort of community assessment so that we are clear on what people in our communities *actually* need. In some cases, they may need a smoking-cessation clinic, but they may have a greater need for an after-school care program. On a more personal basis, ministering to specific needs involves the capacity to provide ongoing support services rather than mere Band-Aids. It is about developing the capacity to serve so that the things we do have a sustainable impact.[16]

Ellen White goes on to explain that Jesus "won" people's "confidence" through this sort of ministry. Winning people's confidence really is the key to this entire process. It is the intended outcome. If people trust you, then they care about what you have to say. If they think you are just "being religious," they turn away. Ellen White reminds us that the life of faith includes connecting with people where they live so that they see our witness as representing true spiritual insight and character. It means that the sum total of what we are doing and saying compels the attention of the community so that they are utterly convicted that we are on their side and that we will stick with them through thick and thin. In all candor, we do not always have this sort of a relationship with our communities. Studies show that many people do not know who we are, and some even hold us in contempt, due to what others have said about us. But the way we win people's confidence is by contributing to the community over and over until we are identified with service in ways that gradually erode prejudice. People need to be able to say, "Those Adventists are always here to help."

Ellen White shows where the process is going, as Jesus finally invited people to "follow" Him. Jesus called people to a point of decision. He knew from the moment He started *mingling* that He would also be *inviting* them. But He took the time to engage first. An invitation for a deeper spiritual life was given, but it was at the end of a long process, in which people observed how Jesus ministered and had reason to trust what He said.

We may not be able to perform miracles of healing in the same way that Jesus did, but we can live lives that seem miraculous to others, because our lives are filled with generosity, faith, and humility. Throughout the process, the invitation part of Jesus' method must be understood and anticipated. Sure, we want to get people in the baptismal tank, and that is a good goal. But the invitation must be preceded by the other parts of the story so that when the invitation is made, people are not surprised by it. Instead, they have been eagerly waiting for it. "I was wondering when you would ask," they say. "I've got some friends I'd like to bring along with me." Jesus was out in the streets, connecting with people in very personal ways that they understood to be based on a commitment to making their lives better. And that is where we need to be, as well, and what we need to mean by the term *evangelism*.[17]

How to engage with the community while remaining Adventist

Now we come to the crux of the conversation. Once we have described the direction the Bible and Ellen White seem to be pointing—where we "mingle" with people and follow Jesus' method—we have to address the challenges that moving down this pathway may produce, given our traditional Adventist culture. Here are some ideas to consider for doing so in ways that do not cause us to lose our way.

First, we need to begin seeing our interactions with people through the filter of mission. Some of us have been taught that our Adventist end-time mission is limited to merely delivering a distinctive doctrinal message. We have not been called just to talk to contemporary audiences about eschatology, theology, or righteous behavior. Rather, our mission is about delivering an in-depth gospel witness, seen through the priorities that shape Adventism. We cannot really discuss any of them properly (eschatology, theology, or righteous behavior) if we do not discuss them in context; by this, I mean a full integration of these themes into the gospel and daily life. These component elements of Adventism are intimately connected, and we will be led astray if we think of them only separately, as abstract concepts, or drop any of them as we construct our end-time witness.

Then, we must become even more specific in telling our "better true stories" in compelling ways. As we try to make our end-time witness more effective, there are a few aspects of the conversation that we dare not miss. "Better true stories" focus on telling the Adventist story persuasively and in terms that an increasingly postmodern and secular audience can comprehend. As a local elder, you may wonder how to tell this story about community engagement effectively to your members and the community. It starts with imagining what might appeal to our selected audiences.

Many of us have been taught to see the end times as mostly about delivering a last-day warning: "Jesus is coming soon; if you don't wake up and smell the Postum, you're going to be dunked into the lake of fire, and that's not going to be fun at all."[18] But the driving force behind this approach is fear: "If you don't join, you're going to burn." This has a tendency to be distracting to secular people, who no longer believe in a personal devil or a fiery hell. Our witness is not just about truth but also about us as truth tellers, who are witnessing to God's intent to deliver us. We must flip-flop on this: God's love transforms, while fear just results in anger and disbelief.

Specifically, we need to be sure we are not allowing ourselves to substitute an apocalyptic vision for the fundamental gospel call, in which we are bent on connecting men and women with Jesus.[19] In order to do this, we must be sure to keep everything in *balance*. While the two can be compatible—we can talk about the sealing, the shaking, the latter rain, the early time of trouble, the later one, and all the rest—it is entirely possible for our commitment to the gospel to be largely, if not entirely, obscured by our infatuation with the more dramatic elements of the end times. It has happened to other groups, and it can happen to us.[20] It is all about dealing with our apocalyptic approaches in context, understanding both what our pioneers brought to the table *and* what we need to add for it to be effective for today's audience. Adventist historian George Knight described it well: "The call is to move beyond beastly preaching and other forms of neutering the apocalyptic vision and toward a renewed examination of the apocalyptic vision in relation to Adventism and the world for the twenty-first century."[21]

Next, in order to address our contemporary world in a distinctly Adventist way, we need to integrate our emphasis on hope and wholeness. A full-blown Adventist approach to the end times is much bigger than the beasts and images to which some of us so often retreat. It must be shaped around hope and wholeness—offering an integrated approach to witness, centered on our connecting with the people of the end times in ways that go far beyond merely warning them of impending doom to featuring a personal witness to our life in Christ.

At the division level, we have made the phrase *hope and wholeness* central to every part of our witness. We have even put it in our mission statement. But more than that, we have asked every department to articulate mission in these terms. *Hope and wholeness* mean presenting every aspect of our witness in personal terms that lead those we approach into an experience that covers all aspects of life, addressing the deepest human needs. It is not just about theology or doctrine but about touching people in ways that give them hope and promise wholeness.

In addition, we need to connect with our communities through the filter of our shared humanity. Specifically, we need to come out of our protected environments. We need to begin connecting with our communities in ways that show people we care about them and that what we are saying to them is backed up by our meaningful engagement with them. Many members of our community are utterly ignorant of our broader Adventist commitments. They know nothing of what we are doing in the community to address human needs and have not seen us through the prism of our extensive health-care emphasis. We have allowed ourselves to be defined by the day on which we go to church and what we do not eat. We have more "better true stories" to tell, and we need to find ways to shift the public's perception of us to what we say when we tell these "better true stories."

Also, we need increasing clarity on just which audiences lie at the center of the Adventist witness. We need to grasp that our true audience for our end-time witness is not just the small sliver of people who care as much as we do about the intricacies of last-day prophecy or structured reforms of behavior but rather the larger audiences that fill our communities. Another way of saying this is by maintaining that we are *Adventist Christians*, not Gnostics. We are not all about escaping the world or establishing a distinctive moral posture but living for Jesus in the world.[22] This means we are sharing life with people, being with them in all the important settings of their lives. We need to develop the capacity to reach secular audiences, not only other religious people.

When we witness, it must be to tell people that it is *Jesus* who is coming, not just the end of the world. We are prophesying about *redemption*, not just finality. Can you see the difference between these two emphases? The

Adventist witness in these end times is one that encompasses people who do not currently believe that religion has anything to say to them—and not merely a debate over competing evangelical interpretations.

Finally, we must pursue an enlightened restoration emphasis that puts the focus where it belongs. Frankly, many of the elements in our distinctive Adventist witness are about restoration, even when we do not always see beneath the surface. It is about what God wants to do in our lives, as He transforms us into men and women whose lives testify to His love and vindicate His character. One important way in which we do this is by allowing God to make us more fully human, capable of connecting with the people around us in ways that reflect our humanity, our compassion, and our generosity so that they are drawn to the aspects in which we confirm the very character of God in our lives.[23]

Within the larger evangelical community, Seventh-day Adventists have been consistently seen as those who stressed particular aspects of restoration, such as the Sabbath, our emphasis on the heavenly sanctuary, and our call for healthy living. We have been accused of pursuing these distinctive features of our religious tradition over the gospel; while most of us would reject the accusation, it remains in place. This has been our legacy. But being about restoration is not a rejection of the gospel. It is, rather, a commitment to the idea that the gospel has implications for the quality of ministry we offer.[24]

We must become better at envisioning the *redemptive character* of a revived church. We are talking about a transformed Seventh-day Adventist Church. A church that understands that its mission is to reach out to contemporary men and women in the name of Jesus. We are talking about a church that is committed to doing so with compassion and generosity—reaching modern audiences with humility and on their own terms.

Yes, a part of this approach is about community-service activity. But not *just* about community service. It is not *just* about health programming. It is not *just* about expanding our educational system.

It is about individual Adventist members engaging with other members in new levels of collaboration for ministry. It is about Adventist members turning our churches into places of help and healing, of hope and wholeness, where people who are lost and confused can come and know they will be loved and cherished. It is about Adventist pastors who preach sermons that build people up and give them courage, rather than issue the typical "hate of the week" on this theme or that.[25]

The story we elders need to lead out in telling has a number of traditional elements to it, but it also includes a number of specifics in areas that may seem new to us. It is about Adventist members becoming engaged, serving on community-action committees, running for local office, and rolling up their sleeves to clean up the streets and plant flowers. It is about offering ourselves to serve in redemptive ways, without worrying about who gets the credit. When talking about a witness of hope and wholeness, it may be as mundane for some of us as leaning over a fence and talking about a garden or a local sports team with a neighbor. It is about becoming *part* of the community.

Tying it all together

Here, at the end of our conceptual conversation on the local elder in Adventism, I want to be sure to make one last call for balance. The local elder, in order to fulfill the call of God, must be focused on what works today in advancing God's mission. It is not about the exotic or extreme—or pushing out to the edges of our church in some effort to ignite a dampened fire. True revival and reformation are about an Adventism that impresses contemporary audiences with its agility and relevance.

Your larger role as the local elder is just emerging. You are both a leader in the local church and a member. Because of this, you are positioned in such a way that God can use you and your "better true stories" in similar ways as in New Testament times. I believe the apostle Paul was referring to us, as local elders, when he wrote, "The whole creation is on tiptoe to see the wonderful sight of the sons of God coming into their own" (Romans 8:19, Phillips).

---

1. For a more comprehensive discussion of these values, I recommend a section in my book *A Deeper Look at Your Church* (Lincoln, NE: AdventSource, 2011), beginning on page 101. In discussing this, I need to give credit to my lifelong friend Ray Tetz, who was instrumental in helping codify it.
2. Ellen G. White, *Gospel Workers* (Washington, DC: Review and Herald®, 1915), 43.

3. I am using the phrase *ministry of engagement* in very specific terms to encompass far more than mere community service, as important as that is to Adventists. A *ministry of engagement* means each of us engages with those who live and work and play near us—using our friendship and example of service to verify the witness we are delivering.

4. Jonathan Dodson, *The Unbelievable Gospel* (Grand Rapids, MI: Zondervan, 2014), 25.

5. Dodson, *The Unbelievable Gospel*, 34.

6. Ellen G. White, *The Ellen G. White 1888 Materials* (Washington, DC: Ellen G. White Estate, 1987), 830.

7. I admit to having endured both training exercises for witnessing as well as going out on the streets to intercept unsuspecting community members with our pumped-up certainties and simplistic formulas. I did this and learned from doing so. But it was not authentic Christian witnessing of the sort that brings lasting results.

8. Even the most biblically correct language may be seen as "meaningless chatter" to someone without our background. It is *our job* to find language that makes sense to our audience, not their job to get up to speed.

9. Robert Putnam, *Bowling Alone: The Collapse and Revival of American Community* (New York: Simon and Schuster, 2000), 61, 100.

10. A recurring theme throughout this book is that what worked for Adventists 155 years ago is not necessarily what will work today. Our doctrines do not need revising, but the language we use in applying them and the methodologies we employ must be constantly adapted.

11. Ellen G. White, *Selected Messages, vol. 1* (Washington, DC: Review and Herald®, 1958), 404.

12. Ellen G. White, *Christ's Object Lessons* (Battle Creek, MI: Review and Herald®, 1900), 127.

13. Dodson, *The Unbelievable Gospel*, 36.

14. Let us be clear that these sorts of meetings *do* appeal to a defined segment of our audience—namely, people who are already Christians who are in some ways unhappy with what their religious experience up to this point provides. The point is there are fewer and fewer of these people, and we Adventists need to develop approaches for reaching the majority populations, who are increasingly secular and postmodern.

15. Ellen G. White, *The Ministry of Healing* (Mountain View, CA: Pacific Press®, 1905), 143.

16. Again, in one of my iFollow books—*A Deeper Look at Your Church*—I list five key values that have characterized Adventists (under the title "The Freedom Framework"). These include (1) our commitment to community; (2) our determination to advance capacity; (3) our support for freedom; (4) our intent to provide service; and (5) our emphasis on witness. I urge you to read more about this because it lies at the center of our effective end-time approach.

17. Some readers may still be dubious about the significance of Jesus' method as I have described it. "Well, that's just one side of the story," you may be saying. I agree. It *is* only one side of the story. But it is the part of the story that distances us from others in the

religious marketplace. By this emphasis, Ellen White is not trying to diminish the distinctive doctrines of the church. Rather, she is telling us where our priorities must be placed if we want contemporary audiences to find anything else we say to be compelling.

18. Trust me when I say this, I have done it myself, and while I was doing it, I thought I was the cat's meow. But as a pastor, I was failing my members because I was not enabling them to see the deeper implications for their own witness. I was letting them off the hook by focusing on propositional truth, rather than a dynamic relationship with Jesus and His people, who have to see Adventism as bigger than this.

19. Some may find it offensive to suggest that some Adventists may be confusing our apocalyptic vision with the gospel. But we have to face the danger squarely and be ever more careful. If we fail to do this, we will not be the first group to have allowed this to happen during the years of Christian history. But our witness will be severely compromised.

20. This confusion was at the root of the Gnostic error, against which many scholars believe much of the Gospel of John was written. Their apocalyptic fervor was fed by misconceptions about Jesus, which led them down some very strange paths. We do not want to go down those paths but rather declare clearly the gospel of Jesus Christ.

21. George Knight, *The Apocalyptic Vision and the Neutering of Adventism* (Hagerstown, MD: Review and Herald®, 2008), 26.

22. Some Adventists do not understand how differently we view the end times compared with the typical evangelical. We use some of the same language—including some of the same texts of Scripture—but we mean quite different things by it. For example, many evangelicals believe Jesus will come to rapture us away, *before* the great tribulation. Believers will be safely in heaven, watching the trouble below. Adventists, by contrast, believe Jesus is coming, but that it will be *after* the great tribulation and that "every eye will see him" when He comes (Revelation 1:7, NIV). Because of their biblical literalism, many evangelicals believe that final events will circle around the Jewish state in the Middle East. Adventists believe that the prophecies apply to "spiritual Israel," as defined by the apostle Paul, and are not geographically defined.

23. We make it very difficult for our witness to connect with contemporary audiences when we make only moralistic arguments. We set up lists of things we should or should not do and allow them to become our watchwords, by which people know us. There is a truth here about the transformation God will make in us. But far too often we get the categories wrong. It is not about what we should do or quit doing but about the deeper changes God wants to make in us, where kindness, compassion, and generosity make us into more transcendent witnesses.

24. The Adventist witness to restoration is something we discussed earlier in some detail. But we need to recognize that while a restoration theme appears in many religious groups, our emphasis is on how God wants to use us to restore a full understanding of His loving character.

25. Over the years, I have encountered several pastors who felt compelled to preach what my family termed "hate of the week" sermons. In these sermons, the pastors used the Sabbath hour to beat us over the head about whatever area they thought we needed

correction in. What they were doing was in no way building up the church or giving their members hope. As believers, we do not require just an endless string of pep talks on better behavior. We need a call to Jesus and to mission, along with the promise that God will be in our lives. Anything short of that hopeful testimony causes listeners to go away sorrowfully (see Matthew 19:22).

CHAPTER 7

Skills for the Local Elder, Part 1

Brethren, I count not myself to have apprehended: but this one thing I do, forgetting those things which are behind, and reaching forth unto those things which are before, I press toward the mark for the prize of the high calling of God in Christ Jesus.
—Philippians 3:13, 14, KJV

As described in the introduction, the final two chapters of this book are a bit different from the first six in that they build conceptually on everything we have said about the local elder. They then attempt to translate the concepts into a number of very specific skills that the elder needs to master. In these two final chapters, there will be six clusters of "skills conversations": three in chapter 7 and three in chapter 8. Each of these clusters covers specific topics that are part of what elders do.

In addition, the specific intent in these final two chapters was to parallel the route taken in the General Conference Ministerial Association's *Elder's Handbook*. As a result, I have made a special effort to cover a similar list of topics, though my approach may be shaped more by what I have covered in the first six chapters of the book. This is done in order to clarify the specific issues in North American terms.

The first cluster of skills the elder should master
The group of skills that we will discuss in this section encompasses some of the big things the pastor and the elder work to shape in the local congregation. These include leading worship, preaching the sermon, setting congregational goals, and motivating.

In the typical Adventist church in North America, part of what shapes what the elder does is the history of local elders in that particular church. If there has been an aggressive elder who expanded the role to encompass a broader ministry, the elders who follow that person almost certainly play a larger role in the church than might be true in some other churches. But if previous elders saw their roles only in a limited set of expectations ("we do this, but we don't do that"), the succeeding elders will probably continue to reduce expectations for their roles. One local elder told me, "I just do what the guy who trained me did; only there were a few things I don't do as much of, because he didn't give me as much training on how to do them."

Additionally, a new pastor might have a set of rather specific expectations for the elders. One elder told me that he had been an elder for several years when a new pastor arrived who had expectations that the local elder was not comfortable addressing, so he resigned. Our primary goal during this conversation is not to present an exhaustive list of responsibilities—with an eye to telling you precisely how to do the job—but rather to focus on the broader challenges behind the specifics that lead to success. Principles will be emphasized. For a more detailed listing of specifics, see the *Elder's Handbook*,[1] which tends to provide at least a paragraph on every traditional area of service.

Leading worship

We expect to see the local elder on the platform, leading worship. Depending on the size of the church, there may be a schedule of worship leaders, with different elders in charge during the schedule period. As the worship leader, the elder may also play specific roles. He or she may offer prayer, take up the offering, or give the benediction. But the primary task to be achieved by the elder is usually to give whatever announcements need to be made and then set the tone for the entire worship experience. Even when the pastor is on the scene and prepared to preach the sermon, the local elder is typically the one who is responsible for the people who will be on the platform, including contacting them, prepping them for any unusual circumstances, and instructing them on the roles they will play.

One of the innovations in many of our larger, more contemporary churches has been the role of the worship leader. This may be one person who holds a permanent commission or the responsibility may rotate among several people.

When I was the director of the NAD Church Resource Center, one of the things we began was an e-magazine for local pastors, titled *Best Practices*. We started a similar publication titled *Best Practices for Adventist Worship*. This publication specifically seeks to provide an expanded understanding of the tools and processes available to worship leaders to make the worship experience more compelling for Adventist audiences.

This resurgent emphasis on worship in the church parallels a similar development in other evangelical denominations. It is tied to a growing understanding that our sincerer members want to be participants in worship, not just a passive audience for a religious performance.

Admittedly, in the typical small Adventist church, aspirations may not be as high for creating the same type of dynamic worship service that larger churches envision. But even smaller churches can benefit from an ongoing conversation about how the local elder—who may be the worship leader in his or her church—can help make the worship experience more meaningful. There are a number of general principles on helping elders better lead the worship experience that have to do both with process and outcome. Let us discuss some of them.

First, keep the focus on the congregation's expression of worship to God. Worship really is not about us, except in terms of what we want to say to God about our acceptance of His grace and our desire to worship Him well. In some congregations, for example, the announcement period is handled before the worship service actually begins, in order to emphasize this dynamic of dedicating the entire service to giving worship to God.

Adventists understand what worship is about; but if we do not make that intent explicit, there is a tendency for the service to become both routine and irrelevant. This will happen inevitably unless we are intentional, which means that those in leadership (often the local elder) should periodically take the time to make an emphasis on the character of worship during prayer meetings and worship services.

Then, be intentional about drawing a clear line between performance and worship. In some churches, the elaborate organ playing, the professionalism of the choir, or other dramatic worship elements introduced into the service have the potential of detracting from a full-bodied sense of worship. The performers are at the center of the experience, rather than the congregation's worship of God. The elder has a role to play in this, along with the pastor, in determining just how dramatic or complex the worship experience is allowed to become.

Sometimes it will be necessary for local leaders to back down the intensity of performances in order to be sure the focus is on God and not on the performers. Those carrying on the various roles in worship may not be well positioned to make judgments about this, so the local elder may need to work toward simplifying the experience. In some of our smaller churches, the local elder may need to address the other side of this conversation—where he or she urges a more colorful worship experience when it has been allowed to become drab or predictable.

Finally, be sure that the worship experience results in the congregation leaving the service with a sense of hope for daily living. The worship experience is, most decidedly, about the adoration of God, and the most important outcome is that God is worshiped. But we also show our faithfulness to God in the worship service by making sure the experience does not ignore His intent for humankind but instead enables participants to grasp His hand in faith. God is worshiped best when His people are blessed and motivated, prepared to face the challenges of another week of living in their complex circumstances.

Preaching the sermon
Because so many of our churches in North America are small district churches, which seldom have a pastor on the scene, one of the responsibilities of the local elder is to see that the preaching service is carefully orchestrated. In many smaller churches, videos or PowerPoint presentations are sometimes used to assure that what might be termed *quality preaching* exists during the worship service. Even audio recordings are used to help fill the gap. In a few places, a central pastor preaches online (on a television screen) to several sister congregations.

In some churches, one of the tasks of the local elder is to call around in the weeks prior to a given service to find well-respected preachers—from the conference, a school, or other Adventist institutions. But the fact is that the local elder may be called on with some regularity to preach a sermon. There are some helpful resources for sermon preparation from the General Conference Ministerial Association that can be accessed online, including some CDs and DVDs that may be purchased. I have reviewed these and assure you that they are quite useful. More are available at the NAD offices and AdventSource.

Still, the local elder should not view the preaching part of his or her responsibility with trepidation but with a sense of opportunity. It is a chance to allow God to speak through him or her. Here are some suggestions to help an elder do this in a more intentional manner and feel more optimistic about how it will all turn out.

First, make sure that whenever you speak to the congregation that Jesus is at the center of your message. I realize that on some level such a reminder should be unnecessary. We are Christians after all. But intentional efforts are sometimes required, to be sure Jesus is lifted up.

Sermons should be thoughtful, sometimes humorous, and clearly well researched. In other words, do not use the sermon as your personal hobbyhorse, to set off on some obscure theological safari. Keep it all about Jesus. Far too many Adventist sermons, even when given by experienced pastors, launch out into rather irrelevant topics, rather than reveal the love of God in sending us His Son to redeem us. As you begin your sermon preparation, ask yourself: *Will what I say help establish in the minds of the congregation that God loves them?* As you think about the upcoming sermon, pray for guidance in making certain that the people who leave the service are more hopeful, more eager to dig into God's Word, and more determined to allow God to lead them than they were before the service began.

Then, allow your understanding of the local congregation to shape your sermon. One of the distinct advantages of the local elder in the preaching role is that he or she knows the congregation better than a guest speaker, or even the pastor at times. Do not abuse this knowledge by identifying people by name or embarrassing members with stories too close to home, but allow your knowledge of them to speak in ways that are local and helpful.

Each faith community has a character. There are issues facing members of your group that you could help them meet if you do so in a thoughtful manner. It is possible that a text of Scripture, discussed thoughtfully, could help a member see a brighter set of possibilities or cling to his or her faith when despair might otherwise be the case. Remember, God is involved, and He can take even the poorest of our offerings and use them to touch the hearts of those who are with us in the moment.

Next, be specific, practical, and very clear as to how your message can be implemented in a life of faith. Far too many of our sermons are on topics that do not lead the congregation toward hope for daily living. Having someone praise you at the door ("Great sermon!") is not necessarily a positive response. "I think I'm going to give that a try" is far better.

As you prepare your sermon, visualize some of the people in the church whose stories you know. Ask God to help you find the words to give them courage. Then, be sure that at the end of the sermon you provide "next steps" for the congregation, including ideas on how to implement what you have discussed. You are not just giving a talk but preaching a *sermon*, which means it is supposed to move people closer to God, to see the mission God has for them a little more clearly, or to pull them together for some important collective objective. I always try to imagine someone sitting in the congregation who will come up to me at the end of the sermon and say, "OK, Pastor, but what am I supposed to do about that?"

Then, do not aim for elegant, wordy discourses, but seek to speak personally and from the heart. Rarely will the local elder be a professional public speaker, able to leave audiences spellbound. More commonly, the gift you bring to the sermon is that you speak out of your personal experience in the things of God. The sermon is primarily a place where your witness to God's presence in your life can be expressed with powerful confidence.

By our very theological heritage, Adventists tend to be people who want to make a point or argue a line of reasoning. Some of that will almost certainly be part of your preaching as a local elder, but you have to be sure that you add into the mix a strong dose of your own story. In the end times, God wants to use Adventists as His expert witnesses, such as those testifying in a courtroom. What He needs from us is not just complex theology but stories about what we have seen God do.

Also, if there is an opportunity to preach a sermon series, use it to explore the more detailed issues and to emphasize God's love for us. As part of the worship experience, the sermon contributes to our collective worship of God. It may take several sermons to explore some of the big themes the apostle Paul discusses in Romans, for example, or lessons from a series of events in the life of Jesus.

Nobody likes sermons that drag on and on. But if you take the time to break what it is you want to say into some thoughtful segments, you can use a series of sermons to tell your story far more effectively. There may be someone in the congregation, just that day, who God has led there in order to hear what you have to say.

In addition, experiment with preaching styles, including using videos as part of the sermon, or even having people with local stories rise up from the congregation. You may not be a skilled preacher in technical terms. But there are many things you can do in the preaching service that are creative and innovative. It may be said later that the things you brought into the sermon, either in the stories you told or the other innovative elements you introduced, helped God touch the church members' hearts.

The ways we conduct worship services in the Seventh-day Adventist Church are copied from the order of the early Protestants' services. There is no right or wrong here, only tradition. If we can alter those traditions in new ways that capture the imagination of individuals in the congregation, we may be saving a young person who was about to leave the church or touch a professional who was about to abandon God.

Finally, remember that you want to inspire thought and action, not exhaust the audience. When you finish speaking, it is far better to have the congregation say, "I want more," than to hear them moan, "I'm glad *that's* over." Pastors often learn this the hard way. In my case, my wife understands that it is her privilege (or responsibility) to point to her watch when I have said enough.

Remember how *you* felt when you sat in the audience and a speaker just went on and on. Use that insight to limit how long you speak and for moderating how complex the arguments are that you undertake. You want to tantalize the listener, so remember that all-important word, *Amen*, after which you sit down.

Setting congregational goals

As the leader of a small local congregation, or as one of the key undershepherds of a larger church, the local elder should be deeply involved in the critical elements of strategic planning. Let the pastor lead out in this effort if he or she is willing to tackle the task or gifted at doing so. Setting congregational goals is not something that can be left to chance; if your church does not have a carefully considered strategic plan, you are unlikely to be moving ahead in an intentional manner. And if that is the case, you are probably not being good stewards of the opportunities God is giving you. It is fundamental to success.

While strategic planning is a complex discipline, with many professionals writing about it and testing various theories, it can be made quite simple for the local congregation. Here are some of the factors you should be considering:

First, sit down with the other leaders of the church and talk about who you want to be, as an Adventist witness, in your community. You must get some consensus on what your members believe an Adventist faith community ought to be like, so there needs to be an opportunity for support and agreement before developing a more detailed plan.

In some churches, a very small vision may need to be expanded. In others, a vision that is currently too broad—or even misdirected—may need refining. As the local elder, it is not your role to establish all this for the church. But it is your role to get the community talking so that a better future may be imagined. You are simply the facilitator.

Then, begin developing a community assessment that identifies what is distinctive about your community and its needs. You need to know what is broken in your community and how it is broken if you are going to offer Adventist services to help fix it. Every community is different. In one community, there will be a need for Adventists to offer some sort of food bank for hungry people. That may not be the biggest need in another community, but there may be a need for help in providing transportation for shut-ins or help with reading programs for children.

The point is that we need to sit down with community leaders and find out where the real needs are so that we can begin making a difference. Again, as the local elder, it may not fall to you to do the actual community assessment.

But you may be responsible for finding someone capable of doing this—or even to get the congregation to commit to hiring someone.

Then, take a careful look at the distinctive spiritual gifts already manifested in your congregation. It is one thing to know what the problems are in your community, but often another to have resources within the church to help address them. There may be needs in your community that you cannot address. Sometimes it is not so much what the community needs as what your church is good at doing (or some balance between the two). There are numerous resources available for conducting assessments on spiritual gifts, but you need to be careful that you do not get dragged deeper into the process than the church can endure. The truth is, as the local elder, you probably already know many people in the congregation who could make far greater contributions than they are currently making. We live in a time when many of us feel too busy to take on many new things, and typically we are not coming to the church offering our services. But Adventist men and women need to serve. If they are not serving in any capacity, they are probably dying on the vine.

Finally, sit down with the other local leaders in the church and write out a strategic plan. A good plan is a written plan. If you do not write it, you will not be able to measure where you are, relative to where you hoped to be. You cannot hold people accountable, including yourself, if you do not do this. Set goals and targets. You need to list the steps you are going to take to satisfy the need and the time frames you believe it will take. Then you need to put names to the tasks.[2] (If it seems that I am not properly emphasizing spirituality, it is because I want to put the attention on the fact that when we serve, we also grow.)

You will also need to identify a budget to support the plan. You must make certain people know where you are going on this, and that includes the people in the church and in the community. You need to tell a story about what you believe God wants your church to do and what you think it will take to get it done. Those who know the story will be able to remind you to keep at it.

Motivating

In order to effect motivation, the local elder—at a very basic level—has to be a storyteller. He or she has to be someone who is committed to what was developed in the strategic plan and is able to get others to join in to accomplish the goal. Find some good books on motivation and read them. Ever since Tony Robbins wrote *Awaken the Giant Within*, people have been trying to tell personal testimony better and better. One of the more widely read books is Stephen Covey's *The 7 Habits of Highly Effective People*. And one of my favorites is *Strengths Based Leadership* by Tom Rath and Barry Conchie.

We should also make sure that we do not get sidetracked by the manner in which we get things done in the church. We can do stupid things that cause people to walk away from what we are trying to accomplish, such as trying to take the credit for what is done or embarrassing people by failing to give them their due. We can push too hard or just lay back and hope it will work out. But motivation in a Christian setting is a bit of a tricky thing, and we have to think very carefully about what we are doing if we want religious people to jump on board with us. Here are some of the things that play into the effort:

First, check in with God to see if the pathway we are proposing leads to where He wants us to go. We need to start with a lot of prayer. God has a habit of slowing us down when the road we are following is not as good as we think it is. Trying to motivate the church is like trying to push a wet noodle on a plate sometimes. One of the great things about church life is that a seemingly good idea can sometimes be replaced by a better one in the blink of an eye. We need to remember that we are trying to advance God's work, so the details are less important than the movement forward.

Then, we need to temper our expectations and take into account local realities that may be unique. Change is difficult under any set of circumstances, and people are unlikely to move unless we can show them how our proposal contributes to the mission God has set for us. That means we will have to slow down and take all the intermediate steps that we might think we do not need. If you have a great idea, it will be worth taking the time to do the research in Scripture and research in Scripture and Ellen White's writings to show that the proposed plan fits in with what has been in God's mind all along.

Then, once that has been done, we need to make sure the plan feels feasible to the congregation. Doubling the membership in five years of a small church that has not grown in twenty years may seem to some to be bold and full of faith, but it may also discourage other members, who do not see how it can be done. God's plans are bold but not insane.

In addition, we need to make sure that whatever the plan is, it ultimately comes from inside the group. It is hard for some of us to understand just how much the world—and the church—has changed from the "good old days," when we could just point into the future and shout, "Follow me, boys." People do not follow others today. They cocreate and collaborate. They set up teams to study options and work together on common goals.

Finally, we need to keep in mind that a good plan is an adaptable one. No plan survives forever. If we want our strategic plan to work over the long haul, we must build in places where we perform a reality check to see if the situation is the same as it was when we started or if there is a need for the plan to be adapted to changed realities.

If the plan has been working well, it may be time for us to tackle another challenge. Motivation is a bit like fire in a fireplace. It requires new logs from time to time, and it must also be stoked to keep it burning brightly.

The second cluster of skills the elder must master
The second cluster of skills include managing meetings, church elections, church discipline, and working with the conference.

One size never fits all. We will not all do things the same way—and that is a good thing, because it embraces the distinctiveness that God creates within us and the differences among the people to whom we minister, both in the local church and the local community. There are some general principles that will inform how we do things, and these are likely to apply in most circumstances. But even those may need to be tested at their edges during some of our most difficult moments, including some of those we will be dealing with during this conversation.

In Andy Stanley's book *Deep and Wide*, he writes, "One of the perplexing things we face as church leaders is that most church people don't know *what* the church is or *why* it exists."[3] Even Adventists sometimes find it difficult to stay focused on what our church is and why it exists.

Managing meetings
Of all the areas where the local elder may get into difficulty, none is of greater

potential than church-board meetings where decisions are made that affect the church's witness. Jonas Arrais, the editor for *Elder's Digest*, writes, "It is the need for action that produces decisions. When you are going through the process of making a decision as a church leader or administrator you should always ask yourself, 'Is there a need to take an action?' "[4]

The point Arrais is making is a critical one. Far too often we take official actions when the circumstances might be better served by no action at all but rather some personal interaction. One of the most common comments made after someone becomes upset is, "Oh, I didn't mean it to be taken that way," as though our mistake should be ignored due to our bland or benign intent. But that is the very point: we sometimes introduce ourselves and our views into situations where we do not need to take action. Let us look at some of the common mistakes we make:

First, we go into a meeting ill prepared. We can always be surprised by an attitude we encounter from someone in a meeting or a specific reaction that we could not have anticipated. Things *can* come at us from left field, and we have to stumble to recover lost ground. But more commonly, when we encounter these seemingly surprising moments, they are really sides of the conversation we should have anticipated and prepared for.

For example, if we are attempting to change the church in some significant way, we need to ask ourselves a series of questions, such as, *How will this affect the different age groups in the church? Who will be asked to pay for this? What reactions can we expect?* Sometimes there is a specific person in the meeting that we know will be affected by something, and we have not taken the time to discuss it directly with him or her in advance. Instead, organize and plan ahead for upcoming meetings.

Then, we go into a meeting with a specific agenda that is not widely shared. Often, we know that our proposal will create resistance, but we just plow ahead. When we bring something to the congregation's membership (or to the board) with no effort to discuss it beforehand, we deserve the response we get.

Do not *dump* things on people. Have conversations in advance, bringing proposals to key constituencies in order to find out how widely they will be supported. This is one of the areas where the local elder can be of great service to the pastor; he or she may be about to launch some new initiative without taking into account the fact that his or her agenda may not match up with the current comfort zone of the congregation.

Finally, we sometimes intentionally divide the church when other, less controversial pathways exist. It is true that many Adventist communities are polarized today. We cannot always avoid opposition to a course of action that seems otherwise productive to the congregation, or to the church as a whole. But it is usually fairly clear (if we take the time to think about it), where the hot buttons are. If you are proposing something likely to be preferred by one group in the church, it is probably going to be equally disliked by another. Why not include other elements in the plan that will appeal to contrasting groups? It is not about winners and losers but about arriving at a pathway into God's future that sweeps up all or most of us and causes us to feel that progress is being made.

Church elections
Electing men and women to serve in the church is a collaborative effort. But sometimes we fail to understand both the possibilities and the broad sensitivities raised. Andy Stanley writes, "The church needs leaders who are willing to do whatever is necessary to ensure that we hand it off to the next generation in better shape than we found it."[5] What are we who serve in the Seventh-day Adventist Church doing to make sure the church we hand off to the next generation is in better shape than we found it?

Like many other aspects of church life, election processes are fraught with the potential for hard feelings and the loss of confidence in the goodwill and transparency of the leadership. On the other hand, when more spiritually mature believers are not elected to serve at a given point, they will find ways to minister anyway. So election to a church office is merely a support for doing the things God asks of believers.

The *Seventh-day Adventist Church Manual* has an extensive listing of possible positions in church leadership.[6] Not every church fills every position, but there is a general attempt to do so—even if one person holds several positions. As you might expect, given the fact that the *Seventh-day Adventist Church Manual* must serve the entire world church, the current language is a rather direct expression of who does what and why, in an effort to maintain order and to avoid too many personal interpretations shaped by culture. That is one of the strengths of the document. On the other hand, this directive nature becomes more challenging for some contemporary readers, here in North America especially, who do not find much in our current setting that is quite so direct or authoritarian. The elder, when quoting from the book during meetings, may want to filter some of this language. Here are some key ideas about doing it well:

First, appoint a good nominating committee. The nominating committee brings its annual report to the church in business session, where the action takes place. Keep in mind, though, that the nominating committee does not elect anyone. The nominating committee members should be selected toward the end of each year in consultation with the pastor, who will in turn consult with the conference where it may be indicated. The nominating committee can be elected directly from the floor, or the church board can be authorized to nominate.

In either case, the nominating committee bears the responsibility for filling the available positions, beginning with the elder and then going on to all the rest. One of the better ways to be sure the process runs smoothly is to put on the nominating committee men and women with no personal agendas to advance.

Then, keep in mind that being on the nominating committee is not for the faint of heart. The nominating committee should only include experienced members in good and regular standing—people who are prepared to be exposed to information about other members. Occasionally, someone will refuse being nominated for this role because they do not want to hear all the "dirt." Individuals may appear before the nominating committee to make comments or recommendations, but they must leave the room while the committee discusses what has been said.

It is critical to remember that this is intended to be *confidential* discussion. And the elder is especially responsible for making sure that the members of the committee explicitly understand this aspect and are committed to doing so.

Next, be prepared for the likelihood that not everyone will be pleased with every nomination you offer. In the Seventh-day Adventist Church, any member has the right to oppose a nomination. The details of the opposition should be expressed in a private session, in order to protect the people involved. Once the individuals are voted into office, any vacancies that occur during the term should be filled by the church board. Those who are most vocal in their criticisms typically do not know how hard the committee has had to work to get this list approved in the face of the complex demands of life today. But this is one of those places where the local elder can exercise the greatest positive influence by remaining calm.

Church discipline
Church discipline is essential for a smooth-running church experience. Still, it is often ugly and almost always leaves scars. As a local elder, it is great to have a pastor to whom you can leave the knotty issues of church discipline, or a conference office to whom you can appeal for outside help. This is not always possible, however, and it will fall to the local elder to make sure that matters of church discipline are handled in the spirit of Jesus—and with as little collateral damage as possible.

The issue of compliance with church standards is one that preoccupies the minds of some members, perhaps far beyond what a balanced spiritual experience might indicate it should. In the Old Testament, we read, "For the Lord is righteous, He loves righteousness" (Psalm 11:7, NASB); the New Testament reminds us that "all have sinned and fall short" (Romans 3:23, NIV). Balancing these two sides of the same coin demands a prayerful approach. We want to establish high standards and then follow them. But the more mature we are, the more we realize that while these standards are important, we do not want them to become a club to beat down those who are not as successful at observing them as we believe we are. Jesus gave us a pattern. He once said, "Moreover if your brother sins against you, go and tell him his fault between you and him alone. If he hears you, you have gained your brother" (Matthew 18:15, NKJV). In this, He was reminding us that in most situations a personal touch is best.

What is the result you are looking for through disciplinary actions? This question is the core of the discipline issue. Discipline is wholly about advancing the mission of God. It is not about proving publicly that somebody is in the wrong. Ellen White writes, "Human beings are Christ's property, purchased by Him at an infinite price, bound to Him by the love that He and His Father have manifested for them. How careful, then, we should be in our dealing with one another!"[7] And in his wonderful little book *Where Are We Going?* Jan Paulsen, the previous General Conference president, writes, "Rules and their application can be so wooden and insensitive that, in enforcing them, we can inflict such unreasonable punishment on someone that we dishonor God, who made both people and rules. Leadership must always be up front about right and wrong and give clear direction as to how the church should conduct its business. But, as leaders, we must also remember that God is in the business of saving as many people as He can possibly lay His hands on."[8] Given that, we have an entirely different focus as we examine matters of church discipline. Here are some ideas:

First, as a local elder, be sure to discipline others through the filter of grace. We do have members who are blind to their own lack of grace or the flaws in their own behavior. We do have members who seem to believe that they are in a position to criticize everyone else or prescribe what the church ought to do. But you are probably not going to cure them of this malady by pointing it out.

What is essential is that in all matters of discipline we are not being punitive but rather seeking a redemptive outcome. Not even those of us who consider ourselves to be the best of us (and quite capable of judging what is best for others) are really so well positioned. It is essential that we act out of our appreciation of God's love for us rather than our dreams of self-importance or a spotless church. Where discipline is needed, it must be executed, but it is really an opportunity to extend mercy and forgiveness in an effort to effect recovery.

Then, remind the church that discipline should be employed more rarely than some may want. The fact is some of us view the church largely as an exclusive club to which we must maintain our membership privileges, and we want to penalize those who break the club rules. But it should only be done when all other strategies have been exhausted, including engaging people on issues and exercising long-suffering patience.

By saying that discipline should be rare, I am not asserting that it should never be applied. But it is a last resort, not a common strategy. And it should never be imposed as a way of assuring that our own version of political correctness is maintained.

Also, it is essential to pursue discipline in order to advance our gospel witness, not merely to safeguard the church. The protectiveness that some of us display toward the church—where we are self-appointed defenders of the church's reputation—is far too often misguided. This is God's church, and He is well able to guard its reputation. Those who want to protect the church say, "We're just trying to keep the church clean." But they are often operating out of a misconception concerning how the mission of the church is achieved. We do not move ahead by purifying ourselves.

Our job as God's end-time remnant is to deliver an expert witness to the power of God in our lives by displaying His mercy, His grace, His forgiveness, and His hopefulness. We should be about helping people grow in Christ, not about figuring out who gets to stay in the church and who has to go. Those who lead out in discipline should be filled with sadness, not self-righteousness.

Then, discipline should never be allowed to serve in place of forgiveness. Sometimes in the church, we just get tired of somebody or simply run out of ideas for helping the person survive the life of faith. Some members are seemingly more trouble than they are worth. But when we discipline because we have run out of hope, we have lost sight of our mission. The church is not a perfect organization, manned by spotless men and women. If it were, it would have closed down long ago because none of us fit the requirements. The church is here to be a redemptive community, and discipline represents the last resort. We in the church should be the last to give up on people. When Peter asked Jesus how many times he should forgive someone, Jesus' response, in effect, asked Peter how many times *he* would like to be forgiven (see Matthew 18:22).

Finally, the discipline process is not just about the individual being discussed but also about the church's overall health. The ways in which discipline is handled by the local church, and the local elder, is an opportunity for the church to discover something about itself, revealing its own spiritual maturity. In the *Seventh-day Adventist Church Manual,* under the section on church discipline,

Ellen White is quoted as urging God's people "to follow the instruction given by the Savior in the eighteenth chapter of Matthew."[9] This, of course, is the statement where Jesus asks us to deal with those in trouble by going to them as brothers, seeking a reconciliation. Ellen White also writes, "The Lord desires His followers to exercise great care in dealing with one another."[10] The greatest danger in church discipline is not that we will not catch and punish an offender, but that we will drive this person deeper into sin and despair.

Working with the conference
The original Greek word for the Christian church was *ekklesia*, which meant "a gathering of people with some common identity for some common purpose." It did not mean a building set aside for religious purposes—let alone an organization set up legally to hold property and pay preachers. Much later, the Germanic word *kirche*, which was transcribed into English, became the word *church*—the common term we came to use. The church itself has undergone a rather complex transmutation from a very simple meeting in homes, where people gathered to share meals and discuss things of a spiritual nature, to the rather formalized structure we see today.

It continues to be a gathering of people with a common identity for a common purpose, which is to share with our communities the good news of a loving God. Today, the Seventh-day Adventist Church structure is quite complex. For the local elder, the next church entity with which most communication is carried on is the local conference. At the conference are a number of "experts" in various aspects of ministry, along with a number of individuals who carry out complex duties having to do with matters such as payroll, insurance, and investments.

When you as a local elder are contacted by these individuals, there is often something they need the church to do or some change in protocol that might enhance the church's effectiveness. One of the major challenges in these exchanges is that it involves people in a business setting interacting with people who are volunteers, doing mission. Typically, these people will work through the pastor, who is also an employee of the conference and their agent at the local church. Occasionally, however, a direct contact with another leader in the church may be indicated, such as the church clerk, the Sabbath School leader, the treasurer, or the elder. Whatever the nature of the contact, there are several key facets of these interactions that are worth discussion.

First, remember that the person at the conference office has the same ultimate objectives that you have. The Adventist mission is accomplished at and through the local church. Reaching your community for Jesus must be done through you. The people at the conference office cannot effect *their* mission except as they persuade *you* to accomplish certain things and assist you in others. It is very easy to believe that the people from the conference are just adding burdensome tasks, requesting the local church to provide information or promote programming. But what we at the local church may forget is that the interactions with the conference are being carried out through men and women who want us to succeed—and who can only succeed when we do.

Then, keep in mind that whatever the conference employees are asking you to do has probably been sent down to them from those above them. Our church has many layers and is filled with people trying very hard to make a difference. The conference committee, for example, is made up of pastors, conference administrators, and lay leaders who are seeking to advance the work of God in your territory. They provide a gatekeeping function and are typically very protective of the local congregation, scrutinizing any who would impose new ideas or programs—let alone new demands. So they have to be persuaded that what those above them in the church structure are suggesting to you or requesting from you is worth the investment.

Working at the division level, I see how many proposals created for new programs never make it to the local church because someone, somewhere along the line, stopped them. If an idea or request does reach you, it has passed several layers of scrutiny. As a result, it is probably worth a fair consideration.

Finally, consider the request from the conference as simply one part of God's larger effort to advance His mission. What is effective in ministry changes over time, though some of us are sometimes reluctant to embrace change. We want to protect what is traditional and proven. That is normal, and everyone in the system is cognizant of this. But the people at the conference—or in the layers of church governance above them—are all trying to effect the changes God has led them to understand are needed. They know that the only way to advance the work is to try new things. It is often one step forward, two steps backward, but it ultimately serves God's purposes.

The requests that come your way are not inconveniences but opportunities. In reality, you may be able to take those ideas and adapt them to fit your local situation far better than those who originated them would ever have believed possible. You are the local elder; you can do this.

The third cluster of skills the elder must master

The third group of skills that we will discuss in this cluster includes support for other local leaders, world church growth, local church growth, reclaiming missing members, and holding new members.

While our focus in these pages is on the local elder in North American Adventism, he or she is not alone in accomplishing mission. The pastor is at the head of this procession of local leadership. When we refer to the elder as a lay pastor, we are emphasizing three critical things: First, in the New Testament, it was the local elder to whom pastoral leadership was assigned, with the expectation that the apostle who founded the church would be moving on.[11] Second, most of our churches are small and are part of districts, so the local elder will need to be the point person much of the time. And third, even in larger churches—with a number of paid professionals on staff—the local elder is the longer-term leader, still in place to implement strategies when the pastors have moved on.

Under these working realities, the local elder will be called on in many, if not most, circumstances to carry out a number of what might be termed pastoral responsibilities. While it is true that the local elder may not have the professional training the pastor has had, he or she is not limited by that lack. Rather, by this local, voluntary status, an even greater access to the congregation is indicated, and some distinctive possibilities for ministry come to the fore. The following are some examples.

Support for other local leaders

The leadership team at the local church is made up of a number of key people. These are men and women who have chosen to commit their time and energy to some part of the congregational ministry. Some of the more obvious of these leaders include the church clerk, deacons and deaconesses, the church treasurer, leaders in various church ministries—lay activities; Sabbath School; communications; Christian education; health and temperance; stewardship; literature evangelism; children, youth, and young adult ministries; family ministries; women's ministries; social planning; small groups; music ministries; and many others—and those serving on a number of boards or planning groups. Your particular list of officers and leaders may be somewhat unique, but here are a few key perspectives on how to do your job with regard to these people:

First, remember a key job for local leaders is putting "fresh heart into the disciples" (Acts 14:22, Phillips). Understand that high morale and encouragement of the various church workers is central to the role of local elders. We saw in the book of Acts that early church leaders got this: "They put fresh heart into the disciples there, urging them to stand firm in the faith, and reminding them that it is 'through many tribulations that we must enter into the kingdom of God.' They appointed elders for them in each Church, and with prayer and fasting commended these men to the Lord in whom they had believed" (Acts 14:22, 23, Phillips).

Putting "fresh heart" into people is not something that we are able to do without some thought. We have to keep in mind that even those with the best intentions get tired and discouraged at times. Calls for people to do their duty get old after a while, if not supported by various forms of encouragement. We do this by being optimistic, by expressing confidence in people, and reminding them how God will be with them through whatever they are facing. Choosing to be someone who puts "fresh heart" into people is a very intentional commitment. We have to understand how important this role is and stay at it, even when we are struggling ourselves.

Then, keep in mind your role in helping establish an overall training pattern. The local elder may not be equipped to offer specific training for leaders in various ministries, but he or she can help these people get the instruction they need. The local conference may have a number of training options available or can access these from the union office, the division office, or even the General Conference. This can also be accomplished through online sources, such as the Adventist Learning Community, or through AdventSource, where many local leadership materials are available. At the very least, the elder can make sure that those who are newly elected to various responsibilities are informed concerning where such resources can be found and then assist these individuals in gaining access to the needed help. You may not feel qualified to do this, but you can facilitate it by connecting new leaders with older ones or even contacting neighboring Adventist churches, where those who are currently doing a particular job can offer help in training the new person.

Finally, local elders must call for the establishment of systematic discipleship training. One of the key opportunities now available to the local church is the iFollow Discipleship Resource, offered at AdventSource, and the many books on discipleship from iFollow that can be purchased at AdventSource or at your Adventist Book Center. The iFollow resource was created because of requests from local pastors and elders; these pastors and elders asked the division to develop a distinctively Adventist resource for doing discipleship training at the local church level. The division spent more than seven years researching, developing, and then distributing this resource, utilizing the very best of Adventist theologians, writers, editors, and graphic designers. The iFollow resource also includes a free downloadable set of more than 120 digital lessons, along with a group of discounted printed books and study guides. These resources are a powerful addition to what is available to the pastor and local elder in leading the church into spiritual maturity.

World church growth
Adventism has always been somewhat unique among evangelical churches, with our strong emphasis on a mission to the world. We are recognized as having a ministry in more countries than any other Protestant denomination. This is supported by several key perspectives:

First, we tie the gospel commission to the Adventist mission. The early Christian church grew because the believers understood the demands of the gospel commission to "make disciples" throughout the entire world (Matthew 28:19, NIV). When the disciples of Jesus began to organize His church, their vision was more limited than God wanted it to be. In some ways, they saw themselves as John's disciples had seen themselves, as a reformation of Judaism, intent on reviving the Jewish religion. The apostle Paul was instrumental in helping the earliest Christian leaders understand that it was not Jesus' intent to limit the mission to Jews.

Paul and Barnabas went to Jerusalem, where their ministry to the Gentiles received recognition. But even though the gospel went to the Gentiles, the battles in the early church resulted in repeated efforts to define what the church was in increasingly corporate terms, ultimately ending up with the formalism of Roman Catholicism. Our job today is to maintain a balance between corporate and individual witness, making sure we do not forget our New Testament roots.

Then, as local elders, we keep attention on the Reformers' focus on the gospel. The Protestant Reformation reaffirmed the core values of the gospel, driving the church to a more personal approach to spirituality that broke with many established traditions. The earliest versions of Protestantism, however, continued to emulate some of the formal tendencies of Catholic theology and practice, causing an increasing number to splinter into groups who disagreed on various matters of theology or practice. Early Protestant leaders, such as Martin Luther and John Calvin, were great men, but their own rigidity sometimes contributed to the splintering process.[12] Diverse holiness groups brought both helpful and challenging elements with this emphasis, including some tendencies toward emotional extremism.

Millerism, as taught by William Miller, created a specific focus on biblical prophecy. In the end, Millerism broke into a number of smaller groups, including one that became the Seventh-day Adventist Church in 1863. Even though Miller taught a somewhat literalistic version of Christianity, Seventh-day Adventists cling tenaciously to our Reformation roots.

In addition, as local elders, we share with our members the broad vision of service established within Adventism. The Seventh-day Adventist Church saw very early that a broad, worldwide mission of service to humanity was required.[13] Adventism began as a small, regionally based movement in the eastern segment of North America. By 1869, only six years after its founding, the church established its first foreign mission society.[14] This process accelerated to the point where we now have a ministry in virtually every part of the world.

In the contemporary church, global mission is emphasized during the Sabbath School program, where a number of programming innovations have been introduced over the years, including major offerings for world mission, and where ideas such as a local church selecting a particular segment of the world to adopt have proliferated. These are part of an emerging Adventist understanding of what our global mission is in contemporary terms.

Local church growth
While our worldwide mission has been and continues to be a powerful force in Adventism, we have also understood our responsibility for local church growth.[15] Jesus asked us to make disciples of all nations, and we are doing that, but we have also clearly known that we need to make them at home as well. This includes several elements:

First, we must note the powerful impact of public evangelism on the psyche of Adventism. There is no escaping the degree to which church growth has been emphasized as central to the Adventist mission. There are many in the larger church who quite sincerely believe that evangelism is the only appropriate focus for the church. As a corporate group, though, we tend to divide ourselves into various camps, in which we focus on our area of church life as though it is the only one that matters. Many believe that the reason Jesus has not returned is that we have not done our job in spreading the distinctive witness of Adventism to the whole world. Others believe that the reason Jesus has not come is that we have not adequately reflected "the character of Christ," by which we typically mean we have not become sufficiently obedient in our behavior. What we need to do, though, is find a way to balance our fascination with evangelism with a commitment to making the church such a welcoming environment that those we baptize stay in the church.

Then, we need to better understand the impact of an emerging spiritual maturity for sustaining church growth. While there should be no loss of evangelistic fervor, it may be that the pathway to sustainable church growth also features the impact of discipleship training, which leads our members into sustainable spiritual growth.

The challenge of the poor retention we are seeing in the church is not tied merely to methodologies. It also reveals our lack of internal health as a church. We are losing far too many of our newly baptized members within the first year. In surveys, people who used to be Adventists tell us that they just stopped coming and nobody came by to ask them why. So the problem is not with the message but with our ability to nurture those we win. What discipleship training offers is another pathway to sustainable growth.

Reclaiming missing members

One part of an effective discipleship training effort is fostering a quality of church health that attracts back into the church those who have left. The reclamation of missing members has a number of facets:

First, we need to remember that there are many reasons members leave the church. In surveys, we see that a number of things may have happened that contributed to members leaving: nobody challenged them to use their gifts; they developed no meaningful devotional life; they married unbelievers; they had marriage problems; they committed adultery and could not face the church; they quarreled with a church member; they took up habits that led them away from the church; they received church discipline; they became ill and nobody came to see them; they found the church cold and unaccepting; and they found the church irrelevant or boring.

Each person is an individual who did not plan on leaving the church when he or she was first baptized. They started out with great enthusiasm. But something went wrong along the way, and we will never get them back until we know why they left—and do something about it.

Then, we must realize we will be unable to address any of the problems without laying out a specific plan for doing so. There is no question that most of the reasons why people leave are attributable to things the church might have done differently. There are many interactions with missing members that happen as well, and a carefully organized church puts systems in place to make it possible for these contacts to be acted on. People who visit missing members need to be carefully chosen and instructed. Calling on these inactive members is a delicate challenge; one that must be handled carefully and with tact.

Next, we must begin visiting members who are inactive (or nearly so). Here are eight suggestions for visiting inactive members. Remember, your objective is to love them and demonstrate that the church is a healthy place and a place they would be blessed to attend again.

The Role of the Local Elder

1. Prepare before you visit someone. Know in advance what there is to know about the person's circumstances. If there is some particular reason why the person stopped attending, be sure to list it next to the person's name and address on your visitation card or list. People are impressed if you show that you have taken the time to understand what they are facing, or even if you have done some research on how the situation may be improved.
2. Begin with social interaction. Do not just blurt out the issue you came to discuss but take the time to talk at a social level. Do not dwell on this sort of idle communication too long, however, so that the individual wonders if you have anything else to say, but do not omit it either. Be sure to start with some matter of current or common interest. Allow the person you are visiting to share with you some matter or activity that is of great interest to him or her.
3. Move to the spiritual. You may have a text of Scripture that has been helpful to you that you may ask to read, or something the pastor said in the past week that was especially meaningful to you. Make a brief comment about some important theme that the church is emphasizing. And be careful that you do not come across as merely there to get the person signed up for online giving or to support the building campaign. Make sure you emphasize that you are there to encourage the individual's faith.
4. Ask important questions. Ask questions that allow the person to introduce matters about which prayer might be helpful. Ask somewhat general questions that are not too probing. You are not there to launch an inquisition. Rather, you are there to be helpful. Be sure that the individual is allowed to express his or her needs. The visit is about this person and his or her needs, not about you showing how much you know.
5. Keep confidences that are shared. The worst thing you can do is show yourself an "unhealthy Adventist" by taking whatever is shared with you and then spreading it to the rest of the membership or referring to it from the pulpit. Your job is to persuade the person that no sin is too big for God to forgive and then to assure him or her that God promises healing. Your intent is to reclaim the individual, not defend some

action that someone took in the past. As a local elder, you represent the very best of the local church. You are not paid to come and visit. You are there because you care and truly believe that the church is diminished if this person is not part of it.

6. Invite the individual back to church. You are not visiting just to gather information about a missing member. You are there to make a specific invitation for that person to come back to church. You are demonstrating by your invitation that the church is now healthy enough to reach out to him or her (however it may have been when the person previously attended). Do not pressure the person but show your personal interest in having the individual begin his or her walk with Jesus again.

7. Be sure to pray before you leave. Ask the family if it would be all right if you prayed with them. Few people are unwilling to have their family members prayed over. And doing so verifies the nurturing character of your visit. Be sure that you are praying for the family and not for some matter of your personal interest or something facing the church. These prayers should be brief and specific. Do not leave the family wondering if this is the only time you have prayed this week.

8. Leave before you are asked to leave. This may seem obvious, and perhaps even a bit humorous, but some of us simply outstay our welcome. When this happens, it is typically not because we are naturally offensive or indifferent to when we have worn out our welcome, but because we fail to think through what our plan is, including getting in and getting back out in a timely manner. If people want to talk longer (which they sometimes may), suggest a visit at the church or a repeat visit just for that purpose. Timeliness matters. It is better for people to say, "He left too soon," rather than, "She stayed too long."

Holding new members

While this topic is quite similar to reclaiming missing members, some elements require a slightly different emphasis. Jesus once said to His disciples: "I have chosen you, and ordained you, that ye should go and bring forth fruit, and that your fruit should remain" (John 15:16, KJV). These are powerful words in the ears of the local elder. It is not just about the early stages of growing the church, where we interest people in how Adventism might change their lives, but also the later stages, where we keep them active and involved in the life of the church. Our new members are typically spiritual "babies," and they need special guidance and protection during the stressful times following baptism. It has been found that the first eighteen to twenty-four months is the most dangerous time for newly baptized members.

Retention is key to overall ministry success. Healthy churches do not lose their members but rather help them grow into mature Christians. Here are some ideas on how to do this:

First, new members need to be befriended. People who do not make friends in the church leave the church. Research suggests that during new members' first six months in the church those who make six to eight friends in the church almost always stay. Make this an intentional part of church strategy and life. Be sure that no one is lost in the shuffle.

Choose suitable members and challenge them to make this a ministry they will stick with, which is to say they will continue to befriend select new members over an extended period of time. You can even put some structure to this, creating a spiritual guardian program, in which strong members of the church take care of newer or weaker ones. Check to be certain your people are doing well. Be sure they are coming to church each Sabbath, sit with them, take them home for dinner, and invite them to join your Sabbath School class.

Then, new members need to be taught with some depth what it means to be an Adventist. Remember that not everything will have been taught to the newly baptized member during the initial evangelistic effort. Indeed, some critical parts of what it really means to be an Adventist may have been omitted. Commonly overlooked issues include such things as stewardship and Sabbath-keeping protocols. The broad themes may have been covered, but the important details that the new member is expected to master may not have been provided at all. Another topic rarely covered during the evangelistic series is the role of the Holy Spirit and the discovery of spiritual gifts. Still another area infrequently dealt with in detail is the process by which a new member establishes a meaningful devotional life.

One way some of this information on what it means to be an Adventist can be delivered is by creating a new members' class, taught by the pastor, the local elder, or some other experienced leader in the church. Another key part of this story is connecting the new member with the various forms of literature that are available in the church, from the *Adult Sabbath School Bible Study Guide* to the *Adventist Review*.

The next key to holding new members is to visit them. There is often an abrupt shift from being prospects to being members. Going from the center of attention to forgotten is a common story told by those who have left the church. Here are a few suggestions: On the list of people the elder plans to visit, the newly baptized should have a special place. The visitation team should be trained to help the newly baptized establish a life in Christ; it may also be useful to continue Bible studies with the newly baptized, in order to establish the next phase in their integration into church life. Again, this is all part of a systematic discipleship-training approach. Some have established a discipleship-training program in their churches primarily to lead new members deeper into spiritual maturity. The iFollow Discipleship Resource was developed as a program for the entire church, but it is a good way to begin with newly baptized members. As a local elder, one of your best methods to connect with new members is to invite them into your home. In this way, you can demonstrate what it means to live as an Adventist.

Finally, if you want to keep your new members, involve them. Some of our healthier churches have put in place specific programming to immediately involve new members in certain parts of the church's ministry. As the local church grows during its discipleship-training process, these parts of the program will be increasingly made intentional. Make sure the new members are specifically invited to all church activities, including youth events, Bible-study groups, outreach and community-service programs. It is important to remember that new members do not necessarily understand the routines of the church and are unlikely to invite themselves to activities. It is unwise to appoint new members into heavy leadership responsibilities. Rather, let them be part of what the church is doing but do not expect them to lead.

It may seem counterintuitive, but new members are probably at their very best point for involving them in soul-winning activity. At that moment in their lives, most of their friends are non-Adventists, though that will change with time. This is certainly part of the reason why Jesus said to the demoniac,

The Role of the Local Elder

"Go home to your friends, and tell them what great things the Lord has done for you, and how He has had compassion on you" (Mark 5:19, NKJV).

---

1. Ministerial Association, *Seventh-day Adventist Elder's Handbook* (Silver Spring, MD: Ministerial Association, General Conference of Seventh-day Adventists, 2013). In developing this book, I had a fairly extensive conversation with the publishers of the *Elder's Handbook*. Even though the handbook had a fairly extensive update in 2013, a revised, electronic version was released in 2016.

2. In order to receive help with this, take a look at www.reachnorthamerica.org. You will find some very helpful resources for strategic planning, and many of them are aimed directly at local church use.

3. Andy Stanley, *Deep and Wide: Creating Churches Unchurched People Love to Attend* (Grand Rapids, MI: Zondervan, 2012), 51; emphasis in the original. Stanley is the son of television preacher Charles Stanley, and his book is very deliberately about establishing a new kind of church—a place where people who would hate the traditional church find an experience that speaks to something inside them. He founded two very large congregations of this type and tells how this was done and what the keys to success are.

4. Jonas Arrais, *A Positive Church in a Negative World* (Silver Spring, MD: Ministerial Association, General Conference of Seventh-day Adventists, 2007), 28.

5. Stanley, *Deep and Wide*, 55.

6. For more information, see Secretariat, General Conference of Seventh-day Adventists, *Seventh-day Adventist Church Manual* (Silver Spring, MD: Review and Herald®, n.d.).

7. Ellen G. White, *Testimonies for the Church* (Mountain View, CA: Pacific Press®, 1948), 7:260.

8. Jan Paulsen, *Where Are We Going?* (Nampa, ID: Pacific Press®, 2011), 23.

9. White, *Testimonies for the Church*, 7:260, quoted in Secretariat, General Conference of Seventh-day Adventists, *Seventh-day Adventist Church Manual*, 19th ed. (Silver Spring, MD: Review and Herald®, 2016), 56.

10. White, *Testimonies for the Church*, 7:264.

11. Remember that the pastor, as a professional employed by the conference and put in churches for temporary assignment, did not exist in New Testament times. His or her role today emerges from the Protestant Reformation, in which the "priesthood of all believers" theme demanded that someone with the vocation for pastoral service be put in place, in contrast with the Catholic priest. The pastor's role was seen as somewhere in-between the priest and the lay member.

12. Please note that it is not my intent to imply that it is proper to ignore the entire history of Protestantism and then jump to Seventh-day Adventism. I am doing this only because our focus is not on history but on the role of the local elder in Adventism.

13. We should note that Adventism arose during a time when this emphasis on reaching the entire world with the gospel was a fire that was driving many church groups. The

Sabbatarian Adventists that became Seventh-day Adventists initially rejected a mission to the world. But when they changed their views on this, rapid growth followed.

14. See James White, "Seventh-day Adventist Missionary Society," *Advent Review and Sabbath Herald*, June 15, 1869, 5.

15. When I say, "We have always understood," that is a bit of an overstatement. Clearly, those who have overseen our mission program at various denominational levels have often viewed the local church as merely a conduit of funds for world evangelism. More so than most other denominations, we have committed local resources to a worldwide mission. And while donations for this purpose have been declining in North America, the wealth and success of mission efforts in the rest of the world are largely more than making up the difference.

CHAPTER 8

Skills for the Local Elder, Part 2

Dwell in me, as I in you. No branch can bear fruit by itself, but only if it remains united with the vine; no more can you bear fruit, unless you remain united with me.

—John 15:4, NEB

As we come to the final chapter in this book, we will move to three more groups of critical functions that the local elder must be able to understand and manage if the outreach of the church in the local community is to be compelling. But we need to be very clear that none of these tasks can be accomplished through our own skill or brilliance. It is only as we remain united with Jesus that our efforts bear fruit. It is only as we turn to Him in times of uncertainty that we discover His plan and find the courage to go on into the future He has prepared for us.

The local elder is not the leader of the church. Neither is the pastor. The leader of the local church is Jesus. He takes our weak efforts and transforms them into powerful results. And even when others give us credit, we know the truth: we would mess it up if it were left to us. But thankfully, it is never left to us.

The fourth cluster of skills the elder must master
The group of skills that we will discuss in the next cluster includes visitation, personal counseling, small-groups ministry, prayer ministry, and social activities.

While the local elder normally is not an ordained pastor, he or she is still ordained and may be asked by the pastor to assist in a specific list of activities—particularly in settings where a great deal of independent action is required.[1] Some of these activities are more likely to be assigned, along with a few that not every elder is asked to carry. In our list of responsibilities for this chapter, we touch on several where dangers exist for the local elder who has not taken the time to imagine how the mission of the church could be advanced.

Visitation

The visitation game is changing in North America. Fewer and fewer families want a pastor or local elder just dropping by for a visit. While many of us are considerably more public with our online and mobile communications, such as Facebook, Twitter, and all the rest, we are increasingly less interested in having our private space intruded upon, even if it is by someone from the church. If you do not wish to unsettle some of your members, make an appointment before you arrive so that people can get the house relatively cleaned up and all the things out of sight that they do not want you to see (just kidding, of course).

Some of us who come from a different cultural matrix (or who have been asleep at the wheel) do not always recognize these changes in contemporary culture, let alone value them (or are willing to respect them). In some cases, our personalities are such that boldness wins over sensitivity, and we manage to barge in, uninvited, without causing too much of an uproar. But for most of us, a visitation plan that makes sense to contemporary members gives us our best opportunity.[2] Here are a few ideas to consider:

First, set up a broad visitation plan that is consistent with your sense of mission. Your plan does not have to be the same as anyone else's, but it does need to match your congregation. Choose visitors for your team who are skilled, mature church members. Not just any member makes a good visitor. It must be someone who understands the mission and who has the maturity to treat the members well and to make the visit about them, not him or her. Do some training to enable those who do the visitations to understand better what they hope to accomplish and how best to do it; try to weed out those who do not have the tact to do this.

Then, follow a few careful guidelines. Here are some ideas that could make your visitation all that you want it to be. Much of this information is similar to what we covered in the previous chapter about visiting members who have stopped attending. But a few items are different in order to fit this part of our discussion; for the sake of convenience, both the new and the old information are included in the following seven points.

1. Prepare before you visit someone. Know in advance what there is to know about the person's circumstances. If there is some particular reason for the visit, be sure to list it next to the person's name and address on your visitation card or list. People are impressed if you show that you have taken the time to understand what they are facing, especially if you have done some research on how their situation may be improved.
2. Begin with social interaction. Do not just blurt out some issue you came to discuss but take the time to talk at a social level. Do not remain on this level too long, however, so that people wonder if you have anything else to say, but do not omit it either. Be sure to start with some matter of current or common interest. Allow the people you are visiting to share what is of great interest to them.
3. Move to the spiritual. You may have a text of Scripture to read or something the pastor said in the past week that was especially meaningful to you. Or make a brief comment about some important theme that the church is emphasizing, but do not come across as merely there to get the person signed up to support the building campaign or the church budget. Moving to the spiritual is not about establishing how holy you are; instead, it is about including the members in the mission God has for the entire congregation, of which they are an important part.
4. Ask good questions. Ask somewhat general questions that are not too probing or that require the person to reveal information that might prove embarrassing. You are not there to launch an inquisition but to be helpful. Be sure that the people you are visiting are allowed to express their needs. The visit is about them and their needs, not to show them how much you know or how faithfully you adhere to the distinct views of Adventism.

5. Keep confidences that are shared. The worst thing you can do is show yourself an "unhealthy Adventist" by taking whatever is shared with you and then spreading it to the rest of the membership or referring to it from the pulpit. Your job is to assure the members that God promises healing. Your intent is to secure their connection with God and the church, not prove some point of argument.
6. Be sure to pray before you leave. Ask the family if it would be all right if you prayed for them. Few people with any level of involvement with the church are unwilling to have their family members prayed over. Be sure that you are praying for the family and not for some matter of your personal interest or something facing the church. These prayers should be brief and specific. Do not leave people wondering if this is the only time you have prayed this week.
7. Leave before you are invited to leave. Some of us simply outstay our welcome. When this happens, it is typically not because we are naturally offensive or even indifferent to when we have worn out our welcome, but because we fail to think through what our plan is, including getting in and getting back out in a timely manner. It is better when people say, "He left too soon," rather than, "She stayed too long."

Personal counseling

Except in a few unique settings, the local elder will not be a trained counselor. Neither are most pastors—and the church has experienced more than a few lawsuits because some pastors have tried to do counseling they are not qualified for and have botched things as a result. Personal counseling is one of the areas where we need to be sure we are only doing what is appropriate for us to attempt and we are extremely careful in what we advise. Moreover, we need to know when we have encountered a situation that requires professional help. Having said that, we also need to understand that one of the most important reasons for people to join the church is that they have personal crises in their lives and they do not know what to do. They need the support that the church can bring. Here are a few guidelines:

First, put your emphasis on listening. Try to understand what the person is actually saying, even when it is not expressed specifically in the words being said. You are trying to help the person move from an emotional level to one where logical action may be contemplated. You need to be sure you are listening carefully so that you can help the person identify where that better level is.

Talking is excellent therapy, so your intent is to allow the person to talk his or her way through the crisis. Be reluctant to give specific advice. You do not know the circumstances well enough to offer advice even after you have spent time listening. But the longer you listen, the better you will be able to move to the next step. If you spend too much time talking, you may miss some of the questions being asked. If the problem is relational, remember that you will probably not receive all the information required from both sides of the issue in order to see a pathway.

Then, focus on broad, spiritual solutions. Move the conversation from the problem to options that remain available to the Christian, given the complexity of the situation. People who are in crisis tend to go back to the same problem over and over, restating it in only slightly different terms. For example, you want to move the conversation away from establishing blame. Determining who is more at fault does little to move to useful solutions. This is especially the case if the problems are marital or are tied to some broken relationship. Sympathize with pain, but do not seek to find a rationale, or especially a pathway to revenge.

Begin identifying feasible courses of action that bring the most helpful possible outcomes. Sometimes the person you are visiting already knows what he or she needs to do but just does not want to face it yet. Do not be surprised if your suggestions are discounted. It sometimes takes years for people to get past these things, so do not go in imagining that you will fix the problem by your overwhelming insight and logic. You are there to establish the support of the church.

Next, help lay out options for the individual to form a plan. Occasionally, people who are in crisis are unable to see clearly what lies ahead of them. While you may not be able to provide professional help, you can help the person think through some possibilities and point to how God can lead him or her into a brighter future.

Once the conversation has reached an appropriate point, begin listing the more obvious available options. This helps the person understand that the moment is not one where there is no hope. Help the person in crisis begin to imagine which of the options promises the best result, without strongly urging one alternative. Seek a commitment on the part of the person in crisis to follow through.

Also, pray with an understanding of the moment of crisis. God's availability to help us in times of trouble has been biblically established. We need to help the person access those resources. Part of the commitment process is praying and asking God to assist the person with follow-through. Prayer validates the fact that the challenges being faced are of such importance that God must be involved. Prayer should be seen as the climax to the counseling session.

Then, understand when referral to a professional is required. You need to know when the moment has arrived for a referral as well as how to do it. You need to be aware of what local resources may be available to help in challenging situations. Note the level of grief, anger, loneliness, resentment or bewilderment. If it is excessive, it may indicate a need for a referral. Pay attention to whether the person is still able to function in the face of the emotion. Assess whether this is a recent problem or something of a long-term scale. Watch for inappropriate responses or illogical verbalizing. This would include extreme depression, the inability to make decisions, belief that others are out to get them, or loss of control over eating or other habits.

Finally, be sure that any counseling setting is carefully constructed with limited objectives. You want to help, but you do not want to be put in a situation where what you have said may be misconstrued or your intentions compromised. Neither do you want the person to put excessive confidence in the help you can provide as opposed to what God can give.

Counseling someone of the opposite sex is particularly dangerous. Do not counsel someone of the opposite sex in total privacy. You want enough privacy to assure confidentiality but also be sure to have someone nearby. Be sure to focus on spiritual help. You are not prepared to offer help that addresses other kinds of psychological needs.

Small-groups ministry

From discussions in earlier chapters, it has been well established that the Christian church began with small groups. The early house churches were small, intimate groupings, where people were known as friends and were supported by the faith community. In our current age of social distance, the need for small groups, where the Christian faith can be nurtured, is perhaps even greater. Whole books have been written about this. Today we experience so much mobility and migration that many of us are in great need of new friends or people with whom we may share a "common life," as Paul put it: "If then our common life in Christ yields anything to stir the heart, any loving consolation, any sharing of the Spirit, any warmth of affection or compassion, fill up my cup of happiness by thinking and feeling alike, with the same love for one another, the same turn of mind, and a common care for unity" (Philippians 2:1, 2, NEB).

The informality of small groups also contributes to the role they can play as a substitute family for those who long for closeness and accountability. There are a number of resources available at AdventSource, as well as your local Adventist Book Center, on setting up and maintaining small groups. The typical resource features ideas such as the following:

First, a time of sharing is central. One of the major strengths of the small-group movement is the opportunity it provides for people to share. Sharing our joys, blessings, and disappointments is central to these meetings and is often the first thing done. To have a successful small group, dialogue is essential. While no one is required to speak, the small-group setting provides an opportunity for people to speak from the heart and for a community to be formed. With this in mind, it is essential that the leader lead by example, encouraging others to speak.

Then, a key to success in Christian small groups is an emphasis on Bible study. Often, a segment of Scripture will be studied by the group and then discussed during the weekly meeting. Ways to make this successful include having a group leader ask probing questions that enable the group to move toward deeper understanding. Members of the group are not Bible experts, but they are men and women who are being taught by God, so what they have to say is relevant.

Also, another key to small groups is the impact of prayer. Often, it is in these small groups that the scope and effectiveness of prayer is discovered. Praying for specific people with specific needs is essential. Group prayer in the small group is a springboard for individual devotions. What we pray for in the small group is also prayed for during private worship. Stories of answered prayer provide encouragement for the group.

Finally, ministry and outreach may be part of the intent of small groups. Not only can the group identify projects they can adopt, but one of the keys to the small group is actively inviting new people to join. Keep in mind that the small group is also part of the larger faith community, sharing with the rest of the church a goal of reaching out to the community in varied ways.

Prayer ministry

Prayer is an essential component in the life of the maturing Christian. One of the ways this has been featured in Protestant churches over the years has been the midweek prayer meeting. While low attendance has caused this part of church life to dwindle in some of our churches, other evangelical churches have been able to revitalize the experience so that the prayer meeting becomes one of the most widely appreciated services offered. Here are several key elements you may want to keep in mind:

First, emphasize the prayer meeting through careful planning. One of the major reasons why so many churches have lost attendance at prayer meetings is that the quality of the experience was increasingly weak and the outcome unsatisfying. Begin by celebrating the prayer meeting outcomes during the Sabbath services, so people feel they will miss something if they are not there. Give the same preparation to the prayer meeting that you give to the worship hour. Even if there is a pastor available for delivering the Sabbath worship sermon, he or she may not be available for the midweek service. This is a place where the local elder can employ his or her teaching gift. Also, consider varying the structure of the midweek meeting, sometimes utilizing it as "Church Night," with a fellowship meal, and other times with specific prayer requests and celebrations.

Then, make the prayer meeting vital through distinctly relevant studies. There are things we can do during the prayer meeting that might be inappropriate during the Sabbath worship time. The topics we address during the midweek prayer meeting can take on a distinctive character, with a depth of discussion that can draw potential audiences. Consider the benefit of a series of presentations in which a more in-depth dialogue can take place than would ever be possible during the Sabbath hour. During the Sabbath service, promote the midweek service as a time that offers a more extensive discussion of some aspect of the topic presented during the sermon.

In addition, take full advantage of the sharing opportunities. Far greater participation in the discussion is typically possible during the prayer meeting than during Sabbath worship. Challenge members to bring insights from their own study. The historic nature of the midweek service is that it is a time when people are able to share blessings and challenges. Be sure to refer to what happened in the prayer meeting during the Sabbath worship hour. Dedicate a special time during the prayer meeting to allow members to share what has been happening in their small groups. This adds quality to the prayer meeting and promotes small groups as well. Be careful to learn a few statements that deflect controversy—phrases such as, "Well, we may need to ask Jesus about that in heaven," or, "Isn't it wonderful that we can have our own opinions on matters like this?" The prayer meeting is for spiritual growth, not dividing the church.

Finally, emphasize the role of prayer. The prayer meeting is about prayer. Take time in the prayer meeting to talk about the character of prayer. You can do this during the worship hour as well and tie it to a promotion for the prayer meeting. Emphasize that prayer should be several things: relevant, specific, intercessory, intelligent, and participatory. In addition, the idea of short prayers is well worth discussing. Ellen White wrote about some of the problems with particular prayer meetings: "Their prayers are long and mechanical. They weary the angels and the people who listen to them. Our prayers should be short and right to the point."[3]

Social activities

One abiding truth about all people, but about Christians in particular, is that we need fellowship. If a person is removed from social interaction for an extended period of time, a measure of spiritual alienation is likely as well. So it is critical that the local elder take a central role in ensuring that the span of social activities in the church is wide. In today's North American culture, we need to make a special effort to provide social interaction that fits our contemporary setting. Here are few of the issues in this conversation that we need to keep in mind:

First, at the root of the social experience is the overall health of the church. As local elders, the health of the congregation is of primary interest to us, and we need to dedicate time to ensure this aspect of church life receives the attention it deserves. We cannot bring in new members if the existing members are not healthy, engaging men and women, who enjoy church life. We need to remember that people do not really experience spiritual growth if they are not involved meaningfully with other people. We need to be sure that we make this a mission-centric emphasis.

Then, part of the reason why we do social activities is that we know our members need to find social acceptance. Isolation from meaningful relationships lies at the root of many of the problems members have. Social engagement of the sort we are describing allows us to know our church members better. This enables us to minister to them in the context of the lives they are living. But social engagement also allows our members to get to know one another and establish context in their lives. The spiritual maturity of the church can be measured in terms of how freely and openly members engage with one another in social settings. Knowing this, you should lead toward it.

Next, at the core of social activities is a desire to bond our members together. There are many ways to contribute to this bonding, but we need to be certain that we do not lose sight of the essential bonding intent. Not only do we get to know our members, but we also are introduced to their families as well. People tend to invite non-Adventist friends and family members to social activities. As a result, bonding between members and prospective members can begin. We must understand that the people we baptize are not merely those who have been persuaded about our beliefs. Rather, they are people who came to see themselves as part of our community. Social bonding facilitates this.

Finally, it is essential to put in place an effective social committee. All the benefits of social engagement are dependent on who we select for our social committee and what sort of charter we give them. It cannot be made up of people who view anything that is fun as un-Christian. And it cannot be made up of people who promote activities that bring our values into question. It is critical that those on the social committee create programming for all ages.

Programs cannot be only for older members or just for younger members. Families have to be considered as well, along with other potential groups, such as singles and young couples. This is a vital area that affects our success in all other aspects of ministry.

The fifth cluster of skills the elder must master
The next group of skills involves the various aspects of the worship service: the purpose of worship, the parts of worship, and the role of preaching in worship.

The worship that takes place during the Sabbath worship service is very important to Seventh-day Adventists. It is when the most compelling group experience for a specific congregation—whatever its size or makeup—is possible.

The worship service is also the time when the broadest possible effort may be made by the local elder to establish in the minds of the congregation what the story of Adventism is all about. God wants His church to understand His love for us and to see Him as a Father, who has sacrificed His Son in order to reach out to us with a compelling story. Above all else, we are a worshiping community who has come together to honor and revere God in a distinctively Adventist manner.

Worship style is a complex matter that must be assessed broadly—with close counsel from key members—and then understood collectively. We have churches within Adventism that are extremely traditional, and some that are quite casual and contemporary. In many churches, there is an attempt to find some middle ground that features different elements in the same service or during the worship calendar. What is most important to keep in mind is that the worship style must be tied to specific missional objectives, rather than merely maintained from some longing for tradition or an argument for reaching only one segment of our audience. Generosity, compassion, and kindness should shape what we do.

The purpose of worship
When we come together as a group of Seventh-day Adventists during the worship hour, we are coming face-to-face with God. We all know that, but we

sometimes lose sight of it in our larger interests. While many other things are going on during the worship time, the focus must be on the development of our relationship with God. There are several aspects of this emphasis on worship as a part of congregational spiritual growth that deserve our attention.

First, we need to emphasize publicly that in worship we are collectively encountering God. During the worship hour, the congregation is coming there to encounter God personally. The specific elements of the service are secondary to the core purpose, which is to put us in God's presence. This is why the service needs to be special in its design and expression. This is time of *encounter*. We need to make sure the moment is not about satisfying the ideas of any group or individual but about our corporate encounter with God. It is not about the choir. It is not about the pastor. It is not about the worship leader. It is about a community of believers expressing worship to God. We need to be more explicit in understanding that the moment is not about us but about God.

Then, we need to be certain to express our adoration for God in our collective worship. How Adventists express adoration for God is an issue that deserves some consideration. We are neither a high-church nor a low-church denomination. Our congregations are quite varied in worship styles—from large churches that approach cathedrals in size and feel to very small churches that emulate the early house-church model. We have churches where the members mostly sit quietly, and some where they do a bit more "jumping" around. We have pastors who are lively and full of humor, and those who are more tightly wound.

It is good for us to ask: In what ways does this adoration for God express itself best, in terms of distinctively reflecting who we are and what our mission is as Adventists? Is it defined by the music styles we use? Is it defined by whether we have a praise team on the platform? Is it defined by the elegance of the language the pastor uses? There may not be one answer for any of these questions. But we need to be sure that our intention is clear: God is meeting us, and we want to present ourselves in ways that communicate our adoration.

In addition, a key element in worship is proclamation. In Adventist worship services, a critical component, which we expect to be done well, is the proclamation of God's Word. The members and visitors anticipate a sermon that gives them hope for daily living. Preaching styles differ, both in terms of content and delivery. There is room for these variances in Adventist preaching. Both contemporary and traditional styles have value—and some effort to introduce variety has merit as well. But the common element must be an effort to emphasize the ways in which God's Word speaks to common men and women in terms of their lives and personal experience. We dare not be so elegant in our preaching, or so clumsy, that common people are lost in the shuffle. It is essential for the local elder to take the time to prepare and deliver messages that help the members find the hope to go back to their personal lives with courage.

Then, a part of worship that is sometimes missed is its intentional opportunity for renewal. Worship is a time for the individual member to reflect on his or her life and meditate on God's love and purpose for him or her. These are moments when the deeper outcomes of the worship experience may be established. In general, formal services tend to create space for this opportunity more often than casual services. Whatever the style, make these moments intentional. While casual worship experiences tend to be more participatory—creating broader specific opportunities for a person to express his or her experience of renewal—these worship experiences should not be so casual that structure is forgotten.

Be sure to let members respond to what you have said. It is not just about standing or coming to the front. It is about creating an entire sequence that allows members to make personal commitments to go out of the worship service as renewed servants of Jesus Christ.

Also, remember that an important part of worship is fellowship. As Adventist believers, we do not come to church to sit alone, cut off from others, but to be with the congregation in reverent fellowship. Some would argue that it is irreverent to jump to one's feet over and over, with songs and testimonies, and they would rather sit quietly and enjoy the choir. Others would argue that it is irreverent to have small children with their parents in the pews, distracting other worshipers. Some would demand a highly structured order of worship and that each element was handled with a professional demeanor, so they could hear a pin drop between each portion of the service. Others would prefer a casual worship style, where laughter and expressions of joy are common and where the pastor may leave the pulpit and wander up and down the aisles while preaching.

But one of the major keys to the entire experience is to create moments when true fellowship takes place. We can do this by stopping the service and allowing people to shake hands and greet visitors. But we can also do it by what happens immediately after worship, by what happens during the week, and in helping members find collective engagement with the community.

In addition, worship must be participatory. This is a church service, not a pastor's service or a worship leader's service. People need to be part of worship, not just spectators. Some in the church today tend to believe that worship is performance. A person or group is on the platform, providing professional music or learned preaching. Others in the church see the broadest possible participation from the congregation to be a better expression of true worship. Some of this will be determined by the size of the church and the makeup of the membership. But is it possible for us to celebrate diversity on this issue, where we are able to enjoy differing styles of worship without being critical or doubting the sincerity of those who see things differently?

Participation from the membership can take various forms; some spontaneous and some structured. But the key is to avoid the mistake of thinking that worship is all about process rather than outcome. Our intention must be to ensure that when worship is over, the worshipers have glorified God.

Finally, worship requires thoughtful planning. Nothing good comes from ignoring good planning and just hoping things will work out. Some of us are simply too lazy to plan carefully. But when we take the time to think through how we are going to do things, we are far more able to predict what will happen, let alone how we might recover from accidents or unexpected events, such as a preacher not showing up or a special music composition going missing. Even those who have regularly offered casual worship styles will attest that they only seem casual because the atmosphere has been established by careful preparation. It is better to have planned well and to make adjustments than to have never planned at all.

The parts of worship

While every worship service is unique and no two churches will worship precisely in the same way, there are standard parts of the Adventist worship experience that can be explored in some detail if we want to be certain that we are incorporating them as well as possible. And while the local elder will certainly need to follow the pastor's lead in some aspects of this, the local elder's influence is extremely important in ensuring that each element is handled with care and thoughtfulness.

First, we must understand the impact of music. There are few components of worship that are more controversial for some members of the church than the style of music presented or the degree to which that music is perceived to contribute to, or detract from, reverence. Whatever style of music is offered during the worship service, it should be chosen in an intentional manner. Do not fail to have an internal discussion with the other leaders of the church about what is acceptable, what blesses the congregation, or what will advance the mission of the church. Put someone in charge of church music who is sympathetic to the complex issues associated with it. While this person should be knowledgeable about music, he or she should also be committed to the collaborative role of music in the style of worship your church prefers.

A good choir, for example, is of tremendous benefit. But do not allow the choir to replace congregational singing. One of the keys to effective worship is group participation, and as local leaders, we cannot allow professionalism to overwhelm mission. At the same time, poor-quality music is unlikely to bless the membership or honor God—so not everyone who wants to sing, for example, should be allowed to do so. An approach to this conversation is that the worship hour each Sabbath should reflect planning and pace. Each part of the worship experience should contribute to the overall impact, rather than conflict with it. For example, at a recent service I attended, a band from one of our universities performed; the pastor stood up to preach, paused, and then said, "There is nothing I could add to the blessing we received from what we just heard." He then sat down—allowing the witness of the musicians to serve as the sermon.

Then, there are the announcements. The announcement period is more complex than some of us realize. Virtually every person in leadership in the local church wants to use the announcement period to promote some aspect of his or her ministry (or interest). Yet, except for a few announcements that may be critical to someone in the audience, the majority of the congregation is bored by long strings of announcements during worship and wants them shortened or even eliminated from the worship hour. Put as many announcements in the bulletin as possible. Generally speaking, the announcements given from the podium should be of an inspirational nature; printed information is better as the details are accessible later.

It is essential to think through the plan for opening the worship service. Consider doing the announcements first, before the worship service actually begins, and then have the choir or congregation sing something appropriate for entering God's presence just before the worship team steps onto the platform.

In addition, we need to think about the call to worship. The transition from the announcements to worship must be clearly defined if the members are to be properly prepared to worship. The essence of the call to worship is an invitation to the congregation to begin a more structured worship experience. You may want all of the elders to be present during the call to worship, even if they do not have a specific part to play, or one person may do this. In any case, it is a rather poor beginning to have the worship team enter without the members realizing the worship service has begun. Instead, you might consider having someone step to the microphone to invite the congregation to stand as the elders walk in and kneel or sing an appropriate song. If you are unsure how effective your call to worship is, experiment with a few variations until you are comfortable with what works best in your setting.

Next, carefully think through the role prayer will play. There are usually several prayers that are part of the worship experience. While a measure of spontaneity is desirable, a better understanding of what is happening, and how to do it well, is also of value.

Public prayer is speaking to God on behalf of the congregation. Each prayer during worship should be directed at God and should not be used as an opportunity to issue some form of corrective to the members. Some would argue that all public prayer should be delivered on our knees. Typically, however, Adventists have believed that content is more important than posture. Critical elements in the pastoral prayer include the following seven items:

1. Address God
2. Praise to God
3. Expression of repentance
4. Expression of dedication
5. General intercession
6. Specific intercession
7. Conclusion

Remember Ellen White's admonition: "One or two minutes is long enough for any ordinary prayer."[4]

Also, we need a thoughtful approach to the offering. Simply announcing what the offering will be used for does not qualify as an offering appeal. Here are several keys to make the moment of great significance: The call for the offering should be handled in a worshipful manner. The offering is a teaching moment and should be used to instruct in basic matters of Christian living, such as self-denial, sacrifice, and trust—which are all parts of stewardship. The offering appeal is all about motivation. Be sure the tactics you are using stand the test of spiritual clarity. The offering appeal should include specific information about what the need is, where the offering will be going, and why the individual should provide support.

Then, we need to include a specific ministry to children. While most Adventist children's ministry leaders agree that children should be considered in every part of the worship experience, some of us are more focused on providing a specific event during the worship service that is dedicated to them. One common approach is to invite the children to come forward for a children's story. Consider having the worship team, including the local elder, move to sit with the children while the story is told. Another helpful innovation is to include a handout for children with the bulletin. This could incorporate questions relative to the sermon being delivered. The pastor or local elder could ask the children what they wrote down as answers. Karen Holford wrote a helpful article on worshiping with children for a recent issue of *Ministry* magazine. She asks a question we would do well to consider: "How does Jesus' teaching about children inform our understanding of the role of children in our churches today?"[5]

In preparing the sermon itself, stories or illustrations should be included that will appeal to younger audiences. Consider having a child on the pulpit with you, on occasion, to offer prayer or read scripture. Make sure that worship is memorable for children so that they grow up into young adults who believe they were well cared for by the local congregation.

Next, think carefully about the scripture reading. Among evangelical Christians, Adventists have been particularly committed to keeping Scripture at the forefront. This should be featured in how we worship. Be sure to clearly establish the relationship between the scripture reading and the theme of the day, which should be tied to the sermon. A well-read scripture can contribute significantly to the overall impact of the worship experience. The use of responsive readings can also aid this by expanding the audience participation in Scripture. Experiment with innovative enhancements, such as having appropriate scenes shown on a screen during the scripture reading or using a variety of translations.

If you are preaching on Sabbath, be sure to reference the scripture that has been read, but be especially careful to use the scripture well, rather than merely employing it as a jumping-off point for some argument you want to make.

Also, consider the role of public testimony. While it may be less than ideal to include public testimony in every service, it can play a key role in enhancing worship when used carefully and strategically. Be sure those who will deliver their testimony are prepared for the moment when they will be asked to speak, both in terms of content and timing. The worship service should not be extended merely because someone (including the pastor or local elder) simply could not find a good place to end the service.

Then, a special effort should be directed at congregational participation. It is very important for us to remember that worship is not a spectator sport. It is not supposed to be just a performance by a group of skilled professionals. It is true that God is the audience for our worship. But He is best blessed by the worship of the entire congregation. He has come to the worship hour to accept our corporate adulation and to bless us in return.

Ellen White wrote, "Much of the public worship of God consists of praise and prayer, and every follower of Christ should engage in this worship."[6] What she said implies that one of the local elder's significant roles is to ensure that the worship experience is constructed with an emphasis on congregational participation. Typically, singing and the use of the litany, often in the form of responsive readings, feature the most regular congregational participation. But some congregations are more creative than others in finding ways for this participation to take place. As local elders, it is our job to imagine new ways for our members to find worship more compelling.

The role of preaching in worship
A vital element in the Protestant Reformation was the return to Scripture. We should also realize that the Reformers made preaching a central feature as well. Early Adventists emphasized these same two parts of worship—Scripture and preaching. Preaching has been highlighted in more than one section in this book; but in this skills chapter, the focus is especially on the role of preaching in the overall worship experience of the Adventist congregation. Here are some of the ways in which we emphasize this:

First, there is a logical progression to the worship service, tied to predictable outcomes, and preaching is part of this. Preaching is generally seen as the capstone of the service, but it is not always the most important part. As local elders, we should be most concerned with the outcome of the worship experience, even when we are not preaching. Two questions need to capture our imaginations: Was God worshiped well? And were the members blessed?

As noted earlier, we also want to be sure that congregational participation has been fully addressed as a key element. If the members were just an audience, worship did not happen.

Then, there are several preaching principles that we should note. There are elements in the local elder's approach to preaching that will determine how effective this part of his or her ministry is. For example, your preaching should emerge from *your own relationship with Jesus*. It is your testimony that makes your preaching relevant as an elder. Do not hesitate to introduce the personal. Then, *you should preach biblically*. The preaching you contribute to the worship experience should be based on the Bible in its context, rather than merely pulling out some passage and twisting it to your own topical purposes. Moreover, *you should preach relevantly*. What you are doing is contributing to worship. That means what you say should speak to the overall needs of the congregation. It should take into account who your audience is and include segments that speak to children, young adults, as well as those in particular points of crisis. In addition, *you should preach positively.* Too many of us forget this. As a part of Adventist worship, your preaching should lift up the membership, not simply warn them or chastise them. Your job is to give people hope. Then, *you should prepare early.* Do not wait until the evening before to finish your sermon. Let the preparation of what you are going to say emerge from your life in Christ, not just some theme that fascinates you. Next, *you should organize logically.* Above all else, sermons are about outcomes. You are there to move members of the congregation along in their spiritual journey, not just discuss some interesting text or theme. Additionally, *you should plan annually.* As a local elder, you may not speak every Sabbath. But you should take the time to plan a progression in your preaching over the year in order to accomplish what you want to say.

The sixth cluster of skills the elder must master
The final group of skills that we will discuss in this chapter involves *all special services.* These include baptisms, child dedications, church dedications, Communion services, ground breakings, house dedications, funerals, new parish inductions, prayer for the sick, and weddings.

The life of the church consists of a number of events that carry long-term significance. The local elder will often be called on to ensure that these events happen in ways that bless the membership.

These special services will typically take place with the local elder assisting the pastor. But in an increasing number of instances in North American Adventism, the local elder will need to handle them, or various parts of them, as assigned. These special services are not at all diminished because the pastor may not be available. Each of these special services is part of the web of life in the local church and contributes to its overall experience. Indeed, these special services will be some of the most memorable events in the church calendar and should be treated with all the attention that they deserve.

In this listing of special services, we will address them in the same order as in the 2013 edition of the *Elder's Handbook.* It will also take into account what is described in the *Minister's Handbook*, which exists to guide pastors. This is done as an intentional reminder that the work of the local elder parallels the work of the pastor and that in some ways the local elder serves as a lay pastor. (I suggest reading both of these books for the added insights they offer. There is also helpful information in the *Elder's Digest*, which is published by the General Conference Ministerial Association.)

The entire church is blessed by its participation in these events. Here are some useful insights on how the local elder works to ensure each of these special services functions to advance the spiritual maturity of the members and the overall mission of God in the local community.

Baptisms

In Adventism, baptisms are viewed with a special emphasis that is tied to our overall focus on evangelism and our belief that we are accomplishing mission when we baptize people. It is the moment when a person who was outside the community has chosen to come inside or a young person who has been reared in the church has chosen to declare his or her personal life of faith. The person being baptized may have been an unbeliever coming in from the cold, or he or she may have been a member of another Christian church, which did not baptize by immersion, and who wants to express his or her new step in spiritual growth by rebaptism. As a result, baptism may signal an abrupt change in someone's life, or it may reflect a growing experience, as someone takes this experience as the next step in a life of faith. We need to be careful when we talk about the experience that we acknowledge both perspectives.

With baptism, the elder has a unique position, often tied to the relationship he or she has with the person being baptized. It is often the case that the person being baptized had Bible studies with the elder, or the elder helped prepare the person for baptism in other ways. Under any circumstance, the elder will continue to be a spiritual mentor to each candidate for baptism and will be involved in his or her life into the future. Baptism is a significant event, but it signals the beginning of longer-term relationships within the faith community, featuring the work of the elder, who will help establish them.

In Adventism, most baptisms are carried out by ordained pastors. This is our traditional experience; it is what our policies recommend and will probably continue to be so in the future. But, at times, a local elder will perform the ceremony with no reduction of its significance. By policy, in order for the local elder to do this in the absence of a pastor, he or she must request permission to do so from the conference president and be assigned to perform the baptism.

Acceptance into church membership is also an important part of this conversation. Typically, after baptism, the congregation is asked to confirm the candidate into membership. Welcoming new members is vital to ensuring that the longer-term impact of baptism is established. Different churches have different ways of welcoming members into the fellowship. The key is making this moment of welcome memorable for the new members. In some churches, everyone forms a circle and sings songs of welcome. In other churches, a celebration meal follows the service. Other approaches are used as well. The main element in whatever approach is used is the bonding of the new members with the church as part of a larger effort to retain them in membership.

The local elder should make sure that once a person is baptized that his or her relationship with the church is established well, with the promise of the person entering into lifelong relationships within the congregation. This can be done in several ways, including enlisting him or her into some form of local ministry or continuing in a new members' class. But the key is to ensure the new member in integrated into the life of the church in such a way that the attention delivered during the recruiting process does not simply end with baptism.

Child dedications

Few events in the Seventh-day Adventist Church represent such times of hope for the future of the church as the dedication of a child. In our faith tradition, we do not have infant baptisms or any of the typically related events, such as establishing godparents (though some of us do the latter, nonetheless). But we do have a service where parents and children are set aside in a special moment of dedication, and the church is committed to doing its part as well. There are several reasons why we have instituted this service.

We want the church to express to the parents that we, as their church, celebrate with them just how special this moment is in their lives. We usually do this by having the child and parents come to the front of the church for a dedication service, which will typically involve a brief homily, prayer, and the dedication itself. The dedication service also exists to covenant with the parents and families that they will raise the child to love Jesus and be active in His church. By bringing the child to church for this service, the parents are expressing their intent to raise the child in ways that reflect the good news of Jesus Christ. Often, the commitment to do this results in the child being brought regularly to Sabbath School, where continued efforts are carried on to establish in the child a life of faith.

The dedication service commits the church to providing the support that the family will need to accomplish all these faith-building processes. A faith community supplies parents with assistance and encouragement in rearing their child. The entire faith community is committing to providing the sorts of nurturing and educational opportunities that promise the brightest future for the child. This event in the life of the church is usually confirmed by a certificate that is prepared for the parents, along with congratulations that will be delivered at the end of the church service.

Church dedications

The church dedication is one of the most significant events in the life of the church family. It allows the pastor and the local elder to emphasize to members of the church the larger mission of the local church as a part of what God is doing in the world. It is also a way of drawing the community's attention to the presence and mission of the Adventist congregation in their midst. So it is important to make certain that the church dedication is featured in the community at large, both by more traditional public-relations efforts and by the personal contacts of the local members with their friends and neighbors.

To the congregation itself, the church dedication is a celebration of a difficult project that has moved to a new stage, with promise for even more growth ahead. When the debt is paid, the focus shifts to the future witness with a new set of opportunities in the community.

Guests and city officials, along with conference leaders and former pastors, are generally invited to this event. The significance of the event in the eyes of the members and the community at large will depend on how well it is organized and carried out. The local elder should feel challenged to make it happen in ways that produce the most compelling outcome. One major element of the event is recognizing those who played an important role in the history of the church, including previous pastors and founding members. Typical parts of the service include a history of the church, a dedication prayer, some sort of consecrative message, and some act of dedication, such as a burning of the mortgage. Both physical and verbal messages should be part of the service, helping make it memorable.

Communion services
While Seventh-day Adventists do not attribute to the Communion service the same level of religious significance that Catholics attribute to the sacraments, we do place great meaning in the experience. Communion is remembering something Jesus did Himself, which He instructed us to do in order to emphasize His significance. It is one of the few services in the life of the church that we view in ritual terms and attempt to make especially memorable for our congregation.

Adventists see the Communion service as an opportunity for renewing relationships. This is one of the reasons why we invest so much significance in it. However often we perform the ceremony, the Communion service lifts the congregation by reestablishing who we are in relationship to one another. Typically, the Communion service is held in Seventh-day Adventist Churches on a quarterly basis, though there is no biblical requirement for this particular frequency. It is also often held at the end of special moments in church life, such as a Week of Prayer, the end of a revival service, or various forms of youth meetings. It is seen as a moment when the vitality of the individual's spiritual experience is enhanced; as a result, the entire church will be moved ahead spiritually.

The preparation for the Communion service is of special importance, particularly how the emblems are handled and how the foot-washing service logistics are set up. While the activity is unusual, and somewhat disrupts the normal patterns of activity, it is repetitive; once the various points of emphasis are learned, they will not be new each time the Communion service is held.

Although there are a number of ways the Communion service may be held, many parts of it are done in the same manner, virtually everywhere, due to the impact of traditional practice in the church. In the *Elder's Handbook*, for example, there is a recipe for Communion bread, along with instructions for preparing it.[7] This means that these items may still be prepared, even if the essential products are not locally available in finished form.

Seventh-day Adventists observe what is called an "open Communion." What this means is that everyone who chooses to participate is allowed to do so. Consequently, it is not the responsibility of local church officers, or the local elder, to determine who may participate. This is left to the conscience of the individual and ultimately to God's control.

The foot-washing service in Seventh-day Adventism is one of our more distinctive practices. Other churches have their own form of Communion, but what we term "the ordinance of humility" is rarely offered as a prelude to the event.

For those who cannot come to church for the Communion service, a visit to the home by the elders and deacons should be arranged, if requested. This is an extremely important part of the church's expression of community and should not be neglected. Typically, for those who are ill, the foot-washing part of the service is omitted. At the end of the Communion service, the emblems should be disposed of in a respectful manner by the deacons, under the supervision of the local elder. Under no circumstances should the food or drink that remains be consumed.

Ground breakings

The ground-breaking service is used to signal the beginning of a significant building project. The pastor, the elders, and the deacons will work together in the planning and execution of the event. The careful work of planning the ground-breaking event assures the best possible outcome. This is an occasion with great promise for the church and community; if you are anticipating a new church building project, be sure to include this kind of an event on your calendar.

Careful thought should be given to the list of invitees. Conference leaders should be invited, along with community leaders. Pastors from other churches could be asked as well. In addition, members of the media should be invited.

If a ground-breaking service is to be offered, the site needs to be prepared so that sufficient space is available for guests and presenters. The event can be casual, but it needs to be done in a thoughtful manner.

House dedications
While house dedications are not as common in Adventist churches in North America as in some other places, the opportunity has potential. Some families will request such a service when they complete the construction of a new home, while others may request it whenever they move to a different home.

Typically, a house dedication takes place after the house is complete and all the furniture is in place. The house dedication is a wonderful occasion to witness to others in the neighborhood. It signals that a Christian family has entered the locale and recognizes an intent to relate to the community in redemptive ways.

Be sure to invite friends and neighbors to the event. Remember that there will be non-Adventists attending, so the character of what is said and done must reflect sensitivity to the audience and care should be taken that the language used does not include phrases that only members of the Adventist Church would understand. No license is required for this service, so it can be officiated by the local elder.

Funerals
The funeral service is an event that is closely tied to culture. That is to say, in many of our Adventist churches in North America there are members who come from widely diverse cultural backgrounds, and they may desire to employ some of the funeral approaches that are consistent with those heritages. These traditions are used to express grief and show respect for the deceased. But if these services are held in an Adventist church, we must also be sensitive to who we are and what we believe. If the members want the service in an Adventist church, they will understand this.

Families may expect a local Adventist pastor to lead out in the funeral service, even if it is at a funeral home. If that is impossible for any reason, the local elder may ask the pastor for permission to fill his or her place and then handle the service himself or herself. Two aspects of this service must be maintained. First, it is our responsibility to conduct a service that respects the distinctive culture and traditions of the family. This will require a visit with the family to identify which of these traditions they expect to see observed. But the second area of responsibility is ensuring the family understands that the local elder will present a Christian service, reflecting the values and perspectives of Seventh-day Adventism. As a result of this second feature, some traditions may not be appropriate. In other words, do not send people off to heaven either in prayers or in the sermon. If the family wants an Adventist to lead out, we should feel empowered to speak in terms of the distinctive Adventist beliefs about men and women resting in their graves until Jesus comes—though it is not necessary that we elaborate on this.

As soon as possible after the funeral, we should visit the family of the deceased. Our presence will bring comfort and support. Offer the church's assistance in whatever way the family would find appropriate and that the church is capable of delivering.

New parish inductions
As Adventists, we tend to be less sensitive to ritual and more used to taking things for granted. One of these is when a new pastor arrives at a church. The new parish induction is a specific ceremony to heighten awareness of the fact that a moment of significance is taking place. It is designed to help the new pastor win his or her way into the hearts of the members. This service is unique in that it is best performed by the local elder and cannot be handled by the pastor (unless it is by a pastor who is leaving and wants to welcome his or her replacement). It is the elder's way of welcoming the new pastor into the life of the local congregation.

At the root of this service is a deeper recognition of the stress involved in transition. While the local congregation may be experiencing the loss of a loved previous pastor, the new pastor and his or her family are enduring significant changes as well, including the loss of friends, the demands of setting up a new household, and even the challenges of a spouse finding a new job. The service should involve both expressing regret over the old (but softening the impact) and celebrating the new. Ideally, the parish induction service should be held during the Sabbath worship hour, when most adult members are in attendance. There is a written litany in the *Elder's Handbook* that features some of the responsive elements that can be included in the service.

At the close of the service, a nice touch is to have the entire church welcome the pastoral family, recognizing that it is the other members of the pastoral family who are the most in need of being welcomed.

Prayer for the sick

The book of James specifically suggests that those who are sick should "call for the elders of the church, and let them pray over him, anointing him with oil in the name of the Lord" (James 5:14, NKJV). The passage then asserts that when this happens, not only will the person be healed but his sins will also be forgiven. The elder is to be a man or woman of prayer, so in this conversation, it is assumed that people who are ill will be a continual subject of the elder's prayer.

The implications of this service are such that it should be reserved for moments when someone is seriously ill and in such dire circumstances that other courses of action seem inconsequential. But we need to be careful that we do not turn the anointing service into the last rites, as performed by Catholics. We anoint expecting healing to result.

It is assumed that this service will involve the pastor, the local elder, and the person's family members, though if other non-Christian friends are attending, it is not necessary that they be asked to leave. The anointing service should be brief, but a few Bible passages relevant to the service should be quoted. The message that follows should refer to the promise of healing, the confession of sins, and the hope for healthy living.

Adventists do not see the anointing service as a substitute for receiving proper medical care. While the service requests God's intervention, it does not attempt to determine what God's will may be, except in terms of hope. Sometimes God heals immediately, and other times He does it over time. At times, physical healing is not part of God's plan. Thus, immediate healing is not to be presented as the necessarily expected outcome of the service.

The anointing with oil is symbolic of the Holy Spirit's involvement.

Adventists do not practice the placing of the oil on the part of the body where the healing is needed but rather pursue a more general approach. There is time for socializing prior to the actual service. When the oil has been administered and prayer offered, the service is over, and the elders should leave with the reverence of the moment held in place.

Weddings

Few services in the Christian community are more joyous than weddings. They are times when both those being married and their families are experiencing great hope and happiness. The local congregation, led by the local elder, should do everything possible to ensure the event takes place in the most positive manner possible.

While the local elder may play a vital role in the wedding ceremony, the wedding is one of those services that denominational policy requires a pastor to officiate. In many places, this is also a state requirement. Denominational policy allows some deviation from this, but only when the division specifically approves it. The wedding is one of the few services where the denomination exercises itself to limit whether an Adventist pastor may officiate. It is important for your local leadership group, under the direction of the pastor, to study the denominational guidelines as stated in the *Seventh-day Adventist Church Manual* and the *Minister's Handbook* and then write their own guidelines—which should be handed out to couples.

In some settings, the pastor's own sense of what is appropriate—given what he or she knows about the circumstances—may require him or her to refuse to officiate. In situations where the pastor or local elder must communicate to couples or families that a requested marriage cannot be held in a Seventh-day Adventist church, or be officiated by an Adventist pastor, it is important that written policies—with larger denominational support but written and approved by the local congregation—stand behind it.

The wedding is both a social and a spiritual occasion. It involves both a legal contract and a spiritual commitment. For an Adventist wedding to take place, it must happen in an entirely positive context. Only rarely should exceptions be made to what the church's written policies describe. The wedding should be a time of hope, not one full of conflict and controversy.

1. Again, in Adventism, we do not indicate by ordination that some special endowment of spiritual qualities is in place. Rather, ordination acknowledges what God has already bestowed and represents the authority the church gives to individuals to assume specific roles in church life.

2. When I was a young man, studying to be a pastor, one of the requirements was that I spend a season as a literature evangelist. I remember well the man I was assigned to work with; he was utterly insensitive to the people who lived in the houses we solicited. He taught me every trick he knew about getting through the door or overcoming obstacles to sales. I learned a great deal, but much of it I later had to unlearn.

3. Ellen G. White, *Testimonies for the Church* (Mountain View, CA: Pacific Press®, 1948), 4:71.

4. Ellen G. White, *Testimonies for the Church*, 2:581.

5. Karen Holford, "Worshiping . . . With Children?," *Ministry*, April 2016, 18.

6. Ellen G. White, "Acceptable Worship," *Signs of the Times*, June 24, 1886, 1.

7. Ministerial Association, *Seventh-day Adventist Elder's Handbook* (Silver Spring, MD: Ministerial Association, General Conference of Seventh-day Adventists, 1994), 168, 169.

CONCLUSION

Ministry of the Local Elder in This Crossroads Moment

We have looked at the role of the local elder in Seventh-day Adventism from many different perspectives. We have discussed it both broadly and in terms of a listing of specific skills and duties to be mastered. We have looked at some of the differences between what the elder does in large, medium, and small churches. We have talked about the local elder specifically in terms of his or her relationship with the pastor and when no pastor is on the scene.

It is not a matter of how much we have said about the local elder but of how little. This is a conversation that could fill several books. Not only that, it is also in the midst of a transformational moment, where our expectations for the local elder in Adventism are adapting to a number of new realities. Just as the larger evangelical community in North America is at a crossroads moment, so is the Seventh-day Adventist Church. Our culture is changing as we speak. The values that drove us for generations are being swept away by new perceptions and expectations.

We all know that a certain segment of the Seventh-day Adventist Church membership are digging in their heels in the face of this. "Not gonna change!" we shout, turning our backs and determining to stand for the good old days. We also know that a younger generation of Adventists—including youth and young professionals—are looking expectantly at those of us who are in leadership, waiting to see whether we care enough to reach out to them. They are not asking us to abandon our distinctive doctrines, but they *are* asking us to find new language for ministering in contemporary culture. They are asking us to look deeper into our own traditions, to see if there is wiggle room for them to be part of the contemporary Adventist conversation.

If you are an Adventist pastor or an Adventist elder, you are in the crosshairs at this moment. You cannot speak for Adventism as a whole, of course; but you can speak for Adventism right where you live. Many of us are very sensitive to the controversies that are sweeping the denomination as we try to figure out how we will engage with our contemporary world. Some of us see pathways to a brighter future, while others of us see only dark images.

A portion of the controversies are about theology, and others are about the application of policy, which is to say ecclesiology. But being Adventists, we tend to throw the Bible and Ellen White at every issue; at times making more passionate arguments than the issues probably deserve. Still, we live in an age of polarization, so we should not expect the church to be conflict-free or that our members will not reflect these passions.

From the very first page, I have argued that mission must drive our conversation. It is not about what used to work but what has the potential to work today. It is about understanding that in these end times we have to anticipate a demand for sharper theological clarity and a more inclusive approach to the Adventist witness. God put us here to do something. He put you in your community to make a difference. And you cannot do that unless you are willing to spend more time listening to people than talking to them. You cannot do that unless you are willing to open your mind to new ways of doing things. You cannot do that unless you begin to see how loving people into the kingdom has a far better chance of reaching them than arguing them into agreement with some interpretations of what the Bible means.

As a local elder, mission demands that you stop confusing Jesus' statement of mission—we are supposed to be out there, reaching those who are rejected by popular society—and Ellen White's description of Jesus' mission as mingling with people and showing our sympathy with more traditional evangelical debates over the rapture, abortion clinics, and protecting our right to bear arms. We *must* get this right. God put us here in these end times to tell the story of a God who wants us to call Him Father. So if we want to make an impact, we need to start telling our "better true stories" and giving up on some of the old, tired debates that have preoccupied us for so long.

When Jesus spoke to the Pharisees of His day, He said, "You're hopeless, you religion scholars and Pharisees! Frauds! You go halfway around the world to make a convert, but once you get him you make him into a replica of yourselves, double-damned" (Matthew 23:15, *The Message*). We need to remember that these people Jesus was rebuking were sincere, religious people. They tried very hard to be what they thought religious people should be. In attempting to get the Romans to put Jesus to death, they thought they were doing God's work. The logic they used to defend their actions made great religious sense. But Jesus called them "frauds" and said the people they were leading into the church were "double-damned" if they followed.

Jesus also said that telling His story in a compelling manner would not always make sense to some people and that we are to keep telling them about a loving Father, no matter how long it takes to sink in. He said, "The kingdom of heaven is like a mustard seed, which a man took and planted in his field. Though it is the smallest of all seeds, yet when it grows, it is the largest of garden plants and becomes a tree, so that the birds come and perch in its branches" (Matthew 13:31, 32, NIV). That is what the local elder in Adventism is being asked to do.

God wants us to plant our "mustard seeds." He wants us to be voices of grace and love in our communities, even when nobody is paying attention or when others are choosing to proclaim darker stories. God wants us to practice forgiveness and generosity, even when people accuse us of not being firm enough in defense of the truth. He wants us to lead our congregations to be expert witnesses of the loving character of God so that the people in our communities—even the secular and postmodern people—will behold the testimony we are delivering and find it intriguing, if not compelling.

That is the mission. That is the sort of "better true stories" we have been called to deliver. Jesus said that when we do this, our witness will grow to become a tree on which the birds of the air will come and perch. We are not assigned the job of creating nets to catch the birds. We are not given guns to blast them off the perch. We are the ones who plant the mustard seeds, and it is God who makes those seeds turn into roosting places that the birds find and where they choose to cluster.

I could go on for pages, talking about what we should do to the soil where we plant the seeds, what to do about watering the growing plants, and all the rest. The part that Jesus wants us to remember is that it is those tiny little seeds we plant that make all the difference. The rest is up to Him.

When we talk to a neighbor about the local basketball team and use redemptive language, that is planting a seed. When we attend a town council meeting on cleaning up the streets and speak calmly and respectfully, welcoming other opinions, that is planting a seed. When we tip the waitress at the local restaurant just a little bit more than average, that is planting a seed. When we smile at the angry lady who wants to kick the leadership out and remind her that Jesus loves her and them, that is planting a seed. When we allow the guy in the church-board meeting to bore everyone with the same arguments he makes in every meeting and thank him for sharing, that is planting a seed.

You get the point. These are all little things that local elders can do better than anyone else. Some of them do not even seem to be religious things. But they collectively witness to the way God is changing us from within, which tells even people who do not believe such things are possible that something special is happening—something they may need to take a bit more seriously. Together, we plant the seeds that God grows big and strong and attractive. This is the process that Jesus described when He said, "Dwell in me, as I in you. No branch can bear fruit by itself, but only if it remains united with the vine; no more can you bear fruit, unless you remain united with me" (John 15:4, NEB).

It is the process the apostle Paul urged us to adopt as we interact with the people in our neighborhoods: "Use your heads as you live and work among outsiders. Don't miss a trick. Make the most of every opportunity. Be gracious in your speech. The goal is to bring out the best in others in a conversation, not put them down, not cut them out" (Colossians 4:5, 6, *The Message*). The local elder is to be cool and collected, sharp as a tack, and always alert for opportunities. The local elder is to be gracious in speech and everything else, putting people above rules, and helping the church choose its better true stories. He or she is building up the people in the church, bringing out the best that is in us. And the local elder is trusting God to take the feeble efforts we offer, transform them into something better than we could ever imagine, and then bring on the birds.

What a joy we, as local elders, experience in having God use us in these ways!

APPENDIX

Resources for the Training of the Local Elder in Adventism

One is tempted to bemoan the small number of specific Adventist materials on the training and ministry of the local elder. We would like to believe that the church understands how vital this role is and provides better resources for it. (An effort is now being initiated to address this.) It is not that there are *no* resources available (you will find several in the following list), but merely that there are too few for the significance of the local elder in the life of the church.

The resources that do exist—while they are well intended and, in some ways, professionally done—are sometimes a bit too mechanical in structure and presentation, or they are less specific than they need to be to support the challenge of ministering as a local elder in North America. Spending several years as the director of the NAD's Church Resource Center, where I helped pastors and others in church life develop good materials, I should have done a better job of finding and getting these resources in place—as should all the others working in various church entities to advance the resource stream.[1]

When I was asked by the administrators in the NAD to research and prepare coursework for this project on the local elder and to work with the Adventist Learning Community in mapping out a pathway for the local elder's training and motivation, one of the distinctive tasks I envisioned was this one—an annotated listing of resources. The listing and evaluating of elders' training materials contributes to the discussion on the local elder by making accessible some of the resources that the local elder (and also other parties, as needed) may want to review as a part of elder training. It will also be useful to existing elders who are seeking ways to expand their effectiveness by further reading.

The truth is Seventh-day Adventists are like other denominations in many ways. But we are not *precisely* like them in what we expect our elders to do. Our history and interactions with those other denominations are complex, and we have a tendency to take what others have done and alter their strategies, even if just a bit, in order to make it work for us. This is often successful; but we sometimes fail to take note of what is said in context, resulting in applications with uneven success, let alone an inadequate filtering of what we have found. So, in these lists of resources, you will find both Adventist and non-Adventist materials, along with some effort to evaluate the contributions they make or, in a few, the elements they lack. The listing is far from complete (and I have probably left off some that should have been included), but it is a good starting place.

General observations about elder's resources

As I said, I wish there were more distinctively Adventist resources on the theme of local church leadership through the local elder from which I could draw. Those in the Adventist Learning Community, who have been attempting for some time to develop materials for the local elder (they were told by Adventist pastors that these sorts of resources were among the most needed in the church), state that a number of people have begun working on such aids but have not yet produced a final product. This book represents an effort to address this. By the time you read this book, other materials may already be available.

Among the existing resources for the local elder, we do have the *Seventh-day Adventist Elder's Handbook*, which the General Conference published in 1994 and updated in 2016. The *Elder's Handbook* is a useful resource and had been needed for a long time when it was first delivered. I am glad we have it, and I am impressed both with the effort it represents and the detail it offers. It includes a brief commentary on a wide assortment of church responsibilities and does give a fairly comprehensive overview of the topic. It is a good book that every elder should read and reread as specific challenges present themselves.

Resources for the Training of the Local Elder in Adventism

Even though it is a useful tool and study guide, and an effort to do some sort of certification, it is really an expression of the broad overview of the elder position rather than something that reflects the changing ministry opportunities for the local elder, especially here in North America and the West. But do not mistake me. As a local elder, you should have a copy of the *Elder's Handbook* and refer to it often. Several experienced hands wrote and edited it, and it will serve you well as a presentation of how the church at large thinks about your role. Since it has been prepared for the whole church, you will find some materials in it that do not relate to your specific situation. For example, early in the *Handbook*, we read, "The tremendous differences between elders in varying parts of the world and in various size churches makes the preparation of a job description extremely difficult. Some Adventist elders can hardly read or write."[2]

This situation probably does not apply as extensively here in North America, where our challenges are less about being sure the local elder can read or write but rather in ensuring that he or she is capable of interfacing with contemporary audiences, who are in some ways unique in their postmodern orientation. Clearly, we have elders whose first language is not English, but our biggest challenge is reaching contemporary audiences.

The other predominant existing resource for the Adventist elder is a quarterly magazine, titled *Elder's Digest*. The *Elder's Digest* is far more agile than the *Elder's Handbook* in that it is ongoing and contains an ever-expanding list of topics. It, too, is a resource that every local elder should be receiving. It, like the *Elder's Handbook*, is published by the General Conference Ministerial Association and deals with many useful topics, including such things as "Tips for Sermon Preparation,"[3] "Elders and the Generational Relay,"[4] and "Proper Use of the Voice."[5] There have been several special issues of the publication that are worth noting, such as the January–March 2008 issue, on "The Ministry of the Elder," and the July–September 2009 issue, with its focus on "Church Administration: The Nomination for the Office of Elder." Archives of the publication can be accessed readily online.[6] Again, it is not tailored directly for the North American audience, since it is a resource for the world field, but that is more a theoretical limitation than a practical one.

Some of the publication's articles are directed toward the pastor or member more than at the local elder. But there are still many good things to be found by the local elder in its pages. As with most of our denominational publications, one of the major challenges the editors face is finding a constant stream of useful material on a topic that has received too little attention. As a result, some of the articles may seem like "fillers," or the sort of things that one would expect to find in the *Adventist Review* or in union papers. This would include matters such as the church's position on alcohol or issues of religious liberty. The articles are often well written and worth one's time, but they may be less than perfectly aimed at the target audience.

Despite this, I have found some excellent stuff here. There was a refreshingly candid article in one issue, titled "I'm Not God: 10 Things Pastors Wish They Could Say to Certain Church Members." The author, who happens to be a pastor friend of mine, has some fascinating language in it. For example, in the first item of the ten things he would like to say to his parishioners, he writes, "I have many parishioners, too many to call every day, so I may not know when you're sick, discouraged, or otherwise in need of pastoral care. If you want me to do something for you, perhaps you might tell me what's happening in your life rather than just complaining to others that I wasn't there for you." The author then goes on: "If you say hurtful, unkind things about me and my family, my feelings can be hurt, and I may even become a little angry. I'm not a punching bag. It is likely that I will minister to you less effectively—and certainly less cheerfully—after you've insulted me."[7]

Ouch! This sort of reality check is vital for the pastor or local elder if he or she is to minister effectively in our contemporary setting and can only be found in a niche publication such as this one. Clearly, this is an article that would be understood best by other pastors, but it still has relevance for the local elder, who sometimes faces similar situations.

Specific Adventist resources for the local elder
The resources annotated below represent materials I found to contain useful information for the conversations on the work of the elder that appear in both the coursework and in this book. The books and articles described are not all directed intentionally at the local elder. Rather, they represent resources I used and that I felt provided some additional value for the elder, should

he or she pursue further reading. These are not the entirety of the resources I used (so do not complain too loudly if I left something off the list) but the ones I felt offered the greatest value:

Arrais, Jonas. "Discovering Spiritual Gifts to Mobilize Church Members." PowerPoint presentation, 2008. https://www.eldersdigest.org/seminars. This is a PowerPoint presentation that can be downloaded from the *Elder's Digest* website. It is helpful in identifying the spiritual-gifts process. Of special benefit is a listing of spiritual gifts that has passed through the filter of Adventist thinking.

———. "Evaluation Process for Local Church Elders." PowerPoint presentation, 2013. https://www.eldersdigest.org/seminars. This is another PowerPoint presentation from the *Elder's Digest* website. This presentation itemizes, in a convenient form, a number of responsibilities that a well-prepared Adventist elder should be handling.

———. "Tips for Sermon Preparation." *Elder's Digest*, January/March 2016. https://cdn.ministerialassociation.org/cdn/eldersdigest.org/issues/ED%20Q1%202016.pdf. A very helpful article that provides ideas on how the local elder can write meaningful sermons for Seventh-day Adventist churches.

Burt, Merlin D., ed. *Understanding Ellen White*. Nampa, ID: Pacific Press®, 2015. In this book are a number of very helpful treatises by Adventist authors who contribute to our understanding of Ellen White in her context. These are apologists, and there is a measure of scholarship on display that will help the local elder have confidence in discussing some challenging issues.

Day, Dan. *A Deeper Look at Your Church*. Lincoln, NE: AdventSource, 2011. While not directed specifically at the local elder, this book was written to "lift the hood" on Adventism for a look inside the "engine" of the church. It was intended to inspire local leadership to seek a more contemporary understanding of what it means to be an Adventist in ministry in North America—especially in terms of how our distinctive Seventh-day Adventist values equip us for discipleship training and a distinctive end-time ministry.

———. *A Guide to Marketing Adventism*. Adventist Heritage Library. Nampa, ID: Pacific Press®, 2014. This is another of my books, and I recommend it because it remains one of the few books Adventism has delivered that steps outside the traditional language of the church to explore strategies for reaching the unchurched in new ways that resonate better with postmodern audiences. To say that the local elder is a "marketer" of Adventism may not roll off the tongue well, but it is still true.

Dedier, Johann. "Elders and the Generational Relay." *Elder's Digest*, January/March 2016. https://cdn.ministerialassociation.org/cdn/eldersdigest.org/issues/ED%20Q1%202016.pdf. This is an interesting personal story of how a young elder finds his footing in the life of the local church. It is of special interest due to its emphasis on team ministry.

Elder's Digest. This quarterly magazine is a noteworthy effort by the General Conference Ministerial Association to keep in front of a more general population a set of conversations that could be relevant to the local elder. Selective reading is recommended.

iFollow Discipleship Series. Lincoln, NE: AdventSource. Each volume in the series of iFollow books is dedicated to some part of the discipleship effort. I have written five of these books, and a number of other authors have written some very important titles. Go to the AdventSource website to see the entire list.

King, Kirk, and Ron Pickell. *The Word on Campus: A Guide to Public College Ministry*. Lincoln, NE: AdventSource, 2008. This book represents an emerging story of how Seventh-day Adventists in local churches are beginning to understand better ways to minister to the 80 percent of our Adventist young adults who are on non-Adventist college and university campuses. This represents one of the underserved roles of the local elder.

Knight, George R. *Angry Saints: The Frightening Possibility of Being Adventist Without Being Christian*. Hagerstown, MD: Review and Herald®, 1998. This book is really about the 1888 General Conference Session, where Adventism actually split into two somewhat diverging strands. The local elder will have in the local congregation representatives of both strands, and he or she must be prepared to understand where they are coming from.

———. *The Apocalyptic Vision and the Neutering of Adventism*. Hagerstown,

MD: Review and Herald®, 2008. This is easily George Knight's most controversial book, in which he attempts to synthesize the loss of apocalyptic fervor, which he believes is endemic to contemporary Adventism.

———. *William Miller and the Rise of Adventism*. Nampa, ID: Pacific Press®, 2010. Much of the early history of Adventism can be found here, including significant insights on how our early history continues to shape who we as Adventists are today. This is one of Knight's best books.

Lake, Jud. *Ellen White Under Fire*. Nampa, ID: Pacific Press®, 2010. Probably the best book about Ellen White that the church has produced up until this time; it includes reasoned responses to all the major criticisms of the work and ministry of Ellen White. Every Adventist elder should have this book, should read it, and should underline key passages.

Land, Gary. *Uriah Smith: Apologist and Biblical Commentator*. Nampa, ID: Pacific Press®, 2015. Understanding the role of Uriah Smith as a major foil for Ellen White within the church is of critical significance for the local elder. Smith was sniping at Ellen White from a leadership position and was the target of some of her most telling criticisms. Many of our members, even today, raise a number of the issues Smith sought to advance but was thrown back by Ellen White over and over again.

McArthur, Benjamin. *A. G. Daniells: Shaper of Twentieth-Century Adventism*. Nampa, ID: Pacific Press®, 2016. McArthur's discussion of A. G. Daniells adds to our understanding of one of the most controversial periods in Adventist history by looking at the righteousness-by-faith controversy and the debate on how Adventism should be governed through the eyes of one of the key players. Daniells is especially important as the primary architect of the governance approaches that continue to shape contemporary Seventh-day Adventism.

Miller, Nicholas P. *The Reformation and the Remnant*. Nampa, ID: Pacific Press®, 2016. This publication is one of the best books on some of the current issues in Adventism that affect the local elder. Miller reflects on a wide assortment of current issues in the church through the lens of Reformation teachings. Miller goes a step further than Knight in analyzing contemporary Adventism from the broadest and most compelling perspective.

Ministerial Association. *Seventh-day Adventist Elder's Handbook*. Silver Spring, MD: Ministerial Association, General Conference of Seventh-day Adventists, 2016. The *Elder's Handbook* is a rather specific publication that attempts to provide a paragraph about every issue in Adventism that is likely to affect the local elder. Its major strength is its broad scope. Its major weakness is that it follows its track rather mechanically and does not pause to discuss surrounding issues. Because of its international audience, doing so would have been impossible.

North American Division, General Conference of Seventh-day Adventists. *Ministry of the Elder: A Quick Start Guide*. Lincoln, NE: AdventSource, 2008. The Quick Start Guides are all brief descriptions of various ministries that give an outline of what that ministry in the local church entails. This is a very helpful place to start your effort to understand the ministry of the local elder.

Oliver, Barry. *SDA Organizational Structure: Past, Present, and Future*. Andrews University Seminary Doctoral Dissertation Series. Berrien Springs, MI: Andrews University Press, 1989. Most of the discussions Adventists have about our current organization, including its flaws, are addressed in this seminal work. The book can be expensive, but there is nothing else that compares with it.

Page, Jerry. "Strategies for Difficult Disagreements." *Elder's Digest*, October/December 2015. https://cdn.ministerialassociation.org/cdn/eldersdigest.org/issues/ED%20Q4%202015.pdf. This is a good example of one of the more useful articles found in the *Elder's Digest*. It lists several key insights into why arguments take place and how to address them.

Paulsen, Jan. *Where Are We Going?* Nampa, ID: Pacific Press®, 2011. This book is part of the conversation not just because Paulsen was a General Conference president but because he is one of the few church leaders who is willing to acknowledge and write about how the church is changing and what some of the implications for the local church, and the local elder, may be.

Rodríguez, Ángel M., ed. *Message, Mission, and Unity of the Church*. Silver Spring, MD: Biblical Research Institute, 2013. What makes this book especially valuable is that it contains scholarly presentations by some of

Adventism's most gifted scholars on the various aspects of mission. Some of the best insights into the biblical local elder appear in these pages.

Sahlin, Monte. "What Is the Role of Elders in Large Congregations?" Paper presented to the Sligo, Maryland, Seventh-day Adventist Church, January 1998. http://www.creativeministry.org/site/1/docs/elder.pdf. This paper addresses not only the topic listed but also the biblical story and history of how Adventism has used elders. It is an excellent work, especially the author's breakdown of various models available to the larger church.

Siebold, Loren. "I'm Not God: 10 Things Pastors Wish They Could Say to Certain Church Members." *Elder's Digest*, January/March 2016. https://cdn.ministerialassociation.org/cdn/eldersdigest.org/issues/ED%20Q1%202016.pdf. Several quotations from this article are used in segments of the coursework. It provides a candid reflection on the challenges a pastor (and local elder) faces in working with real-world Adventists.

Valentine, Gilbert M. *The Prophet and the Presidents*. Nampa, ID: Pacific Press®, 2011. In the pages of this book, there is a more comprehensive picture of the early conflicts that shaped Adventism than you can find anywhere else. One can see Ellen White's growing frustration with denominational leadership and the reasons for her call to a return to more transparent organizational structure and policy. It is a side of Seventh-day Adventism that the local elder should be exposed to, in order to enable him or her to deal with conflict in the contemporary setting.

Whidden, Woodrow. *E. J. Waggoner: From the Physician of Good News to Agent of Division*. Hagerstown, MD: Review and Herald®, 2008. The controversy over righteousness by faith that figures so highly in contemporary Adventism began with the impact of Jones and Waggoner on the church in the late 1800s. The story depicts the rise and fall of a central figure in Adventist thought.

Broader Christian resources for the local elder

There are a number of non-Adventist books that the Seventh-day Adventist local elder should consider adding to his or her library in support of their role in the church. Not all of them will be helpful in every chapter, or without viewpoints with which you might disagree, but they do contain segments that are of great benefit. Here are a few of the better ones I have reviewed—most of which I have added to my own library—and used in the development of a number of resources for leaders in the local Adventist church:

Briggs, J. R., and Bob Hyatt. *Eldership and the Mission of God: Equipping Teams for Faithful Church Leadership.* Downers Grove, IL: InterVarsity Press, 2015. This is a book about a successful ministry that engages pastors and elders in witness. The authors write about "missionaries [who are] cleverly disguised as plumbers, teachers, stay-at-home parents, attorneys and the like."[8]

Holbert, Cary. *The Elder.* Columbia, SC: Dirty Feet Ministries, 2013. This is a very readable discussion of the elder's role in the life of the church. The author is both a pastor and a consultant to churches seeking stronger organizational success.

Ireland, David. *The Ministry of the Elder: Developing Effective Elders to Serve the Local Church.* Verona, NJ: IMPACT, 2004. This is actually a workbook with twelve lessons for individual and group study. It is designed to be an aid for the local congregation in attempting to teach new elders—and may serve as a model for similarly developed tools for your church.

Kinnaman, David, and Gabe Lyons. *unChristian: What a New Generation Really Thinks About Christianity . . . and Why It Matters.* Grand Rapids, MI: Baker Books, 2007. This is the single most significant book written in recent years about the state of the church. As the president of Barna Group, Kinnaman shaped research studies that have revolutionized the way the contemporary evangelical community understands the impact of what is being done to reach younger audiences.

Mancini, Will. *Church Unique: How Missional Leaders Cast Vision, Capture Culture, and Create Movement.* San Francisco: Jossey-Bass, 2008. Mancini, a church-growth consultant, emphasizes how churches can succeed in mission by ceasing to focus inwardly and instead focusing on engagement with their communities and influencing culture.

Newton, Phil A. *Elders in Congregational Life: Rediscovering the Biblical Model for Church Leadership.* Grand Rapids, MI: Kregel, 2005. One of the better books for wrapping your mind around what the biblical role of the church elder was. It also focuses on the fact that the local church may need several elders for ministry to be effective.

Newton, Phil A., and Matt Schmucker. *Elders in the Life of the Church: Rediscovering the Biblical Model for Church Leadership*. Grand Rapids, MI: Kregel, 2014. An excellent discussion of the role the elder is beginning to play in the Southern Baptist Church, where it has previously been largely ignored.

Rainer, Thom, and Eric Geiger. *Simple Church: Returning to God's Process for Making Disciples*. Nashville, TN: B&H, 2011. Based on a study of eighty-eight churches, Rainer and Geiger emphasize the role the simple church movement can make in Christian life, particularly in terms of creating healthier churches.

Schultz, Thom, and Joani Schultz. *Why Nobody Wants to Go to Church Anymore*. Loveland, CO: Group Publishing, 2013. This is a seminal work that every local elder should read. It is popularly written, so the ideas are organized in dramatic form. But the data and its interpretations are extremely useful for understanding what is happening in our communities.

Stanley, Andy. *Deep and Wide: Creating Churches Unchurched People Love to Attend*. Grand Rapids, MI: Zondervan, 2012. Stanley has been called one of the ten most influential pastors in America, with six churches in the greater Atlanta metropolitan area and many others around the globe. His book is about the significance of individual Christians making friends and bringing them to church.

Stetzer, Ed, and Thom Rainer. *Transformational Church: Creating a New Scorecard for Congregations*. Nashville, TN: B&H, 2010. The primary benefit of this book is the way in which it shows data that enable us to move the conversation about success in ministry from numbers to accountability, discipleship, and spiritual maturity.

Strauch, Alexander. *Biblical Eldership: An Urgent Call to Restore Biblical Church Leadership*. Rev. ed. Colorado Springs, CO: Lewis and Roth, 2011. This is a heavy, scholarly work on the biblical background of elders but well worth the energy that is required to read it.

Waggoner, Brad. *The Shape of Faith to Come: Spiritual Formation and the*

Future of Discipleship. Nashville, TN: B&H, 2008. Waggoner, a researcher into the life of the church, describes the processes by which struggling churches may be led into deeper spirituality.

Other books you probably should read

I hesitated to include this section; in the end, I felt I should introduce you to several books that may make a difference in your life, even if they do not directly apply to the work of the local elder. If you are going to communicate with contemporary audiences, you will need to be aware of what is going on in matters of leadership and current Christian thinking. Here are a few books that should help keep you current and informed:

Barna, George. *Revolution: Finding Vibrant Faith Beyond the Walls of the Sanctuary*. Carol Stream, IL: Tyndale House, 2005. This is one of the five most essential books for the elder to own. The Barna Group is the most respected organization researching the life of the Christian church today. The book discusses why so many Christians are abandoning the organized church for a life of faith without it. The elder needs to understand why this is happening.

Beckham, William. *The Second Reformation: Reshaping the Church for the 21st Century*. Houston: TOUCH Publications, 1995. If you want to discover what is really happening in churches today, read Beckham's analysis. He presents a logical discussion of what is wrong and how to fix it.

Chappell, Paul. *Guided by Grace: Servant Leadership for the Local Church*. Murfreesboro, TN: Sword of the Lord, 2000. This book brings a much-needed emphasis on servant leadership. It can sometimes be a bit heavy-handed, but it is still valuable.

Collins, Jim. *Good to Great: Why Some Companies Make the Leap . . . and Others Don't*. New York: HarperCollins, 2001. In terms of establishing leadership, the local elder needs to understand why some churches go from good to great and others do not. This is a key resource for leadership training.

Dodson, Jonathan. *Gospel-Centered Discipleship*. Wheaton, IL: Crossway, 2012. In Dodson's book, he goes to great lengths to draw a distinction between approaches to discipleship that are driven by seeking piety and those that are more clearly oriented to mission and evangelism. He especially emphasizes that the church got into trouble when the early Christian disciples began to focus largely on the vertical dimension (on piety).

Duhigg, Charles. *The Power of Habit: Why We Do What We Do in Life and Business*. New York: Random House, 2014. This is a remarkable study of how we form habits and the ways in which we can alter them to make our lives more successful—a game changer.

Ehrman, Bart. *Lost Christianities: The Battles for Scripture and the Faiths We Never Knew*. New York: Oxford University Press, 2005. This is one of those critical works that show the diversity within the roots of Christianity. The author contrasts these early differences with those between Adventists and Catholics and suggests that the earlier differences were far greater than the current ones. Not a book for the faint of heart, but it is carefully researched.

Jiwa, Bernadette. *Difference: The One-Page Method for Reimagining Your Business and Reinventing Your Marketing*. Australia: Story of Telling Press, 2014. Not a book precisely about Christianity or Adventism, but this is one of the very best books for understanding how we need to tell our stories in the local church if we want the people in our communities to pay attention.

Kinnaman, David. *You Lost Me: Why Young Christians Are Leaving the Church . . . and Rethinking Faith*. Grand Rapids, MI: Baker Books, 2011. This is a book every elder should have in his or her library. It represents the findings of the Barna Group (Kinnaman is its president) on why young adults are leaving the church and how those of us who serve in the church must examine what we are doing to keep them.

Lyons, Gabe. *The Next Christians: The Good News About the End of Christian America*. New York: Doubleday, 2010. In this companion volume to *You Lost Me*, Lyons is describing a new way of worshiping God that moves beyond what is traditional in the Christian church. Seventh-day Adventists are following this route more slowly than some denominations, but the local elder should know where the pathway is leading.

Mouw, Richard. *Uncommon Decency: Christian Civility in an Uncivil World*.

Downers Grove, IL: InterVarsity Press, 1992. One of the most important books for understanding how committed, passionate Christians can interact with the people around them in ways that are civil, rather than confrontational, and improve their chances of getting people to take their witness seriously.

Ogden, Greg. *Transforming Discipleship: Making Disciples a Few at a Time.* Downers Grove, IL: InterVarsity Press, 2003. Ogden makes the point that we are ignoring the example of Jesus and Paul when they took a small group of believers and spent months or years mentoring them into mature Christian disciples.

Pope, Randy. *Insourcing: Bringing Discipleship Back to the Local Church.* Grand Rapids, MI: Zondervan, 2013. This book is the story of a pastor who has spent the past twenty-five years emphasizing discipleship in his congregation and includes insights into how he has done this and where the emphasis has taken the group.

Quinn, Robert. *Deep Change: Discovering the Leader Within.* San Francisco: Jossey-Bass, 1996. This is one of the most significant books ever written on leadership. It continues to be used in classes and business settings. For the local elder, it is vital for a better understanding of how change in the church can be managed.

Rainer, Thom, and Sam Rainer III. *Essential Church? Reclaiming a Generation of Dropouts.* Nashville, TN: B&H, 2008. This book is a highly recommended study of what is happening with our younger members, who increasingly do not find a place for themselves in the local church. It contains remarkable studies and conclusions that every elder needs to ponder.

Roxburgh, Alan. *Structured for Mission: Renewing the Culture of the Church.* Downers Grove, IL: InterVarsity Press, 2015. This is one of those thought-provoking books that address the way culture is changing in North America and how we need to examine the underlying stories, metaphors, and cultures that give the church its contemporary witness.

Stetzer, Ed, and Mike Dodson. *Comeback Churches: How 300 Churches Turned Around and Yours Can Too.* Nashville, TN: B&H, 2007. This is a fascinating study of how three hundred churches turned things around so that they stopped declining and began growing and making a difference in their communities. It contains some great ideas for revitalizing a tired church witness.

---

1. I have had personal conversations with many of those who, by title, should have assured that a broad spectrum of resources was available for the training of local elders. For example, many pastors have conducted this training, developing and utilizing their own materials, since the available resources were scarce. (The places that might be expected to have provided these training aids had few things on their shelves.) We should—prior to this—have assembled these and extracted the best ideas for general use. At any rate, we are now beginning a long-overdue process.

2. Ministerial Association, *Seventh-day Adventist Elder's Handbook* (Silver Spring, MD: Ministerial Association, General Conference of Seventh-day Adventists, 1994), 33, 34.

3. Jonas Arrais, "Tips for Sermon Preparation," *Elder's Digest*, January/March 2016, 4, 5, https://cdn.ministerialassociation.org/cdn/eldersdigest.org/issues/ED%20Q1%202016.pdf.

4. Johann Dedier, "Elders and the Generational Relay," *Elder's Digest*, January/March 2016, 22, https://cdn.ministerialassociation.org/cdn/eldersdigest.org/issues/ED%20Q1%202016.pdf.

5. Ellen G. White, "Proper Use of the Voice," The Art of Speech, *Elder's Digest*, April/June 2015, 23, https://cdn.ministerialassociation.org/cdn/eldersdigest.org/issues/ED%20Q2%202015.pdf.

6. The *Elder's Digest* archives are available at https://eldersdigest.org/archives-en.

7. Loren Siebold, "I'm Not God: 10 Things Pastors Wish They Could Say to Certain Church Members," *Elder's Digest*, January/March 2016, 9, https://cdn.ministerialassociation.org/cdn/eldersdigest.org/issues/ED%20Q1%202016.pdf.

8. J. R. Briggs and Bob Hyatt, *Eldership and the Mission of God: Equipping Teams for Faithful Church Leadership* (Downers Grove, IL: InterVarsity Press, 2015), 17.